Prophetic Dialogue

Prophetic Dialogue

Reflections on Christian Mission Today

Stephen B. Bevans
and Roger P. Schroeder

ORBIS BOOKS
Maryknoll, New York 10545

Founded in 1970, Orbis Books endeavors to publish works that enlighten the mind, nourish the spirit, and challenge the conscience. The publishing arm of the Maryknoll Fathers and Brothers, Orbis seeks to explore the global dimensions of the Christian faith and mission, to invite dialogue with diverse cultures and religious traditions, and to serve the cause of reconciliation and peace. The books published reflect the views of their authors and do not represent the official position of the Maryknoll Society. To learn more about Maryknoll and Orbis Books, please visit our website at www.maryknollsociety.org.

Library of Congress Cataloging-in-Publication Data

Bevans, Stephen B., 1944–
    Prophetic dialogue : reflections on Christian mission today / Stephen B. Bevans
      and Roger P. Schroeder.
      p. cm.
    Includes bibliographical references (p.   ) and index.
    ISBN 978-1-57075-911-6 (pbk.)
    1. Catholic Church – Missions. 2. Missions – Theory. 3. Christianity and
culture. I. Schroeder, Roger, 1951–   II. Title.
BV2183.B48 2011
266'.201 – dc22   2010039668

To
Claude Marie Barbour and Eleanor Doidge
Friends, Colleagues,
Models of Prophetic Dialogue

Contents

5. Unraveling a "Complex Reality"

6. Entering Someone Else's Garden

7. Letting Go and Speaking Out

8. Table Fellowship

9. A Short History of the Church's Mission

10. Church Teaching, Mission, and Prophetic Dialogue

Ad Gentes, Evangelii Nuntiandi, Redemptoris Missio,
and *Dialogue and Proclamation* 138

Frequently Cited Sources

Ad Gentes, Vatican Council II, Dogmatic Constitution on Divine Revelation, 1965.

Dei Verbum, Vatican Council II, Dogmatic Constitution on Divine Revelation, 1965.

Dialogue and Proclamation, Pontifical Council on Interreligious Dialogue and Congregation for the Evangelization of Peoples, 1991.

Ecclesia in Africa, Pope John Paul II, Apostolic Exhortation, 1995.

Ecclesia in Asia, Pope John Paul II, Apostolic Exhortation, 1999.

Ecclesiam Suam, Pope Paul VI, Encyclical Letter, 1964.

Evangelii Nuntiandi, Pope Paul VI, Apostolic Exhortation, 1975.

Evangelium Vitae, Pope John Paul II, Encyclical Letter, 1995.

Gaudium et Spes, Vatican Council II, Pastoral Constitution on the Church in the Modern World, 1965.

Lumen Gentium, Vatican Council II, Dogmatic Constitution on the Church, 1964

Nostra Aetate, Vatican Council II, Declaration on Non-Christian Religions, 1965.

Redemptoris Missio, Pope John Paul II, Encyclical Letter, 1990.

Biblical quotations are from the New Revised Standard Version of the Bible (NRSV). We have made the language inclusive for both people and God, in consultation with the original Greek text.

Introduction

The Acts of the Apostles tells the exciting story of how the Spirit led the early Jesus community to respond creatively and communally in new and surprising situations as it preached the gospel "to the ends of the earth" (Acts 1:8). No one ever expected *Samaritans* to be part of the new community. Certainly not a *eunuch*. Hardly a *Roman centurion*. Ordinary *Greeks?* No way. And yet, time and again, the community marveled that even the Gentiles had accepted the word of God (See Acts 11:1, 18).

At the same time, Acts demonstrates as no other book in the New Testament that the emerging Christian community is not the work of Peter or the creation of Paul, but the work of the Risen Lord and his Holy Spirit. What was inaugurated at Pentecost and came clear at Antioch was that, for all its distinctiveness from Judaism, the church was in radical continuity with the mission and ministry of Jesus of Nazareth. The church found its identity as the first disciples continued to be led and challenged by God's own mission, a mission, they realized, that Jesus embodied, and that they were called to share and continue.

The church is "missionary by its very nature," Vatican II taught.[1] If the church is to be the church today, it must also share and continue in God's healing, fulfilling, challenging, and redemptive work. It must truly be God's missionary People, the Body of Christ in the world, the presence of the Spirit as God's Temple, God's building. The various components of the "single, but complex reality"[2] of mission today should be faithful, creative, and communal acts that reflect the breadth of God's mission — *faithful* to the essential missionary identity of Christianity, *creative* in responding to changing contexts, and *communal* in engaging God's Spirit in tradition, history, and human experience.

In our book *Constants in Context* we offered a description of the theology and practice of mission throughout the history of the world Christian movement, and the way mission might be understood and practiced now in the twenty-first century.[3] We have been truly honored

and humbled by the broad reception and use of our work since its publication in 2004. We are amazed that it has been translated into Chinese,
Indonesian, Italian, and Spanish. Of course, the communal process of
theological reflection on mission continues among scholars and practitioners of mission. In that light, the interest in our work has thankfully
generated further writing, reflection, and discussion in reviews of the
book, more extensive articles, and many stimulating workshops and
discussions.[4]

In the final chapter of *Constants in Context* we proposed the idea
of "prophetic dialogue" as a synthesis of the three major theologies
of mission that had been articulated in the last half of the twentieth
century: (1) mission as participation in the mission of the Triune God
(*missio Dei*), (2) mission as liberating service of the Reign of God, and
(3) mission as proclamation of Jesus Christ as universal savior.[5] "Prophetic dialogue," as we developed it originally, was a term used by the
2000 General Chapter of our religious congregation, the Society of the
Divine Word (SVD), currently the largest explicitly missionary congregation of men in the Roman Catholic Church. The term was the fruit
of a process of Chapter delegates from all over the world who drew on
their theology and experience of mission in many different contexts. It
has proved a controversial but ultimately very helpful concept for SVDs
to speak of the way we would like to do mission in the many countries
and contexts in which we work.

We ourselves adapted and developed the idea of prophetic dialogue as
an expression of a comprehensive theology of mission. Furthermore, we
suggested that the phrase can serve as an overarching umbrella for an
understanding of the various elements in the practice of mission — witness and proclamation; liturgy, prayer, and contemplation; justice, peace,
and the integrity of creation; interreligious dialogue; inculturation; and
reconciliation. Each one of these components can be understood from
a "dialogical" perspective, and each can also be understood from a
perspective of prophecy.

Perhaps more than a theology, however, we began to be conscious
of the fact that — to paraphrase Robert Schreiter — prophetic dialogue
functions much more as a *spirituality* than as a *strategy*.[6] In this way, it
is similar to what the great David Bosch described as the "bold humility" that Christians bring to the practice of mission — a boldness in
proclamation that is tempered by a deep humility for the harm that

mission has done and a deep respect for the God who was there before the missionary's arrival.[7]

Many questions and challenges have been raised regarding our choice of the term "prophetic dialogue." How, for example, can one engage in sincere dialogue, particularly interreligious dialogue, while also being prophetic in the articulation of one's beliefs? How can dialogue have any role if one takes a prophetic stance against injustice? Is prophetic dialogue more a creative tension than a synthesis? How could the prophets of the Old Testament be associated in any way with a spirit of dialogue? How can prophetic dialogue be described with more theological depth? Has not, in fact, prophetic dialogue *always* been the ideal of missionary practice throughout Christian history? Is not prophetic dialogue really a contradiction, and so impossible to practice? These are all questions raised by Asians, Latin Americans, Africans, North Americans, Europeans, Australians, New Zealanders, and Pacific Islanders, students, biblical scholars, theologians, missiologists, and — not the least! — missionaries themselves, in conferences, classes, workshops, and many one-on-one conversations.

IT IS IN RESPONSE TO and in conversation with such concerns and questions that we have tried to reflect further on prophetic dialogue in the years since *Constants in Context* was published, and it is this further reflection that this volume represents. Several of the chapters in these pages were published even before we hit upon the idea of prophetic dialogue as a synthetic theological and missiological concept. What we realized as we were challenged and inspired by our various audiences, however, is that the idea of prophetic dialogue had been brewing in our own thinking for a long time before we adopted the expression. Several chapters were written and published in the years since 2004, but, as in the case of earlier articles, we have thoroughly revised them for this book. A number of other chapters have been written specifically for this book and are published here for the first time. These chapters — especially chapters 3 and 8 — represent our latest thinking about the theme, although they have inspired many of the revisions in the other chapters.

The first five chapters present what we believe is a more developed and systematic understanding of prophetic dialogue by drawing upon Scripture, theology, and history, and by incorporating images and practices of mission. Chapter 1, "The Mission Has a Church: An Invitation

to the Dance," suggests that God might best be described as a verb —
a flow, an embrace, a movement, a dance — and this is the basic reason
why we can speak of God as Mission. Faith in such a God is participation in God's mission, and the community that consciously participates
in God's mission is the church. The following two chapters are more
in-depth reflections on the two aspects of dialogue and prophecy — how
God's mission needs to be lived out in today's world. As such the two
aspects of mission are inseparable. For the sake of deeper understanding,
however, we try to focus on one at a time, thus employing the classic
scholastic dictum of *distinguishing* while not *separating*.

Chapter 4 aims to bring the two aspects of dialogue and prophecy
together again in the context of the history of mission and through the
lens of contextual theology. While dialogue and prophecy are *always* to
be employed in the practice of mission, what emphasis needs to be placed
on one or the other, like any good contextual practice, always "depends
on the context."

Chapter 5 briefly reflects on the six elements of mission treated more
in depth in the last chapter of *Constants in Context.* By this point in the
book, our hope is that the reader will recognize that each of these elements should be understood and practiced from the perspective of *both*
dialogue and prophecy. The emphasis on one or the other will depend
on what the concrete context demands. Thus, for example, *witnessing*
to the gospel might be practiced dialogically in an Indian context by a
deep respect for Hinduism or Islam and taking care to immerse oneself
in the local cultural context — as exemplified by Bede Griffiths. On the
other hand, living a countercultural lifestyle of simplicity and ecological
responsibility in North America can be a prophetic witness in such a context of secularism or consumerism. Mary Jo Leddy and Jim Wallis are
examples of such a prophetic lifestyle. *Proclamation,* working for *justice,*
etc. can be lived out in the same way, according to what circumstances
demand.

Chapters 6 to 10 then unpack some of the interrelated implications
and aspects of prophetic dialogue. In these chapters we reflect on prophetic dialogue through the image of entering someone else's garden
(chapter 6), through the spiritual asceticism of discerning how and when
to "let go" and "speak out" (chapter 7), and through the powerful
practice of Jesus and the early church of boundary-breaking table fellowship (chapter 8). The final two chapters trace the practice of prophetic

dialogue in the actual history of the church's mission (chapter 9) and in the teaching of the Roman Magisterium of the Catholic Church in the last half century (chapter 10).

THIS BOOK WAS ORIGINALLY INTENDED as a collection of essays. However, as we worked on and revised the essays we began to realize that there was such a clear pattern in them that it made much more sense to shape them into a proper book. Originally, some of the essays were written by each of us individually (chapters 1, 4, 5, 6, 7, 8, 10), and others were written together (chapters 2, 3, 9). In a crucial decision, we decided to rewrite *every* essay in the first-person plural, using the third person for individual experiences when necessary. The only exception to this is in chapter 6, which involved such a personal reflection by Roger that we had to leave much of it in the first-person singular. Like we did with *Constants in Context,* we read every essay out loud to each other, and revised and rewrote everything together. The experience of doing this was invaluable, and we had many "magic moments" when ideas took us places we never had imagined going.

As we worked together we also tried to make many more references to and reflections on prophetic dialogue than were present (with the exception of chapters 2 and 3) in the original essays. What we are presenting here, therefore, is a new book, not a mere collection of essays, that we hope will advance theological and missiological thinking on prophetic dialogue as the key to understanding mission theology and practice today. Naturally, some of the original contexts of the chapters will show through, especially in a certain amount of repetition of key ideas and favorite quotations. But what we have written in these pages is quite different from what we had originally intended. We were the first to be surprised by where the Spirit led us!

WHILE WE ARE UNABLE to acknowledge everyone whose challenges and affirmations have contributed to our further reflections on the concept of prophetic dialogue, we would like to mention at least the following venues and persons as somehow representative of the wide network of inquiry and scholarship to which we belong and for which we are truly grateful.

In 2006 we led a two-week workshop at the Divine Word School of Theology in Tagaytay City, Philippines, on the teaching of *Constants in Context*. Present were some forty professors and other academics in mission studies who work in the Asia-Pacific region. We are grateful for the support of the SVD Asia-Pacific Zone (ASPAC) for making this workshop happen.

Roger Schroeder presented and discussed the idea of prophetic dialogue with the Midwest Area directors and staff of Diocesan Mission Offices meeting in Milwaukee, Wisconsin, in the fall of 2006, and in four workshops given in the SVD China Province in the summer of 2007. He also engaged Catholic theological faculties, Muslim graduate students, and Christian missionaries on the topic of prophetic dialogue while on sabbatical in Indonesia in 2009. In 2010 Roger was privileged to be the keynote speaker and respondent at a conference on prophetic dialogue sponsored by the University of South Africa (UNISA), where David Bosch had served on the faculty. Forty percent of the conference participants were Pentecostals, and most of the rest were of the Reformed tradition.

Stephen Bevans developed much of his own further thinking on prophetic dialogue in presentations to SVD confreres at the 2006 Chicago Province Chapter and at East Troy, Wisconsin, in the fall of 2006. He was also able to hone his ideas in presentations in Brisbane, Sydney, and Melbourne, Australia, in 2009, at a retreat for SVD confreres in Ireland and in a workshop for members of the Missionaries of the Precious Blood in Salzburg, Austria — both of these latter in July of 2009. He was also privileged to try out ideas in various presentations throughout Great Britain while serving as missiologist in residence at the Church Mission Society (CMS) in the fall of 2009, and in a workshop for members of the Manila Vice-Province of the Redemptorists in May of 2010.

Among many individuals who have been important conversation partners on this topic, we would like to mention the following: Thomas Ascheman, Klippies Kritzinger, Ennio Mantovani, Larry Nemer, Tim Norton, Gary Riebe-Estrella, Lazar Stanislaus, Cathy Ross, Tim Daikin, Jonny Baker, Ross Langmead, Mike Gable, Tim Naish, Marcina Stawasz, Lenny Mercado, Ben Beltran, Cobus Wyngaard, Ariel Lubi, Caloy Ronquillo, Katalina Tahaafe-Williams, Donatus Sermada, Paul Klein, Raymund Sudhiarsa, Leo Kleden, Elizabeth Inosensia Loghe Pati, Bernadette Edgecombe, Paul Han, Jacques Kuepers, Brad Hinze, Mary Ann Hinsdale, Lucas Cerviño, Bill Nordenbrock, and Nico Botha.

Many thanks to Julián Fernández, SVD, main translator of *Constants in Context* into Spanish, for giving us the original idea for what developed into this present work. Sadly, Julián died tragically in a traffic accident in Mexico in the Fall of 2010, when this book was in production. We mourn the loss of a confrere, a collaborator, and a friend.

Melody Layton McMahon, director of the Paul Bechtold Library at Catholic Theological Union (CTU), along with the entire library staff, has been unfailing in assistance, especially as we reached the final stages of working on our book. We also want to acknowledge the constant support of our community of the Society of the Divine Word, especially that of our provincial, Mark Weber, and our rector, Stan Uroda. We are who we are because of family, friends, and colleagues at CTU.

Our book is dedicated to two very special colleagues at CTU — Claude Marie Barbour and Eleanor Doidge. Perhaps more than anyone we know, Claude Marie and Eleanor embody the spirit of dialogue, but also prophetic dialogue. Their commitment to what Claude Marie has called "Mission in Reverse" has inspired thousands of students in the last thirty years. It is a practice and attitude — indeed, a spirituality — that has dialogue at its heart, but the way it is lived out in Claude Marie's and Eleanor's lives gives a challenging prophetic witness to anyone who dares to proclaim the gospel. We refer to the idea Mission in Reverse often in these pages. We count ourselves fortunate to be their friends, mentees, former student (Roger of Claude Marie), and teacher (Steve of Eleanor).

Special thanks to the editors and staff at Orbis Books, especially our editor Susan Perry, publisher Robert Ellsberg, and amazing production coordinator Catherine Costello. Bill Burrows, now retired managing editor, has been a constant stimulus for thought, and Steve's best friend and conversation partner for fifty years.

The illustration on our cover has a very special meaning for us. It expresses beautifully the dance of the Trinity into which Christians are called to join in prophetic dialogue. Originally, a photo of the sculpture was given to Steve by our beloved colleague, Barbara Bowe, RSCJ, as a birthday present several years ago. Barbara died in March 2010 of a brain tumor, and we miss her presence at CTU terribly. The title of the sculpture is "Homage to Matisse." It is a work by noted artist Paula Mary Turnbull, SNJM, MFA. Sr. Paula has graciously given us permission to use a photo of this work, as has photographer Herman Marciel.

We also want to acknowledge the help of Sr. Mary Boys, SNJM, and Sr. Jere Mansfield, SNJM, in helping us to contact Sr. Paula.

Our book is the fruit of respectful engagement with many people of different nationalities, contexts, perspectives, and ecclesial traditions. We have a deep sense that our conversations over the past several years have been calls to fidelity, creativity, and community as we work and think together to fathom the mystery of God's call to participate in God's own mission. These have been conversations involving both listening and speaking, challenging and being challenged. They have been instances, in other words, of prophetic dialogue.

STEPHEN B. BEVANS
ROGER P. SCHROEDER
December 22, 2010

Chapter 1

The Mission Has a Church

An Invitation to the Dance

God Is a Verb

A few years ago Steve Bevans began to realize that God — the God revealed to us by Jesus of Nazareth through the power of the Holy Spirit — might be best described as a *verb,* not a noun. What this means is that the God we know from revelation might be best imagined not as a static kind of "person" — sort of like us but wiser and more powerful — who is "up there" or "out there." Rather, in a way that is much more exciting and worthy of our adoration and love, God is a Movement, an Embrace, a Flow — more personal than we can ever imagine — who is always and everywhere present in God's creation.[1] God is present in the very warp and woof of creation, working for its wholeness and healing, and calling creation to its fullness. Even more amazing, God invites women and men on a small planet in a minor galaxy in this vast universe — billions of years old, billions of light years in extension — into partnership in God's work. These women and men, Genesis tells us (1:26–27), God created in the divine "image and likeness."[2] They are to be, as Nigerian Old Testament scholar James Okoye tells us, stewards, caretakers, "greeners," viceroys of God on earth. We do not know, although it is surely possible, whether other creatures — perhaps in a far-off galaxy and perhaps many times more intelligent than we — have been entrusted by God with the same task. What we do know from revelation is that *we* have been.

Nothing about our God is static. One of our greatest theologians, Thomas Aquinas, spoke of God as pure act.[3] And the equally great theologian Bonaventure speaks of God as self-diffusive goodness and love.[4] In the great Western medieval tradition, Mechtilde of Magdeburg spoke of the "restless Godhead," an "overflow . . . which never stands still and always flows effortlessly and without ceasing."[5]

God is not even static within Godself as such. God in God's deepest identity is a relationship, a communion. "In the remotest beginning," Brazilian theologian Leonardo Boff writes of the Trinity, "communion prevails."[6] This life in communion spills out into creation, healing and sanctifying, calling all of creation, according to its capacity, into that communion, and once in that communion, sending that creation forth to gather still more of it into communion. It is as though God as such is a dance (a great conga line, one might imagine) moving through the world, inviting the world — material creation, human beings — to join in the dance. And the more that join the more attractive joining becomes.[7]

This self-diffusive, gathering, and sending nature of God hints at what the true nature of reality is. What is real is not what is concerned with itself or turned in on itself (this latter is Luther's definition of sin!). What is real is going beyond oneself, being in relation, calling others to relation. The British philosopher Alfred North Whitehead suggested that God, rather than being the *exception* to the laws of the universe, is really their greatest exemplar. And so God is perfectly related to the world; in fact God is relation itself. God is perfectly involved in the world, and rather than being unable to change and suffer with the world, God is infinite in God's ability to be affected by the world and is, in Whitehead's famous words, the "fellow sufferer who understands."[8] Benedict XVI describes God in a way far from Platonic and Aristotelian thinking: God is "a lover with all the passion of true love."[9]

God Is Mission

Another way of saying all this is that God is Mission. Not that God *has* a Mission, but that God *is* Mission. This is what God is in God's deepest self: self-diffusive love, freely creating, redeeming, healing, challenging that creation. God, as my colleague Anthony Gittins once said in a lecture, is "love hitting the cosmic fan." Or, to be a bit more prosaic, God is like an ever-flowing fountain of living water, poured out on earth through the Holy Spirit and actually made part of creation through the Word-become-flesh. As Vatican II's document on missionary activity (*Ad Gentes*) puts it, God "generously pours out, and never ceases to pour out, the divine goodness, so that the one who is creator of all things might at last become 'all in all' (1 Cor. 15:28), thus simultaneously assuring God's own glory and our happiness."[10]

God Inside Out

There has never been a moment when God has not been present to and in creation. From the first nanosecond of time, God has been there, in the fullness of God's Mystery, through the presence of the Holy Spirit. The Spirit is, as it were, God "inside out" in the world. She is God's complete presence, palpable, able to be experienced, and yet elusive, like the wind. Or, as she is described in a best-selling book today, *The Shack,* she is perhaps best seen from the corner of our eye rather than visible straight on.[11]

In our own tradition, with its roots in the Old Testament, the Spirit is described as breath or wind, *ruach* in Hebrew. She broods over the primeval chaos in the first lines of Genesis, like a mother bird brooding over her nest. She is the breath that God breathes into the "earth creature," *ha adam,* that we call Adam. She is the spirit that stirs up prophecy, that brings the dry bones in Ezekiel chapter 37 to life. She is the water that pours out of the Temple in Ezekiel's great vision in chapter 47, the water that gives life to healing plants and abundant fruits. She is the ointment in Isaiah chapter 61 that brings good news to the afflicted, to bind the wounds of the brokenhearted, that proclaims liberty to captives, that frees those in captivity. U.S. feminist theologian Elizabeth Johnson beautifully sums up the Spirit's role in history: "Whether the Spirit be pictured as the warmth and light given by the sun, the life-giving water from the spring, or the flower filled with seeds from the root, what we are actually signifying is God drawing near and passing by in vivifying, sustaining, renewing, and liberating power in the midst of historical struggle."[12]

God Is Like Jesus

"In the fullness of time" (Gal. 4:4), the Word of God became flesh and gave the Spirit, God's complete yet elusive presence, a human face. Jesus continued the work of the Spirit, but now God is present in a visible, audible, and concrete way. Jesus was a man led by God's Spirit. All three synoptic Gospels begin their narrative of Jesus' ministry with Jesus being led — or in Mark "driven" — by the Spirit into the desert to prepare for his ministry (see Matt. 4:1, Mark 1:12, and Luke 4:1). Luke describes

Jesus' inaugural sermon at Nazareth, as he read from the scroll of Isaiah: "The Spirit of the Lord is upon me, because God has anointed me to bring good news to the poor,... to proclaim release to the captives and recovery of sight to the blind, to let the oppressed go free, to proclaim the year of the Lord's favor" (Luke 4:18–19). The work of the Spirit in Isaiah is now the work of Jesus, and this is the program of his ministry.

In this ministry Jesus reveals the God who is a verb: God is a God who reigns, and God reigns by forgiving, healing, saving, reconciling, being in relation. "God is like Jesus," Uruguayan liberation theologian Juan Luis Segundo writes.[13] Note that what Segundo says is *not* that Jesus is like God, as if we already know who God is; rather, it is Jesus who shows us what God is like. When we see the way Jesus taught and acted and suffered, we see the way God teaches and acts and suffers. Three hundred years after Jesus' resurrection, when the church was embroiled in the controversy with Arius, this is what was at stake. If Jesus wasn't truly God (*homoousios to patri*), then we don't really know what God is like. The truth is, though, that we do.

Jesus taught, especially in parables. He taught about forgiveness in parables of the lost sheep, the lost coin, and the lost son in Luke 15. He taught about God's generosity in the parable of the generous employer in Matthew chapter 20. He taught about how all are called to salvation in the parable of the wedding feast in Matthew 22, and about God's persistent quest for justice as portrayed by a persistent widow in the face of an unjust judge in Luke 18.[14]

Jesus' message was a message of joy. It's too bad that Christian artists have for the most part portrayed Jesus as a serious, even somber character. How could he have attracted children if he didn't smile? How could he have held the crowds if his parables were not humorous — even though ultimately deadly serious? Recently one of Steve's students in Chicago put him on to a wonderful Internet exhibition on the "Laughing Jesus," sponsored by the Major Issues and Theology Foundation based in Queensland, Australia. Jesus portrayed as a dancer, a comedian, a juggler and in abandoned conversation with the disciples at Emmaus (where he appears as a woman) helps visualize and better imagine the God of joy that Jesus revealed.[15]

Jesus healed and drove out devils. His healings and exorcisms were parables in action. Making the lame walk, the blind see, the deaf hear, the dead return to life, those caught in the grip of evil experience liberated (see, for example, Matt. 11:2–6) — these were all ways of saying that God's salvation was not just something spiritual, but fully and completely involved with living in this world.

As Edward Schillebeeckx and others have suggested, Jesus himself was a parable.[16] His own personal freedom in interpreting the Law, his fun-loving lifestyle (e.g., drinking wine), and his scandalous, inclusive behavior all pointed to the nature of a God who is a God of life, a God who cared for all, a God of freedom.

Of course, we know where all of this got Jesus. Although his message was deeply rooted in the Jewish tradition — particularly that of the prophets — it proved to be too much for the Jewish leaders of the time. They interpreted Jesus' joy and freedom and inclusiveness as an affront to their tradition, even a blasphemy to the God of Israel (see, for example, Matt. 9:2–8). And they intuited, probably correctly, that if people continued to take Jesus' message seriously it would prove a threat to the Roman occupation of their country (John 11:45–53).

And so they killed him. But even here Jesus reveals the nature of God. God is vulnerable; God will not override human wickedness, but will suffer because of it. In many ways, the image of Jesus on the cross is the dearest image we have of God. God will go to such lengths to reveal a love that so deeply respects human freedom.

But you can't kill God! You cannot stop the Movement that is overflowing life and love. The Mission continued. The disciples experienced Jesus as alive in their midst, especially when they gathered to break bread and share the cup of wine in his memory. They began to realize now that Jesus had been no ordinary man. Jesus had in one way been taken from them in death, but in another way, one that was even more real, he was still with them, guiding them by the Spirit to whom he gave a face. Gradually they began to realize that his mission, the mission of God, was their mission. The mission began to have a church.

The Mission Has a Church

Gradually. As Jesus' disciples experienced his living presence among them — and especially after the extraordinary experience that took place some fifty days after his death, on the day of Pentecost — they realized that they had been given the task to continue Jesus' mission of proclaiming, demonstrating, and embodying God's Reign. But most probably like Jesus as well, they understood this mission as (1) quite temporary, for Jesus would soon inaugurate the Reign of God when he returned in glory, and (2) only for the Jews. Although Judaism had engaged in some mission to bring Gentiles into the covenant people, the prevailing understanding was that, once God's Reign had been inaugurated, the nations would stream toward Jerusalem and acknowledge the God of Israel as the God of all the earth (e.g., Isa. 2:2–5). The members of the Jesus community almost certainly thought that, after Pentecost, the Jews had been given another chance to accept Jesus' vision of God and the radical change of mind and heart that it entailed, and when the Jewish nation would change its mind and believe the good news (see Mark 1:15), the Reign would be established and the Twelve would be set up on the twelve thrones that Jesus promised to judge (i.e., rule, govern with righteousness) the twelve tribes of Israel that the coming of the Reign of God would reconstitute. The fact that they were having such success — three thousand converts here (Acts 2:41), five thousand there (Acts 4:4), people added every day (Acts 2:47) — probably convinced them that the time was very near.

But soon there began to be doubts about all of this. Stephen, with some Greek-speaking disciples perhaps, may have been the first to intuit that what Jesus meant went beyond Judaism. When he was killed for preaching such a radical, unthinkable doctrine and many Greek-speaking followers of Jesus had to flee the city lest they suffer the same fate, strange things began to happen. One of Stephen's companions, Philip, preached to Samaritans (half-Jews, half-breeds), and they accepted the Lordship of Jesus and his vision of God and of the world. Philip was also led to preach to an Ethiopian eunuch, by law excluded from becoming a Jew, and he was moved to admit him into the Jesus fellowship. Peter was amazed to be led to the house of a Roman centurion — a *good* Gentile but a Gentile nonetheless — and when he preached about the Lord Jesus, the same Spirit that had fallen upon the disciples at Pentecost fell upon Cornelius and his household.[17] This was unbelievable! Peter could only baptize them, even though he had to face the grave doubts of the Jerusalem community when he returned. When he explained they exclaimed that God had given *"even to the Gentiles the repentance that leads to life!"* (See Acts 11:18, emphasis added).[18]

What had started out as a movement *within* Judaism had become something much different. The Spirit was moving the community to another place, taking Jesus' vision to where perhaps even he had not imagined it would or could go. The climax came — according to Luke's theological / historical retelling in Acts — when some unnamed men and women who had fled persecution after Stephen's execution[19] arrived in the great urban center of Antioch in Syria (the third largest city in the world at the time) and preached not only to Jews, but also to Gentiles. The result was that "a great number turned to the Lord" (Acts 11:21).

Our contention over the last several years has been that it was here in Antioch that the church was born. We often speak of the day of Pentecost as the "birthday of the church," but we don't think this is true. We think it is here in Antioch, where the disciples were first called "Christians" (Acts 11:26). Our reasoning is that before Antioch — although the realization was growing all through Acts up to this point — the disciples saw themselves as Jews, not as members of a separate, discrete religion. Now, however, at least in germ, they began to see that in Jesus something new had begun, that God's mission in the world — begun in the Spirit from the first moment of creation and continued concretely in Jesus — had been handed over to them. And now they were called to continue this mission to the ends of the earth — in every nation, in every culture, in every time period. Now it became clear — or at least they saw glimmers of it — that God had chosen a particular people to carry on the divine mission, to be the face of the Spirit, the bodily presence of Jesus in the world. At Antioch and thereafter, what began to become clear is that God's mission has a church.

The Mission Has Us

The church comes to be as the church engages in mission, as it crosses the boundary of Judaism to the Gentiles and realizes that its mission is the very mission of God: to go into the world and be God's saving, healing, challenging presence. This is why we can say, with Vatican II's document on missionary activity, that the church is "missionary by its very nature."[20] Mission precedes the church. Mission is first of all God's: God inside out in the world through the Spirit, God in Jesus teaching, healing, including, suffering. Almost incredibly — as an act of grace! — God shares that mission with women and men. Mission calls the church into being to serve God's purposes in the world. The church does not have a mission, but the mission has a church.

Imagine what our church would be like if Christians really understood this and took this seriously. What it means is, first, that the church is not about the church. It is about what Jesus called the Reign of God. We are most church not when we are building up the church, but when we are outside of it: being good parents, being loving spouses, being diligent and honest in our workplace, treating our patients with care if we are health workers, going the extra mile with our students if we are teachers, living lives responsible to the environment, being responsible citizens, sharing our resources with the needy, standing up for social justice, consciously using inclusive language, treating immigrants fairly, trying to understand people of other faiths, etc., etc. What we realize too is that people in the church don't have a monopoly on working for the Reign of God. Maybe people don't call it that, and maybe some people are even repulsed by the church. Nevertheless, they are our partners, our allies, and need to be our friends. St. Augustine said it wonderfully, "Many whom God has, the Church does not have; and many whom the Church has, God does not have."[21]

Imagine what the structure of the church would be like if we recognized that it is mission that needs to be first, and not the church. We need structure in the church, for it is a human institution, and all institutions need to be ordered. But if the mission has a church, then it is the mission that has ministry, not vice versa. Ministry would exist for the mission and not for itself. So many things that bog us down today would simply fall away: clerical privilege, restrictions on lay people's ministry, the role of women in the ministry and decision making in the church. What would be important is not people's roles in the *church,* but how ministers might equip people for ministry in the world.

If mission precedes the church, and constitutes it as such, there will be no "passive" Christians. Baptism will be understood as the main "ordination," giving every Christian the privilege and the duty to minister through a life lived in witness to the gospel in the world. Mission will be understood as part of Christian life. It certainly includes, but is not restricted to going overseas, or immersing ourselves in exotic cultures or dangerous situations. Many people in the church are called to this. All Christians, though, are called to minister in ordinary and extraordinary ways in their daily lives, both within the church and in the world.

Imagine how the sacraments, especially the Eucharist, might be celebrated. It would be the celebration of all the people of God, and it would
be the result of, a preparation for, and an act of mission. As U.S. lay theologian Gregory Augustine Pierce has beautifully said, we don't so much
go to Eucharist as *come back* to Eucharist, to celebrate, be strength-
ened for, and share our participation in God's mission in our everyday
life. We bring our weaknesses in God's service, the needs of the people
whom we meet, and the needs of the people of the whole world — even
the wounded cosmos itself — to share with our Christian community. We
receive consolation and inspiration from the Scriptures and the paschal
mystery for our work in the world. We welcome strangers, we celebrate
beautifully, we always have something in our homilies for those who
might be visiting, or "putting their toes in the water" by coming to our
parish. The climax of the Eucharist is the dismissal rite, when we are
once again sent forth on mission.[22]

Imagine, finally, how recognizing that the mission is primarily God's
would ease our anxiety in the church. God has certainly given us the
privilege of being co-workers, sacraments of God's movement of healing,
reconciliation, and life-giving in our world. Ultimately, though, the work
is God's. We do our best, we work with all our hearts, but we can realize
that it is not all up to us. We don't have to burn ourselves out in ministry,
we don't have to worry so much about our children not going to church,
we don't have to worry about the millions who will never belong to the
church. As Vatican II says wisely (and the phrase is one of the favorites
as well of Pope John Paul II) the Holy Spirit, in a way known only to
God, offers all peoples ways of participating in the paschal mystery.[23]

Do You Want to Dance?

Do you want to dance? Do you want to join in that great Conga Line
that has moved through the world since the beginning of time and that
is also the heartbeat of God's deepest self? The dance will go on without
us. It does not need us to continue its joyful progress among all peoples
and in all times. But if we do join, we won't regret it. As we dance to
bring wholeness and healing and peace in the world, we ourselves will
become whole, be healed, and be graced with peace. Even if we don't
join in the dance, we will be its beneficiaries. But the dance goes on,

the movement that is God continues to move, God continues — joyfully, indefatigably — to be in mission.

The way God engages in the dance of mission, and the way Christians are called to engage in it as well, is through the practice — the dance! — of what we call "prophetic dialogue." Because of God's presence in the world from the first moment of its creation, all of us are called to honor that presence through dialogue: openness, listening, and care for all God's creatures. But because of the incredible news of the gospel, especially in the face of human sin, we are also called to be God's prophets: calling creation to its complete fullness, warning women and men when they live in ways that lead to their own and others' destruction, living ourselves in ways that give witness to the life that the gospel gives. In the chapters that follow we will reflect more deeply on this way of doing mission as prophetic dialogue, joining God in the dance of mission.

Chapter 2

"We Were Gentle among You"

Christian Mission as Dialogue

An army of youth flying the standards of Truth,
We're fighting for Christ, the Lord.
Heads lifted high, Catholic Action our cry,
And the Cross our only sword.
On Earth's battlefield never a vantage we'll yield
As dauntlessly on we swing.
Comrades true, dare and do 'neath the Queen's white and blue,
For our flag, for our faith, for Christ (our) King![1]

Daniel A. Lord's rousing hymn "For Christ (Our) King," was a song that many Catholics (including ourselves!) sang with gusto in the halcyon days of the 1950s; and it was a song, we believe, that captured the spirit of the way Christian mission was often depicted and imagined as "an assertive Christianity...aiming at conquest."[2] This was not, of course, the way the best thinkers about mission and many missionaries themselves thought about mission; our own study of mission theology and our own friendship with missionaries of that era certainly would bear this out.[3] Even Dan Lord, it will also be noticed, does speak about the *cross* as "our only sword"!

Nevertheless, to imagine and to preach about mission in military terms was — and sometimes still is — very much part of the vocabulary of the church's mission. In the 1920s, Divine Word missionary Clifford King founded the Catholic Students' Mission Crusade; student mission clubs were named "*militia orans,*" or the "praying army"; missionaries often spoke of "conquering the world for Christ"; and we remember being told as high school students that we Divine Word missionaries — and missionaries in general — were the "marines of the Catholic Church"! As Jean Yves Baziou describes this attitude: "it was usual to speak in

19

terms of territory to be conquered, or occupied, and in terms of peoples or individuals to be converted and baptized.... Obsessed with frontiers, mission was perceived as pastoral work in pagan territory where the Church had yet to be established."[4]

Mission theology and practice today, however, have undergone what can only be described as a radical shift in understanding and motivation. To use Baziou's language, that shift is from understanding or imagining mission as "expansion" to understanding and imagining mission as a genuine and deep "encounter." Instead of envisioning people who are to be evangelized as "objects" or "targets," contemporary mission theology and practice is struggling — and we mean struggling, because this is "no small death...to be endured"[5] — to acknowledge people as genuine "others."[6] Mission today, in other words, needs to be thought about and carried out in the spirit and practice of *dialogue* — recognizing that, in the famous words of Max Warren, "God was here before our arrival," or in the words of Donal Dorr: "There is a two-way exchange of gifts, between missionaries and the people among whom they work.... Mission is not just a matter of *doing things for* people. It is first of all a matter of *being with* people, of *listening* and *sharing* with them."[7]

Mission today must still be possessed by St. Paul's urgency for witnessing to and proclaiming Christ — "for an obligation is laid on me, and woe to me if I do not proclaim the gospel!" (1 Cor. 9:16; see Rom. 1:16 and 2 Cor. 5:14). And in its *annunciation* of the gospel, the church must be equally passionate about its *denunciation* of injustice and evil.[8] The gospel is good but disturbing news in a profoundly sinful world. But for all his boldness and passion, Paul speaks of his ministry as done in vulnerability and weakness, and he describes himself as a "slave to all," "all things to all people" (1 Cor. 9:19, 22; see 1 Cor. 2:1–5; 2 Cor. 12:8–10). In the passage that inspired the title for this chapter Paul writes about his arrival among the Thessalonians not "with words of flattery or with a pretext for greed," nor making "demands as apostles of Christ." Rather, he says, "we were gentle among you, like a nurse tenderly caring for her own children.... We are determined to share with you not only the gospel of God but also our own selves, because you have become very dear to us" (1 Thess. 2:5–8).

It has been pointed out that the "who" of mission — Jesus — is not in doubt; what concerns mission today is the "how," the *way* mission is conceived and lived out, the *method* of mission.[9] In this regard, then, as the late Archbishop Marcello Zago has expressed it, "The dialogue method must be manifested in the whole of missionary and pastoral activity."[10] Ultimately, mission must witness to and proclaim the name, the mystery and the gospel of Jesus Christ; it must be conceived of and practiced as *prophetic dialogue* (which we will treat in the final section of this chapter, and which this and the next chapter attempt to understand more deeply). But in today's world mission needs first of all to be imagined, thought about, and practiced as "gentle among" women and men — *as dialogue.*

Dialogue as Spirituality

The term "dialogue," as the 1991 document entitled *Dialogue and Proclamation* points out, can be understood in a number of different ways.[11] In the first place, it can refer to a practice that leads to good communication between or among persons, or even to a sense of intimate communion between friends or lovers. Second, dialogue can mean "an attitude of respect and friendship, which permeates or should permeate all those activities constituting the evangelizing mission of the church," an attitude that can be called "the spirit of dialogue." Third, dialogue can be understood as the practice of openness to, fairness and frankness with, respect for, sincerity toward and appreciation of people of other Christian churches or other religious ways, those who hold to a particular ideology (e.g., Marxism), those for whom faith commitment is meaningless (e.g., secularists), or those who have no faith at all. This latter meaning of dialogue is what is known as ecumenical, interreligious, or interideological dialogue,[12] and — in regard to the last two types — is one of the elements that make up the "single but complex reality" of the church's evangelizing mission as a whole.[13]

Dialogue and Proclamation says specifically that it is the third understanding of dialogue that it focuses on in the document. Our focus, however, in this chapter is the second understanding, which "permeates or should permeate...the evangelizing mission of the church." Our focus, in other words, is a basic attitude, something that not only is practiced in the specific *practice* of dialogue, but one that gives direction to each and all of the elements of mission, whether it be the way Christians give witness or proclaim the gospel, celebrate liturgy or pray, do deeds of justice and peacemaking, engage in inculturation or in the process of reconciliation. Dialogue as used here is "a style of living in relationship with neighbors."[14]

In a certain sense, when we speak of "mission as dialogue" as we will here, we are speaking of dialogue as a "spirituality," a sense of "contemplation" that enables the minister or missionary to perceive a particular context in a new way. As *Dialogue and Proclamation* expresses it, mission "always implies a certain sensitivity to the social, cultural, religious, and political aspects of the situation, as also attentiveness to the 'signs of the times' through which the Spirit of God is speaking, teaching, and guiding. Such sensitivity and attentiveness are developed through a spirituality of dialogue."[15] When we speak of mission as dialogue, therefore, we are saying that this "spirit" or "spirituality" of dialogue "is the norm and necessary manner of every form of Christian mission, as well as of every aspect of it.... Any sense of mission not permeated by such a dialogical spirit would go against the demands of true humanity and the teachings of the Gospel."[16] There is a real need today to recognize that mission should be done in vulnerability, in humility, with a sense of being open to be evangelized by those whom we are evangelizing — a kind of "mission in reverse."[17] Like Paul, missionaries need to be "gentle among" those to whom they are sent, sharing not only the gospel of God but their very selves (see 1 Thess. 2:7–8).

When we speak of mission as dialogue, then, we are about as far away from imagining mission as "conquering the world for Christ" and missionaries as "marines of the Catholic Church" as we probably can get. There has indeed been a radical shift, both in the world in which the church does mission and within the church's own consciousness of the goodness and even holiness of that world.

Although we would not fully subscribe to the radical pluralism he advocates, Leonard Swidler points out the significant changes that have taken place in human thinking about the nature of the world and the adequacy of language to express that truth. Language is a thoroughly contextual reality, and no language or even doctrinal expression can fully capture the human experience of transcendence. Truth, in other words, may exist in powerful expressions *outside* the boundaries of any culture or any religion, and so it behooves visitors to another culture or missionaries engaging in intercultural ministry to pay close attention to linguistic forms and cultural ways.[18] In addition, the last half of the twentieth century saw the collapse of a colonialism that had its roots in the "Age of Discovery" beginning in the fifteenth century, but that was practiced with particular intensity in the "Age of Progress" in the nineteenth and early twentieth century. No longer could the cultures and peoples of the world outside Europe and North America be conceived as the "White Man's Burden," but — especially with the rise of nationalism and the renaissance of local religions — they had to be taken seriously and treated with respect. Such new attitudes, of course, were the result of the West's "turn to the subject" at the dawn of modernity and the subsequent realization of universal human dignity and of peoples' right to participate in the processes of their own governments. Tied to this new attitude as well was the discovery by the new science of anthropology of what Bernard Lonergan has called the "empirical understanding of culture" — that culture was not a norm held up by an elite but a universal reality in which every human being takes part and to which every person contributes.[19]

Within the Catholic Church in particular, a number of theological shifts were taking place in response to these shifts of consciousness in the world at large. Christian theology had always had a strong, if perhaps subaltern, tradition of the possibility of grace and salvation outside the boundaries of the church and explicit faith in Jesus Christ — from the second-century theologian Justin Martyr through Thomas Aquinas to Pius XII in the 1940s.[20] However, the documents of the Second Vatican Council, Paul VI's *Evangelii Nuntiandi*, John Paul II's *Redemptoris Missio* and documents like *Dialogue and Proclamation* represent an authentic breakthrough in the church's openness to and reverence for other religions, to the presence of God in history, and to the goodness and holiness of the world's cultures. Vatican II's *Nostra Aetate* speaks about the existence of "rays of the Truth which enlightens all human beings" within religions other than Christianity. The document on the church in the modern world — *Gaudium et Spes* — recognizes that the concerns of the world are indeed the concerns of the followers of Christ, and that Christians must seek to discern the "signs of the times" as they are manifested in the warp and woof of history. The Council's document on missionary activity speaks about the fact that missionaries can learn "by sincere and patient dialogue what treasures a bountiful God has distributed among the nations of the earth."[21] Jacques Dupuis traces a particularly positive development at Vatican II in terms of the possibility of salvation not only *despite* peoples' participation in other religions, but *because* of it. *Dialogue and Proclamation* puts it clearly: "It will be in the sincere practice of what is good in their own religious traditions and by following the dictates of their conscience that members of other religions respond positively to God's invitation and receive salvation in Jesus Christ, even while they do not recognize or acknowledge him as their savior."[22] Paul VI in *Evangelii Nuntiandi* speaks about the importance of the evangelization of culture, not just in a superficial way, as in a veneer, but by a mutual penetration of faith and culture.[23] In a famous line, Pope John Paul II says that faith that does not become culture is not really faith.[24]

In 1964, Paul VI said in his first encyclical, *Ecclesiam Suam,* that there are a variety of valid ways for the church to approach today's world — one might say to approach the way of doing mission. However, "it seems to Us that the sort of relationship for the Church to establish with the world should be more in the nature of a dialogue." It is this method, the pope goes on to say, that "is demanded nowadays by the prevalent understanding of the relationship between the sacred and the profane. It is demanded by the dynamic course of action which is changing the face of modern society. It is demanded by the pluralism of society, and by the maturity women and men have reached in this day and age."[25] We can no longer march through the world as "an army of youth." We must bear our "standards of truth" with gentleness among the women and men of our time, offering not only the message of the gospel, but our very selves.

But the deepest reason for mission as dialogue is not found in accommodation to new thought forms or new appreciation of the world's religions, or of human history or human culture. Mission must be lived out in dialogue because of the nature of God as such, and because mission is participation in that divine, dialogical nature.

Trinitarian Foundations

Although there are only a few hints in official church documents and in the writings of theologians, the ultimate foundation for mission to be thought about and practiced in a "dialogical spirit"[26] is the doctrine of God as Trinity. Christians have experienced God in all God's "unapproachable light" (1 Tim. 6:16) as "inside out" in the ebb and flow of human history as God's Spirit gives and restores life, raises up prophets and calls women and men to freedom and communion with one another.[27] This mysterious yet palpable presence of the Spirit "present and active in every time and place"[28] was "in the fullness of time" (Gal. 4:4) — a particular time: 4 B.C.E. — concretized in the particular and limited body of Jesus of Nazareth. By the way he talked, the way he cured illness and exorcised demons, the way he included all and excluded no one, and the way, finally, he was vulnerable "even to death on a cross" (Phil. 2:8), Jesus revealed the very face of God and gave concrete reality to the Spirit's always and everywhere life-giving work. Jesus' words, deeds, and person announced and sacramentalized the way God was present — "reigned" — in creation; through Jesus and in the power of the Spirit, the Mystery at the center of the world was calling humanity into a "kingdom" or communion (some call it a "kindom") of "truth and life . . . holiness and mercy . . . justice, love and peace."[29]

Through all this, God's and Jesus' method was one of dialogue. As Paul VI teaches in *Ecclesiam Suam,* dialogue has its origin in no less than the mind of God, and says that "the whole history of humanity's salvation is one long, varied dialogue, which marvelously begins with God and which God prolongs with women and men in so many different ways."[30] The Spirit's presence was (and still is in some cases) a "secret presence,"[31] a gentle and persuading presence calling women and men to participation in what would be revealed in time as the "Paschal Mystery,"[32] within the context of peoples' histories and cultures. Jesus, too, is remembered in the Gospels as a man of dialogue, open to foreigners, to people of non-Jewish background like the Samaritan woman (the story is a model of dialogue) and the Canaanite (Syro-Phoenician) woman, responsive to the pleas of the centurion, of Jairus and blind Bartimaeus.[33] Through the working of the Spirit and the ministry of Jesus, God does "not force his mystery on us," to quote a line from the Scottish theologian John Oman. Rather, God works with "the final might of the world," which is "truth and character and service and the spirit of love."[34]

What theologians have recognized — particularly in the last several decades, but building on insights going back to Gregory of Nyssa in the fourth century — is that the communion of wholeness or "salvation" into which God calls women and men to participate is the very communion that God is in Godself. God works for communion in the world because God as such *is* communion and wants to be "all in all" (1 Cor.

15:28; Eph. 4:7). In other words, God's very *nature* is to be in dialogue: Holy Mystery ("Father"), Son (Word) and Spirit in an eternal movement or flow of openness and receiving, a total giving and accepting, spilling over into creation and calling creation back into communion with God-self. Relationship, communion and dialogue, therefore, is the ultimate goal of all existence. As Vatican II's document on revelation puts it: "through this revelation...the invisible God...speaks to women and men as friends...and lives among them..., so that God may invite and take them into communion."[35]

What *missiologists* have recognized in the last several decades is that if God's *inner nature* (what theologian Karl Rahner calls the "immanent Trinity") of dialogue and communion is the same as God's *outer movement* (what Rahner calls the "economic Trinity")[36] of acting in dialogue and calling to communion, then the very nature of God as such is missionary; God in God's deepest triune nature is a communion-in-mission. The same Spirit who is Holy Mystery "inside out" from the first moment of creation and who is manifest in the flesh of Jesus of Nazareth has been bestowed in a new and dynamic way by the Risen Christ on those who have found a new wholeness and breadth of vision in his name (see Acts 4:12). That Spirit, given in baptism, unites women and men to Christ in such a way that they are a "new creation" (2 Cor. 5:17). Now that work of reconciliation that God has done in Christ has been entrusted to them (2 Cor. 5:19), and they now live in the world as Christ's body (1 Cor. 6:15; 12:13; Eph. 4–7), created by the Spirit as God's temple — i.e., God's visible presence — in the world (see 1 Cor. 3:16; 6:19). And so the *church,* because it participates in God's life as communion-in-mission (*missio Dei*), is *itself* "missionary by its very nature."[37]

What follows from this reality, then, is that the church — rooted in the Trinity and therefore committed to mission as its "deepest identity"[38] — takes its lead in mission "from the divine pedagogy,"[39] engaging in its evangelizing mission in the same dialogical, vulnerable, gentle way in which Holy Mystery is made known by the Spirit's "secret presence" and in the life and person of Jesus the Christ. *Evangelii Nuntiandi* says that the church seeks to convert women and men to Christ through "the divine power of the message"; as John Paul II writes, in other words, *"the Church proposes; it imposes nothing."*[40]

The Scope of Dialogue

Perhaps the understanding of mission as dialogue as so foundational to the nature of the church has been best understood and best articulated in the documents of the Federation of Asian Bishops' Conferences (FABC). In fact, the word "dialogue" summarizes the whole attitude of the Asian church, its mode of evangelization, as the understanding of mission in Asia has developed since the 1970s.[41] Reflecting on the thought of Edward Schillebeeckx in the light of the FABC's documents, Malaysian theologian Edmund Chia speaks of the church as a "sacrament of dialogue"; in a similar way Malaysian theologian Jonathan Tan images the church in his reflection on the FABC as a "community of dialogue."[42]

Since its beginning, the FABC has spoken of the mission of the church in Asia as an engagement in a threefold dialogue. A passage from its Fifth Assembly is representative of what is constantly repeated in its documents as "a new way of being church" in Asia:[43]

> Mission includes: being with the people, responding to their needs, with sensitiveness to the presence of God in cultures and other religious traditions, and witnessing to the values of God's Kingdom through presence, solidarity, sharing and word. Mission will mean a dialogue with Asia's poor, with its local cultures, and with other religious traditions.[44]

This articulation of mission, we believe, is Asia's gift to the entire church. Like the church in Asia, the church in all parts of the world should be engaged in a dialogue with the poor, with particular contexts, and with the other religions, ideologies, or secular value systems among which it lives. In addition, we might extend this basic attitude of dialogue to the way the church witnesses to and proclaims the gospel message, to the way the church engages in its ministry of reconciliation, and even to the way it celebrates its liturgy and practices its prayer and contemplation. Space does not allow us to go into detail here. However, in chapter 5 we reflect in some brief detail on each of these themes or "elements," and in our book *Constants in Context* (chapter 12) we deal with them more fully.[45] Here a short reflection on each of these elements as a way of dialogue is certainly in order.

First, then, there is the *dialogue with the poor,* a dialogue that can also be widened to a dialogue with any marginalized people, such as women, people of color, the disabled, gays and lesbians. As a "sacrament" or "community" of dialogue, the church gets its vision from a solidarity with the world's poor and marginalized. Latin American theologians have spoken of the need for the church to be not only a church *for* the poor, but also a church *of* the poor and *with* the poor.[46] This will also involve a close and deep listening to the poor, taking the needs of those on the margins of society seriously — developing, in novelist Alice Walker's phrase, "a heart so open that you can hear the wind blow through it."[47]

Second, we may speak about *dialogue with particular contexts.* We use the word "contexts" here instead of "cultures" in order to point to the wider arena in which the church engages in mission, and so by context we mean any particular situation in which mission takes place: in dialogue with people's particular experiences (death in the family, or a social experience like a hurricane), with people's social location (again, an attention to people of color, to gender, to wealth or poverty), or to culture and the various changes happening within a culture (for example, globalization). We do not do mission in a vacuum, and so we need to be sensitive to the environment in which we minister, to listen, hear and see, be open to difference and vulnerable to awkwardness in strange situations, willing to learn. We have to learn to "let go" before we "speak out."[48]

In the section on *interreligious dialogue* in *Redemptoris Missio,* Pope John Paul insists that such dialogue "does not originate from tactical concerns or self-interest." Rather, dialogue with other religions demands "a deep respect for everything that has been brought about in human beings by the Spirit who blows where He wills."[49] Such dialogue demands a deep commitment to learn from the other, to be ready to be changed by the other, to be fully prepared for conversation by studying the other's religion and to try to "get into its skin" as much as possible, and, when necessary, to take the other seriously enough to "agree to disagree." Leonard Swidler offers a "dialogue decalogue," ten principles that are the conditions for the possibility of true dialogue.[50] We might add here that, according to *Dialogue and Proclamation,* part of the church's mission in regard to interreligious dialogue is to encourage dialogue of the world's religions and ideologies among themselves.[51]

Witness to the gospel is almost by definition dialogical. One "preaches the gospel," to allude to the saying attributed to Francis of Assisi, but one does it by example, by kindness and gentleness, by service rather than the words of an explicit message. But even *proclamation,* says Marcello Zago, "presupposes and requires a dialogue method in order to respond to the requirements of those to be evangelized and to enable them to interiorize the message received."[52] A stunning example of a lack of such dialogue is that of the fundamentalist missionary in Barbara Kingsolver's novel *The Poisonwood Bible* when the missionary zealously proclaims "Jesus is Lord!" but because he has not learned the language sufficiently he actually tells the people "Jesus is poison" — and so the people recoil in horror!

What might the attitude or spirituality of dialogue have to do with *liturgy, prayer, and contemplation?* A community never celebrates liturgy, first of all, in a vacuum. It is always done in a context of particular concerns and a particular cultural group, and these factors need attending to. And one never knows who might be in the liturgical assembly: people visiting for the first time, people attending because of a particular crisis in their lives, people coming to church out of curiosity. What this means is that the assembly — from greeters to lectors to the presider — needs to be a welcoming one, an attentive one. Prayer and contemplation, of course, are also deeply dialogical, because before we pray we must listen to God's stirrings within our hearts, and such attentiveness and centering is also the sine qua non of contemplation.

Finally, as Robert Schreiter urges, the church's ministry of *reconciliation* is much more a spirituality,[53] a disposition of openness and readiness, than it is a strategy, a set of steps toward a goal. Those engaged in the work of reconciliation need to have patience, courage, and genuine vulnerability. They need to be hospitable, offering safe places of refuge and sharing for those who have been wounded and scarred by untruth and oppression. Perhaps more than any other aspect of mission, ministers of reconciliation need to be gentle among whom they minister, giving not only the *message* of reconciliation, but their very selves.

Characteristics of Dialogue

The preceding section has certainly pointed to several characteristics of authentic dialogue: respect, openness, willingness to learn, attentiveness, vulnerability, hospitality, humility, and frankness. But we might also name a few more as well, so as to understand this basic attitude for mission even more deeply.

A first characteristic — not often mentioned in the literature of dialogue from our own reading — is that of *repentance*.[54] Mission, as Peter Phan has remarked, is not an "innocent word," but one that evokes anger and even disgust.[55] Christians have a lot to apologize for — to peoples formerly colonized by the West, to native peoples in North America, Latin America, Australia, and New Zealand, to women, to other Christians — and we must do it. Otherwise there is no way that these cultures and peoples will be able to listen to the good news that — despite their malpractice in the past — Christians have to share with the world.

A second characteristic of dialogue must be *orthopraxis*. Edmund Chia expresses this well when he speaks of the importance of the "principle of graduality" urged by the Asian bishops. "Evangelization," he says,

> must be engaged in one step at a time. The early steps are the most tedious, yet easiest and most important. The Christian witnesses through love, service and deeds in the *dialogue of life*. It is through simple acts of caring, sharing, and attending that others see Christ and come to accept the Church and Christianity.... That accounts for why Mother Teresa has been so well accepted in Asia. Hers is a mission of touch, of love, and of service. That also accounts for why the Asian bishops stress that evangelization in Asia must begin with the "way" before preaching the "truth." Presence, deeds, and service are key words the Asian bishops use most often when speaking about evangelization.[56]

Pope Paul VI in *Ecclesiam Suam* offers several other important characteristics that underlie the basic attitude or spirituality that should inform all missionary activity. The first of these is *clarity* — "before all else; the dialogue demands that what is said should be intelligible.... In order to satisfy the first requirement, all of us who feel the spur of the apostolate should examine closely the kind of speech we use. Is it easy to understand? Can it be grasped by ordinary people? Is it current idiom?"[57] Dialogue, in other words, demands an attitude that is "listener oriented" rather than "speaker oriented."[58]

The pope goes on to speak of the fact that dialogue must be carried out in the same spirit of *meekness* that characterized Jesus himself. Dialogue, in other words, needs to eschew all arrogance or bitterness. What gives our mission authority is its authenticity and transparency. "It is peaceful, has no use for extreme methods, is patient under contradiction and inclines toward generosity."[59]

A third characteristic mentioned by the pope is *confidence* — not only in the effectiveness of one's own ability to communicate, but also in "the good will of both parties in the dialogue.[60] Mutual trust, in other words, is absolutely essential. Dialogue as mission is first and foremost about establishing and maintaining relationships.

The fourth characteristic mentioned is similar to the Asian bishops' "principle of graduality." In paragraph 87, however, even though it is not included in the section on "characteristics," the pope speaks eloquently of a kind of *discernment* that characterizes any and all dialogue: "Before speaking, we must take great care to listen not only to what people say, but more especially to what they have it in their hearts to say. Only then will we understand them and respect them and even, as far as possible, agree with them."

There are probably more characteristics that might be mentioned here, but we think we have named the principal ones. Basically, however, these characteristics point to the fact that mission is never about imposition or conquest. On the contrary, it is about the love of God for all peoples and all of creation, and that such love is expressed first and foremost in a gentle presence and an offer of self.

Images of Mission as Dialogue

A powerful way to speak about mission as dialogue is through a number of images that evoke the kind of thinking and practice that the method of dialogue requires. In a line that one of us (Bevans) has quoted a number of times in his writing, theologian Jack Shea insists that we do not so much *see images* as we see *through* images.[61] Images, we believe, especially a constellation of images, help us to move beyond the conceptual and the abstract to the level of the emotions and the imagination, where we can be motivated to think in a way that leads more immediately to action. Here we'd like to speak about four images of mission as dialogue: the missionary as treasure hunter, as guest, as stranger, and as someone entering into someone else's garden.

Treasure Hunter

First, the missionary might be imaged as *treasure hunter.* This is an image first used a number of years ago in an article by Robert T. Rush.[62] Rather than the image of the missionary coming into a particular place already bearing a treasure, this image highlights the fact that — while she or he *does* bring something of inestimable value — the missionary's task is also to search for the treasure that is already present there. Missionaries need to look long and hard for the treasure. They do not know *where* to look, but they know because of the treasure they *already* bear that there is, indeed, a treasure buried in the context into which they have come. They need to study the "local maps" with care: they need to learn the language, proverbs, and the traditional wisdom of the people. Most of all, they need to befriend people, engage them as guides, be taught by them. If they can, they recruit the people to help them in their search. As a result of the search, both missionaries and people are changed. Had the missionaries not come, the people may not have discovered a treasure in their own soil of such richness and abundance, and so they are enriched. But also, had the missionaries not come, they would not have been enriched by a new people and a new wisdom, nor, ironically, would they have grown in as great an appreciation of the treasure they already possessed. Arriving not to impose or conquer but to be enriched and enrich in return has made all the difference.

Guest

As treasure hunters in a foreign land, missionaries are deeply aware that they are *guests.* A guest is always a blessing, for a guest brings new ways of seeing and understanding the world. But guests, in turn, have to always be aware of the graciousness of their hosts. They need to learn the etiquette of the context in which they are being hosted; they need to learn to appreciate the local food and customs; and they need to recognize the value of the gifts, large and small, that their hosts lavish on them. Guests also need to be sensitive to the fact that learning to accept hospitality gratefully and graciously is perhaps the best way to be of service to their hosts; this goes hand in hand with knowing the best time to offer them a helping hand.

Stranger

As guests, missionaries always remain *strangers.* Strangers, too, are blessings, but they also are sources of challenge and uneasiness within a group or society. And so strangers have to be very careful not to impose their strange ideas on the people among whom they have come. They need to act with care and respect, and take care to ask about customs and ideas that are foreign to them, while trying to explain their own customs to the people among whom they have come. The stranger is always going to make mistakes of language or cultural etiquette, but she or he can apologize for them and constantly try to do better. Bevans reflects that his own experience as a missionary is that, although he could increasingly feel comfortable with Filipino culture, he recognized that he was always going to be awkward, an outsider. Soon after he arrived he heard a story of an old Spanish priest who had spent most of his life in the Philippines. He was asked if, after all those years, he had come to understand the people. His reply was "el alma del Filipino es un misterio" — "the soul of the Filipino is a mystery." And yet, that recognition of ignorance seems to be a kind of *docta ignorantia,* a "learned ignorance" that is born of deep respect and that yields a very important kind of knowledge. His own sense was that the more he recognized his strangeness and foreignness among the Filipino people, the more accepted and closer to them he became. Being a real stranger, ironically, is a way of coming close. As missiologist Anthony Gittins wisely reflects:

> If a newcomer honestly presents herself or himself as a stranger, thus showing respect for the hosts and allowing them to take certain necessary initiatives, this facilitates the interaction, even though the price may be some uncertainty and powerlessness on the part of the stranger. But only by doing this will missionaries be able to indicate their openness, integrity, and willingness to engage in relationships.[63]

Entering into Someone Else's Garden

In his writings, Roger Schroeder has proposed a fourth image: *entering into someone else's garden.*[64] This draws together aspects from the earlier images. One enters another's garden not to compare its beauty and variety with one's own, but to appreciate another way of gardening, another way of arranging the flower beds or vegetable patches, another way of pruning and weeding. One can always learn from another gardener, and although one may want to give advice for growing roses or tomatoes, it is probably best that one waits until asked. One can call attention to the existence of weeds in the garden, but she or he had better be careful, for what is considered an undesirable weed in one gardener's mind might be in another's a beautiful flower or a plant that serves medicinal purposes. A garden is a person's special place, and so one has to be respectful of the gardener's particular tastes and talents, and the experience that he or she brings to his or her work there. When one develops a relationship with the gardener, one can learn a lot and perhaps even teach a bit as well. On a deeper level, the plants valued as bearing life-giving fruit in that particular garden represent how God is already present and nurturing them, the seeds of the word of God, or using the term from above, the treasure buried in this ground. Those plants considered weeds sap and destroy that which sustains life and represent those elements of evil and injustice that need to be denounced in the face of the gospel. Of course, all gardens have their share of weeds and life-giving plants, and the gardener has the primary responsibility for his or her own garden. A missionary who enters into someone else's garden needs to do so very gently and respectfully and to remember that she or he is a guest and stranger there. A missionary needs an attitude and spirituality that allow the gardener to share one's unique garden at his or her own pace with the missionary. With time, trust, and in response to an invitation, a missionary can accompany the other in tending to the others's garden. At the same time, the missionary can learn so much about gardening in general and about the life-giving plants and weeds in her or his own garden.

Inspirations for Mission as Dialogue

In 1927, Pope Pius XI proclaimed St. Francis Xavier and the newly canonized Thérèse of Lisieux patrons of the church's missionary work — a wonderfully balanced choice of a man who was a tireless worker in the field and a woman who, though confined to a small Carmelite convent in a small town in France, brought the whole world with her into the cloister and prayed passionately for missionaries. Although we balk a bit at the word "patron" because of its patriarchal overtones and perhaps would prefer to use the term "inspiration," we think it is appropriate to suggest a few women and men as "patrons" or "inspirations" for mission as dialogue. We have already mentioned Mother Teresa and, in note 3 on page 159, several others. Let us suggest here, however, from a rich choice of examples, three more: Francis of Assisi, Charles de Foucauld, and Pandita Ramabai.

Francis of Assisi (1181–1226)

In the midst of the Fifth Crusade in 1219, Francis of Assisi and several companions set out for Damietta in Egypt, where the crusading army, under the command of Jean de Brienne, king of Jerusalem, had pitched camp — although Brienne was under the watchful eye of Cardinal Pelagius, legate to Pope Honorius III.[65] After spending several days at the Crusaders' camp, Francis and his companion, Brother Illuminato, crossed the battle lines, and after some mistreatment it seems, were brought into the presence of the sultan, Al-Malik al-Kamil. The sultan, who legend has it was a highly educated and sensitive man, sick of war, received Francis with great hospitality and spent several days listening to Francis's gentle words about Christianity, after which he had him escorted back to the Christian camp after asking that Francis pray for him. It was clear that Francis certainly intended to convert the sultan to Christianity, but he went about it not with the military violence of the Crusaders, but with the gentleness and vulnerability of Christ himself. Obviously Francis did not succeed in converting the sultan, although some legends have it that the sultan was "secretly" converted; nevertheless in several ways Francis *himself* was converted.[66] Francis most likely had believed that the sultan, and all Muslims for that matter, were evil, violent men. That idea vanished as he met the man face to face. And Francis was so deeply impressed by the Muslims' periodic call to prayer that he proposed the same thing for Christians. As missiologist Mary Motte puts it, "Having no need to exert power over the other, Francis was able to learn more about prayer from the followers of Islam."[67]

Francis seemed to have learned a lot about mission as well. In his rule of 1221 he addressed "those who are going among the Saracens and other nonbelievers," explaining that Christian presence and witness might be done in two ways. A first way does not start with "arguments or disputes," but on being "subject to every human creature for God's sake" (1 Pet. 2:13). A second way is to preach the gospel openly and explicitly, but it depended on the particular context, Francis said, whether one would choose the first way or the second. In either case, mission was about "living spiritually" among people, and Franciscan scholar Cajetan Esser says that both ways of mission are ultimately interrelated.

"The preaching of the Word, as Francis saw it, availed little without the sermon of one's life."[68] Or, in the phrase often attributed to Francis, "preach always and, if necessary, use words."

Charles de Foucauld (1858–1916)

On November 13, 2005, Pope Benedict XVI beatified Charles de Foucauld, whose rule was the inspiration for the founding of the Little Brothers (1933) and Little Sisters (1936) of Jesus. After a rather decadent life in the French army, Foucauld underwent conversion and spent a number of years as a Trappist monk in Syria, and then as a handyman in a convent of sisters in Nazareth in the Holy Land. It was only in 1901 that he found his true vocation when he was ordained a priest and decided to live as a hermit in Algeria. Foucauld was murdered in 1916 at his hermitage in Tamanrasset in the Ahaggar Mountains by a young man "in what was probably a tragic accident."[69]

In all his ten years in Algeria, Foucauld baptized only two people — a child and an old, blind woman. As Little Sister Cathy Wright says, "If missionary 'success' was to be measured in numbers, Charles was a miserable failure."[70] And yet, in many ways, Foucauld pioneered a whole new way of doing mission: the mission of *presence*. What attracted people to him was his great kindness and holiness, his "unspoken imitation of Christ, in which they recognized the Qur'anic portrayal of *Isa* (Jesus)."[71] Foucauld practiced hospitality, bought the freedom of seven slaves, and nursed the wounded from battles between the local people and the French colonizers. Toward the end of his life Foucauld wrote that he was "not here to convert the Tuareg people at once, but to try to understand them."[72] Direct preaching, he wrote, was not the method Jesus wanted in his situation. "We must go very slowly and gently, get to know them and make friends with them."[73] His apostolate, as he wrote in 1909, "must be one of goodness. In seeing me one must say, 'If this man is good, his religion must be good.' If they ask me why I am good I must answer, 'Because I am the servant of one who is so much better than I. If only you knew how good my Master, Jesus, is.' "[74]

Although he had written a rule and had dreamed of founding a community that would live out his own ideals, Foucauld attracted not one follower in his lifetime, and it was only some twenty years after his death that men and eventually women began to form the community he had hoped for. Although rooted in the theology and missiology of his time, his commitment to authenticity, simple presence, and deep reverence for Islam make him a marvelous "inspirer" of mission as dialogue today.

Pandita Ramabai (1858–1922)

Our third "inspirer" is a person who will most likely be unknown to most Catholics today. Dongre Medhavi Ramabai (Ramabai was her first name) was born a Hindu in India in 1858. She was the daughter of a wealthy Brahmin scholar who, much to the shock of his friends, taught her to read the Sanskrit classics of Hinduism. After her father's death she toured all of India's holy shrines and amazed audiences by her knowledge of Sanskrit poetry. As Robert Ellsberg writes, "Her knowledge of Sanskrit, the sacred language of Hinduism, eventually won her fame and honor. She was given the honorific title 'Pandita,' mistress of wisdom."[75]

Ramabai married at twenty-two, but her husband died after only sixteen months of marriage, leaving her a widow with an infant daughter. As she traveled around India she now became sensitized to the plight of widows and orphans, and so she began to dedicate her life to women's rights in India. Such commitment to social justice brought her into contact with Christian missionaries, and, on a journey to England, she asked to be baptized a Christian. When she returned to India amid angry reactions from Indian Hindus, Ramabai continued to be involved in much charitable work, "founding a center for unwed mothers, a program for famine relief, and a series of schools for poor girls."[76] But now it was her fellow Christians who were her bitter critics. They were angered because she made no efforts to convert the women she served. But Ramabai continued in her work and refused to be intimidated. She strongly believed that "to serve women and the poor was a religious and not simply a social work,"[77] and so was a real expression of preaching the gospel. In the 1890s she underwent a second conversion that was evangelical and Pentecostal in nature, and in 1905 the school she had founded experienced a Pentecostal style renewal.[78]

Ramabai had a real aversion to the cultural insensitivity of foreign missionaries in India and was convinced that one could be a Christian and not betray Indian culture and values. In her later years, Ellsberg writes, she "prayed not for the conversion of Hindus but for the conversion of Indian Christians"[79] — not obviously a conversion back to Hinduism but to the gentle way of Jesus, and what we would call today his "dialogue method."

Mission as Prophetic Dialogue

Although this chapter has been an extended reflection on "mission as dialogue," and although dialogue "must be manifested in the whole of missionary and pastoral activity,"[80] mission simply *as dialogue* is not enough. Ultimately, we believe, mission is best done in *prophetic* dialogue.[81] To reverse the emphasis of what we have said at the beginning, Paul certainly becomes "all things to all people," "a slave to all," but this is because "woe to me if I do not preach the gospel" (see 1 Cor. 9:16–23). Paul writes that he was "gentle among" the Thessalonians, and that he gave them his very self, but he also gave them "the gospel of God" (1 Thess. 1:7–8). South African missiologist David Bosch speaks of mission done in real vulnerability and humility, but he also speaks of mission done in "bold humility," or with a "humble boldness." We do not have the "corner" on God's love and mercy when we offer the gospel. "We know only in part, but we do know. And we believe that the faith we profess is both true and just, and should be proclaimed."[82]

To say mission must be done in *prophetic* dialogue is to take back not one thing that has been said in this chapter. Mission must first and foremost be done with openness and respect for the other, recognizing that God was present before our arrival, that the Spirit has sown the seeds of the word among all peoples and all cultures, and that we missionaries need to be evangelized by those whom we evangelize. However, as we will explain further in the following chapter, we *do* have something to say, and we speak, like the prophets of the Old Testament, not in our own name, but in God's. As God sent Jesus, so Jesus has sent us, to be his witnesses to the ends of the earth (see John 20:21; Acts 1:8). Dialogue is the "how" of mission, and in many ways the "what" of mission as well, because it is a sacrament of the way God is. Being prophetic develops and makes explicit that sacrament and gives it a shape and a name. Christians must speak in the context of dialogue, but we *must* speak, for we indeed have something to say: we are not ashamed of the gospel, because "it is the power of God for salvation to everyone who has faith" (Rom. 1:16).

Conclusion

Yes, the gospel about which Christians are not ashamed "is the power of God for salvation for everyone who has faith." It is the *power of God,* which is not a power that overwhelms or forces, but a power that leads patiently and gently to freedom and abundant life. This is why Paul, with all his confidence in the gospel, came "gently among" the Thessalonians and gave not only the gospel, but his very self. This is why, although the task of mission clothes Christians with the mantle of the prophets — especially the mantle of the great prophet Jesus — it also bestows on them the yoke of him who, in his prophecy, was "gentle and humble in heart" (Matt. 11:29).

Chapter 3

"I Am Not Ashamed of the Gospel"

Mission as Prophecy

Some years ago on a visit to Boston, one of us (Steve Bevans) found himself riding on the rapid transit system Bostonians call the "T." At one point in the trip, a young woman boarded the train and walked up and down the aisle, chanting over and over again an appeal to save the whales, to safeguard the environment, to treat the earth and all its creatures with responsibility and love. After apparently walking through all the cars on the train, the woman got off and waited for the train going in the opposite direction so she could continue proclaiming her important and urgent message. The people on the train seemed rather embarrassed or, in more cases, indifferent. They may well have heard her appeal before. Probably, for several hours or for the whole day she simply repeated her message about ecological responsibility to the passengers of every train she rode.

Although he was one of the embarrassed ones, Steve suddenly realized that what the woman was doing on the Boston T was not all that different — in form at least — from what the prophets did in Israel. The prophet Jeremiah once walked through Jerusalem wearing a yoke (Jer. 27–28), entreating Judah to submit to Yahweh's will by accepting defeat by Babylon. Although this action was hardly popular with the king or with the people in general, Jeremiah spoke nevertheless "the word of the Lord." In season, out of season, despite opposition, derision, and persecution, the prophet is the one who discerns the meaning of daily events and speaks God's word to God's people. The prophet, too, is the one who is impassioned by that word, who feels its urgency, and who sees its implications for the future. Such were Jeremiah and Amos and Isaiah and Hosea; such was the Lord Jesus; and such must be the church, missionary by its very nature.[1] Indian missiologist Michael Amaladoss suggests that prophecy might be the best single word to express the reality of mission in today's world.[2]

Mission, of course, as we spoke about it in the previous chapter, is also an activity done in dialogue. It is dialogical because it is the participation by Christians in the very mission of God, and God in God's life and activity is dialogical. It was in dialogue that God offered and constantly renewed the Covenant with the chosen people of Israel, and it was in dialogue that God fully manifested Godself in the life, ministry, teaching, death and resurrection of Jesus of Nazareth.[3] "Dialogue is . . . the norm and necessary manner of every form of Christian mission, as well as of every aspect of it, whether one speaks of simple presence and witness, service or direct proclamation. Any sense of mission not permeated by such a dialogical spirit would go against the demands of true humanity and against the teachings of the Gospel."[4]

But if mission is an act of dialogue it can still be characterized as an act of prophecy. If mission is and must be dialogical because God is dialogical both in God's deepest nature and in the way God acts in the world, mission is and must be prophetic because God's inner nature is also prophetic, and because God is prophetic in dealing with creation. In the dialogue that is the Trinity, Holy Mystery eternally "speaks forth" the Word and, through the Word, breathes forth the Spirit. From the first moment of creation, that Spirit has been breathed forth upon the whole of creation and has been made concrete in the incarnate Word. It is the Spirit who comes with power upon the prophets and anoints them to speak God's Word faithfully, to bring good news to the oppressed, healing to those who are discouraged, liberty to captives, release to prisoners, comfort to those who mourn, but condemnation to those who have betrayed the covenant (see Isa. 61:1–4). As we read in 2 Peter 1:21, "no prophecy ever came by human will; but men and women moved by the holy Spirit from God." It is this same Spirit who comes upon Jesus at his baptism in the Jordan (Matt. 3:16; Mark 1:10; Luke 3:22), "drove" him into the desert to be tempted (Mark 1:12), and anoints him for his ministry of bringing good news to the poor, proclaiming release to captives, healing the blind, liberating the oppressed (see Luke 4:18). As Edward Schillebeeckx and many others have argued in their works, the best way to understand Jesus and his ministry is to understand him as he understood himself: as a prophet, the eschatological prophet who

preached, demonstrated, and embodied the Reign of God, the fulfillment
of all the hopes of Israel, and through Israel, humankind.[5]

If, then, God is a God of prophecy and the church shares in God's
mission, mission must be lived out as prophecy as well. It is our task,
as members of Christ's body and conformed to him in baptism, to
preach, demonstrate, and embody the Reign of God in our ecclesial and
individual lives.

The Nature of Prophecy

What, however, does it mean to be a prophet? First of all, and perhaps
somewhat ironically, being a prophet means to be someone who is rooted
in dialogue: someone who listens, who is attentive, who sees, who has
a sensitivity to the world and to women and men.[6] Prophets are women
and men who have listened carefully to God, who are able to discern
the signs of the times, who are attentive to people's expressions, tone
of voice, body language. Jesus, the great prophet, was also a person of
dialogue.

Second and etymologically, a prophet is someone who "speaks forth"
(Greek: *pro ephein*), and this in two senses. In a first sense, once having
heard or discerned the Word of God, the prophet faithfully announces
a message, either in words (e.g., the message of consolation in Isa. 41;
Jesus' Sermon on the Mount in Matt. 5–7, or amazing parables) or in
deeds (Jeremiah and the loincloth in Jer. 13:1–11; Jesus' healings and
exorcisms). In a second sense more associated with popular notions of a
prophet, the prophet "speaks forth" the future. Such predictions of the
future, however, are not mere "fortune telling," but the setting out of
a vision of what God has in store for people in God's plan of salvation
(e.g., Isaiah's marvelous imagery of the "mountain of the Lord" in Isa.
2:2–4, or Ezekiel's memorable prophecy over the dry bones in Ezek. 37;
Jesus' promise of blessing for those who live the values of the Reign of
God in Matt. 5:1–11).

Third, prophets speak *out* in God's name when people refuse to live
lives worthy of their calling. Thus Amos railed against the injustices that
Israel committed against the poor (Amos 2:6–7). Hosea and Jeremiah
call Israel back from unfaithfulness and idolatry (e.g., Hos. 6:1–11;
Jer. 18:1–17), as does Joel in the passage we read every year on Ash
Wednesday (Joel 2:15–17). Jesus condemns any narrow understanding

of Judaism that fails to recognize it as a religion of the heart (e.g., Matt. 12:1–14; Mark 2:13–17).

Speaking out also entails predicting the future, for if Israel continues on the path of unfaithfulness it will see destruction. Joel predicts the coming of the "day of the Lord...a day of darkness and gloom" (Joel 2:1–2) if Israel does not repent. Jesus laments over Jerusalem as "the city that kills the prophets" and predicts the destruction of the temple (Matt. 23:37–24:2). Such news of destruction is something the prophets deliver not so much in anger but in sorrow, born out of love for their people. Jeremiah laments bitterly; Jesus weeps over Jerusalem.

Prophecy, like mission itself, is a complex reality. It has several aspects, often intertwined. It is accomplished through words, and it is accomplished through deeds as well. The prophet is someone steeped in God's Word. The prophecy that she or he delivers is never her or his own word, but God's. Sometimes prophecy is a joyful task (Jesus rejoicing in the Spirit in Luke 10:21–22); sometimes it is difficult (as when Jeremiah complains about his task in Jer. 20:7–18). It is always a task done out of love for God's people, and never out of disgust or hatred. As Gregory Nazianzen powerfully says, Christians sometimes must correct their brothers and sisters, "but this with gentleness and love, not as an enemy but like a doctor who is precise and knows where to cauterize and cut." And he also cautions those who undertake this prophetic action to be aware of their own weakness.[7] But the prophet must be faithful to the task, even to the point of persecution and death.

Mission as Prophecy

"Speaking Forth" without Words: Witness

Always listening, always open, always learning from the peoples among whom it works, the church witnesses to the truth, the joy, and the life-giving power of the gospel. Pope Paul VI says that the "first means of evangelization is the witness of an authentically Christian life."[8] In the same document, the pope speaks famously about the power of witness. People today, he says, do not listen very much to what people *say* — to teachers. They listen rather to witnesses. And if they do listen to teachers, "it is because they are witnesses."[9] The pope talks eloquently about how a community of Christians might be witnesses in a way that is a truly prophetic act:

Take a Christian or a handful of Christians who, in the midst of their own community, show their capacity for understanding and acceptance, their sharing of life and destiny with other people, their solidarity with the efforts of all for whatever is noble and good. Let us suppose that, in addition, they radiate in an altogether simple and unaffected way their faith in values that go beyond current values, and their hope in something that is not seen and that one would not dare to imagine. Through this wordless witness these Christians stir up irresistible questions in the hearts of those who see how they live: Why are they like this? Why do they live in this way? What or who is it that inspires them? Why are they in our midst? Such a witness is already a silent proclamation of the Good News and a very powerful and effective one.[10]

The great British missiologist Lesslie Newbigin spoke of the Christian community as a "hermeneutic of the gospel," the way Christians interpret the gospel to the world and the way the gospel is interpreted by others. As Christians live a life of vital community, of community service, of ecological integrity, of shared prayer that is beautiful and inspiring to visitors, they speak forth without words what the gospel is and what human life might be if the gospel is lived authentically. To allude to a phrase attributed to St. Francis of Assisi, already quoted in chapter 2, this is the way that Christians can preach always, but without words.

"Speaking Forth" with Words: Proclamation

Christians in mission prophesy the future — *God's* future. Like Jesus they explain to one another and to the world — if asked (see 1 Pet. 3:15) — what the future of the world will be under God's loving providence. Like Jesus, in other words, they proclaim the message of the Reign of God. They can only use images, stories, or symbols, but they proclaim with conviction that God's plan for creation is one of full flourishing. Women and men will live in peace and justice and will enjoy the fullness of freedom; all creatures, animate and inanimate, will live in harmony. When and how this will come about is not certain, but that it will come about is. It will be a time when "swords will be turned into ploughshares" (Isa. 2:4), when "the veil that veils all peoples" will be destroyed (Isa. 25:7), when people "from every tongue and nation" (Rev. 7:9) will live together in joy and friendship.

Even more, however, humanity and creation can have a taste of this future now. The joy, the peace, the love, the harmony of God's future Reign can be found in faith in Jesus, and in his community, the church. Of course, to prophesy in such a way demands a commitment on the part of the church to be what it is in its deepest essence — God's holy People, Christ's body in history, the community open to the Spirit's creative power, molding it into a temple that shows forth God's presence. The church, as we know all too well, will never fully live the truth that it is, but it can commit itself to try. It can be an open society, confessing its failings and sinfulness. Often that is enough for people — and already a true foretaste of what God has in store for God's entire creation.

Christians prophesy by telling the world about Jesus. It is in the story of Jesus' ministry, death, and resurrection that we come to know most fully, Christians believe, who God really is. "God is like Jesus," Uruguayan theologian Juan Luis Segundo emphasized.[11] The phrase is important. It says that perhaps more important than the truth that "Jesus is God," is that the life and death of this human being is the key to understanding who God is. What Jesus reveals "is a God who is anthropocentric. God's cause is the cause of human existence. God is a God who is for humanity, as creator and thus one who is intrinsically interested and concerned about the well-being of what God creates."[12]

This is good news. This is something that women and men need to hear. So often people are caught up in either worshiping a God who is truly not worthy to be worshiped — imaged as a judge, or a tyrant, or someone who can be manipulated or persuaded with either costly sacrifices or long prayers to come to humanity's or the world's aid. Often as well people rightly deny that such a God exists, and so do not believe at all. But the God of Jesus Christ is a God who is truly on the side of God's creation — a loving God (e.g., John 3:16), a humble God (Phil. 2:6–11), a God who respects human freedom (Gal. 5:1), a God who promises life and joy even in the midst of oppression, suffering, and death (Matt. 1:26–33), a God of unconditional forgiveness (Luke 15), a God of radical inclusion (Matt. 90:9–13), a God who calls women and men to work together with God's plan for a free and flourishing humanity and cosmos (1 Pet. 2:9).

It is especially the image of Jesus on the cross that speaks most eloquently of the kind of God Jesus presents. As U.S. theologian William Placher says powerfully:

If God's primary characteristic were almighty power, then...the crucified rabbi could not be the self-revelation of God. But if God is, first of all, love, then, odd as it might seem, God is *most* God in coming to us in the form of a servant for the sake of our salvation. Starting with love, we can then even see what Gregory of Nyssa said about God's power: "God's transcendent power is not so much displayed in the vastness of the heavens or the luster of the stars or the orderly arrangement of the universe or his perpetual oversight of it, as in his condescension to our weak nature."[13]

To be prophetic in our mission is to share with the world the good news of God's future, the good news of a gracious, gentle God.

"Speaking Against" without Words: Being a Contrast Community

Christian life goes against the grain. It is not *anticultural,* because a faith rooted in the doctrine of the Incarnation loves the created world, loves people, recognizes the deep goodness of human culture. But it is profoundly *countercultural.* Living the values of the Reign of God as Jesus articulated them in the beatitudes or in the Sermon on the Mount (Matt. 5–7; Luke 7:17–49) offers a different vision of the world than what is the natural drift of society. Leading a simple life, standing for peace and justice, learning to forgive people who have offended us, living with the conviction that "unless a grain of wheat falls into the ground and dies it remains just a single grain" (John 12:24), learning to serve not to be served (Matt. 20:28) — these are all prophetic actions in a world that envisions success as being self-centered and having power over others. Christians live life in openness and dialogue, but even these attitudes are ones that often go counter to prevailing cultural values.

Christian community, being church, is also countercultural and prophetic. This is the people who by their prayer, their life together in community, their attempts to live as reconciled and reconciling, their efforts to mirror the justice for which they work in society form what Gerhard Lohfink calls a "contrast society." "The church serves the world best," Lohfink writes, "when it takes with radical seriousness its task of being a 'holy people' in the sense of 1 Pet. 2:9–10. The church is the *salt of society* precisely by living symbolically God's societal and social order."[14] Stanley Hauerwas and William Willimon, echoing Phil. 3:20,

1 Pet. 1:1 and the Letter to Diognetus, speak of the church as a community of "resident aliens" in this world. Christians are to live as a colony of the Reign of God in the midst of the world, showing forth by their lives together and by their care for the world around them what the gospel can be if it is lived seriously.[15] Another prophetic image of the church is offered by U.S. Reformed theologian Craig van Gelder. Van Gelder appeals to his boyhood growing up on a farm in Iowa where a new farming method, seed, or fertilizer was used in "demonstration plots," usually found along a major road in a particular area, to show rather reluctant farmers that these new ways could improve the yield of their crops:

> It was not uncommon for farmers to remain skeptical throughout the summer as the crops grew. But there was always keen interest in the fall when the crop was harvested. Invariably, the innovation performed better than the crops in the surrounding fields. By the next year, many farmers, including my dad, would be using the innovation as if it had been their idea all along.
>
> The church is God's demonstration plot in the world. Its very existence demonstrates that his redemptive reign has already begun. Its very presence invites the world to watch, listen, examine, and consider accepting God's reign as a superior way of living.[16]

Being the church, *truly* being the church, is a prophetic act.

"Speaking Against" in Words: Speaking Truth to Power

In accomplishing their prophetic mission Christians speak out against any form of injustice and against any form of what John Paul II called "the culture of death."[17] Christians do this individually in the workplace, in their neighborhoods, in politics, on blogs, in letters to the editor of newspapers, through participation in demonstrations like the annual demonstration at the School of the Americas at Fort Benning, Georgia. The teaching office of the church does this as well, on all levels. John Paul II's encyclical *Evangelium Vitae* is an example of this, as is the entire tradition of Catholic social teaching. National Episcopal Conferences have issued important pastoral letters, as did the U.S. bishops in 1981 and 1986 with their pastorals on peace and the economy.[18] In 1975, and again in 1995, the bishops of Appalachia in the United States issued two beautiful documents on their region: *This Land Is Home to*

Me and *At Home in the Web of Life.*[19] Both are powerful calls to justice and ecological sustainability. Individual bishops as well have issued important social justice statements, such as Cardinal Francis George's pastoral *Dwell in My Love: A Pastoral Letter on Racism.*[20]

As the "father of liberation theology" Gustavo Gutiérrez famously argued, the *annunciation* of the gospel involves at the same time the *denunciation* of anything that is contrary to it, in society or in the church itself.[21] As John Paul II put it, the "gospel of life" is the "good news" that the church needs to preach with "dauntless courage." But such good news has to be preached and lived out in confrontation with the "culture of death."[22] To speak truth to power in this way is to risk a lot — the church's position of respect in secular society, the continuation of the privileges it has had in many places since the time of Constantine, persecution in many contexts, even Christian ones. The risk no doubt has to be a calculated one, but there is no doubt that having such a prophetic voice for the poor, for human life, and for the integrity of creation is constitutive of its mission.[23]

Images of Mission as Prophecy

Prophecy, of course, is already an image of mission, as are the images of the church as a community of "resident aliens" or as "demonstration plot," about which we reflected above. But because we tend to understand a reality by "seeing through images,"[24] we might explore other images as well. Here we propose to reflect on the images of the missionary as teacher, as storyteller, and as trail guide.

Teacher

A teacher has something to teach. She or he has to be steeped in the subject to be taught and has to find ways to present the topics of a lesson in a clear, accurate, interesting, and relevant way. A teacher has to be open to questions, not threatened by them, and must be able to answer them honestly and as fully as possible. While teaching is often imparting information to students, it is also awakening them to things that they already know but are unaware of, and challenging students to learn to think for themselves, both creatively and critically. As every teacher knows as well, only a part of teaching takes place in the classroom. The teacher has to be available for consultation, to answer questions as they come up in study, to clarify things that have been said in the classroom.

Naturally, too, teaching is much more. It is living an exemplary life, a life of enthusiasm for a subject, and a life of integrity and curiosity. Paul VI says, as we have noted earlier, students will listen to teachers only if they are also witnesses. Teachers also need to be open to their students, and ready to learn from them as well. Teachers are certainly images of a prophetic approach to mission, but they are also in many ways images of the dialogical aspect of mission. The best teaching is not done, as Brazilian Paulo Freire long ago pointed out, by employing a "banking method," but by creating an atmosphere where a real community of inquiry can form.[25]

Mission might be characterized by good teaching. Christians in mission have to know what they "speak forth" in prophecy. They have to be convinced of it, love it, and model it in their lives. They need to find ways to present the teaching in a way that is not the mere imparting of information, to be memorized or learned in rote fashion. Rather, their "speaking forth" is "student centered," aiming for the real appropriation of their message. Their task is to awaken curiosity in people, giving adequate answers when they are asked to give a reason for their hope (1 Pet. 3:15). And not least important, they have to challenge those who seem impervious or indifferent to the precious knowledge that they have to offer. Their "prophecy" must always be tempered with dialogue, but they must always be convinced that they do indeed have something to teach.

Storyteller

In his delightful novel *Ireland*, Frank Delaney constructs his own plot around a *shanachie*, or traditional Irish storyteller, who in the course of the book relates the whole history of Ireland. The main character of the book, a young boy named Ronan, is fascinated when the *shanachie* comes to his home one evening and subsequently spends a good part of his youth searching for and finding the storyteller once again. In the meantime he hears other people tell the stories of the old man, listens to recordings of them, and through them grows into his identity as an Irishman.[26]

Stories have a way of doing that. Whether we listen to stories our grandfather tells after Sunday dinner, stories by old confreres in religious life, stories about the origins of our nation, stories of saints, or stories from the Scriptures, stories not only entertain. They bestow identity, they shake us up, they open us to our own deepest experiences.

A good storyteller is certainly an entertainer. She or he uses words in marvelous ways, knows how to develop suspense in her or his audience, understands how to embed a message and a moral in the most exciting tale. The British philosopher Alasdair McIntyre has characterized human beings as "story-telling animals." We think we could say as well that human beings are "story-hearing animals.[27]

Mission might be characterized as telling a story — the story of Jesus, the story of Israel, the story of the church. Like a good storyteller, missionaries need to know their audience, and they need to find ways of "entertaining" those who hear them. Their witness, their deeds tell a story. Their words, when they are asked, tell a story. The story is informative, it is formative as well, like the *shanachie* in Delaney's novel. It can challenge and convict, as did the singer in Roberta Flack's classic song "Killing Me Softly."

The missionary tells the story with the conviction that it is everyone's story and that, if the story is told well, any person from any culture and context will recognize that it is her or his own story, and can give light and depth to that person's life. At the same time, the missionary works hard to find ways to tell the story that will make sense in the particular context in which he or she works. The *story* is universal; the *way it is told* is contextual. Inculturation, in other words, is an integral part of the prophetic mission of the church.

The prophets told stories — think of Nathan telling David the story of the poor man with the little ewe lamb (2 Sam. 12:1–7), or Ezekiel's story of the dry bones (Ezek. 37:1–4), or Jesus' many parables — and the church engages in mission by telling those stories as well as new ones with courage and conviction.

Trail Guide

Trail guides know the way, and they know how to read maps. The knowledge they have is hard won. It comes from years of experience on the trail, a practiced sense of direction, a fearless self-discipline, and a seasoned ability to lead others. But there is something inborn about a trail guide, too. She or he has been given the gift of being able to read the signs of impending storms, how to stay the course on a path that keeps on

forking, and to offer words of caution or warning in the face of potential danger, like the proximity of a bear or the suddenness of a steep
cliff. When people lag behind, want to wander off, or are distracted by
a beautiful plant or waterfall, the trail guide keeps them going, encourages them to keep moving so that they arrive at their day's destination
on time. When someone insists on taking another way, the trail guide
can give reasons why his or her way is safer and surer. And when someone wants to give up and go back, the trail guide encourages and even
challenges him or her to keep going, and not to give up. Sometimes he
or she can be pretty fierce in calling people to task, but this is always
done for the welfare of the whole group and for the success of the journey. Because of the intimate knowledge of the land through which the
group is traveling, the trail guide is able to point out aspects of nature,
tell stories about the places through which the group walks, or reminisce
about the hundreds of hikers who have gone before them on the trail.
Because of the trail guide's knowledge, the group sees and experiences
much more than it ever could on its own. On the other hand, the trail
guide is open to the fresh perspectives that the group might bring and
often learns a lot from their enthusiasm, their questions, and their own
previous experiences. The ultimate goal of the trail guide is to teach the
group how to walk the trail on their own. The trail guide knows the
way, but the path is not one that she or he has forged. Rather, the path
is one that other trail guides have followed for many generations.

In the Acts of the Apostles, the early Jesus movement was spoken of
as the Way, and so it is quite appropriate that Christians in mission are
like trail guides. They need to have a deep experience of the journey of
faith, and they need to recognize the gifts of discernment and prophecy
that are theirs in baptism, and also present in the ones among whom
they work. They have a sense that the path on which they lead people
to faith is not their own because there is only one Way.

Theirs is a ministry of clearly showing the way, pointing out the paths
that should be taken and paths to be avoided. When people want to take
their own path or want to turn around, Christians who engage in mission
as prophecy call people back to the right direction. When people become
tired and discouraged in a world that ridicules Christian values, the prophetic role is one of encouragement and, if necessary, challenge — even
fierce challenge. But, like the trail guide, any fierceness is grounded in a
deep concern for the well-being of the community and for the integrity

of the gospel. As they journey with a people, Christians in mission show them aspects of life and of the world that only a Christian vision can perceive. It is not that these things have not been there before, but the missionary as prophet helps them see them even more clearly. Christians in mission inspire, challenge, encourage, and enlighten. They are prophets, trail guides on the journey of life.

Inspirations for Mission as Prophecy

In Robert Ellsberg's marvelous collection of saints' lives, entitled *All Saints*,[28] a number of candidates for "inspiration" appear: prophetic figures like Bartolomé de Las Casas, Patrick of Ireland, Lanza del Vasto, Mother Teresa, George Fox, Katherine Drexel, Cesar Chavez, Mary McKillop, Thea Bowman, Chico Mendez, Oscar Romero, and Jerzy Popieluszko. The history of the church and its mission is replete with prophetic figures. Given limitations of space, however, and recognizing that this study is not meant to be exhaustive, we will focus on three prophetic figures in the church's mission: Spanish Jesuit Francis Xavier, Ugandan Bishop Janani Luwum, and American pacifist Dorothy Day.

Francis Xavier (1506–52)

Francis Xavier of the Basque region of Spain was a member of the first group to join Ignatius of Loyola's "Company of Jesus," or "Jesuits." After over a year's sea voyage, he arrived in the Portuguese settlement of Goa on the west coast of India, filled with zeal to proclaim the gospel and "save souls." In Goa, Francis was shocked by the immorality and violence of the colonists and, with all the passion of a prophet, he wrote letters back to Europe condemning such scandalous behavior. He soon moved from Goa and focused his efforts on proclaiming the gospel primarily among the poor and lower castes in southern India. Because of his fervent and effective preaching, thousands converted their lives and were baptized. His missionary zeal would later take him to present-day Malaysia, Indonesia, and Japan.

During his early years in Asia, Francis, a man of his time, did not have much respect for local cultures, but in Japan he underwent a major change or "conversion" through which he overcame his European ethnocentrism and acknowledged the cultural richness of the Japanese people. As a result, he developed a mission approach of accommodation that shaped the foundations of the small but vibrant Japanese Christian communities and the work of future missionaries in Japan. He did this by recognizing that the gospel needed to be preached first to local leaders, the *daimyo,* and so he dressed not in the common cotton fabric of the poor, but in the silk garments more acceptable to the leaders. He also engaged in discussion with Buddhist monks, a small number of whom were baptized. In Japan Francis discovered that his passion for proclamation needed to take on ways that would make it more acceptable and intelligible to the Japanese mind and heart.

After only twenty-seven months in Japan and having baptized one thousand Japanese, Francis then set his sights on entering the vast Chinese Empire to proclaim the gospel there, but he died on an island in sight of the Chinese coast. In 1927, he was named, together with Thérèse of Lisieux, patron of mission, no doubt for his prophetic passion to proclaim the gospel.[29]

Janani Luwum (1924–77)

Janani Luwum was the Anglican archbishop of Uganda during the reign of terror of the dictator Idi Amin. In ways reminiscent of the early years of Archbishop Oscar Romero in El Salvador, Luwum at first wanted to have nothing to do with politics and tried to maintain friendly relations with Amin, frequently saying "We are with you, your Excellency, with all that you do that is good." But Amin was doing less and less good as tens of thousands were executed, sometimes very cruelly. By 1977 Amin began to circulate rumors that the bishops were planning a rebellion against his regime; Luwum responded angrily and demanded proof of the president's accusation. In response to this, government troops surrounded the archbishop's residence and proceeded to search it for evidence of Amin's accusation — all of this while holding Luwum at gunpoint. The Ugandan bishops then issued a strong prophetic statement that condemned the violence that was racking the country in no uncertain terms. Soon after the bishops were called into Amin's presence and accused of amassing weapons to use against him, and when they were dismissed Amin ordered Archbishop Luwum to stay behind.

The Archbishop was never seen again. The government first said that he had been killed in an automobile accident, then as he attempted to resist arrest. Later it was discovered that he had been shot by Amin himself when, knowing that his time had come, he had begun to pray. At the archbishop's funeral, Ellsberg writes, Luwum's predecessor, Archbishop Erica Sabiti, proclaimed the words of the angel at the tomb of the Risen Jesus: "He is not here. . . . He is risen."[30]

Dorothy Day (1897–1980)

The beginning of Dorothy Day's life showed evidence of anything but holiness and missionary zeal. As a young socialist journalist she had an affair with the American playwright Eugene O'Neill, became pregnant by another man and had an abortion, and lived in a common law marriage. When she became pregnant again, however, she decided to have the child, and her relationship with her partner came to an end. She converted to Catholicism because she saw the Catholic Church as the church of the poor, and after she met Peter Maurin, an itinerant French philosopher and mystic, they together published a newspaper called the *Catholic Worker* and founded a house of hospitality by the same name. The newspaper championed socialist and union causes and took a strong pacifist stance, and the house was open to any and all. Day was jailed many times for her demonstrations against U.S. involvement in World War II (a very unpopular cause!), nuclear armament, civil rights policies, and the Vietnam War. If ever there was a prophet, she was certainly one, even though she set a high standard for prophetic activity.[31]

Conclusion: Mission as Prophetic Dialogue

In speaking about mission as dialogue in the last chapter, we offered the beautiful passage from the Second Letter to the Thessalonians, in which Paul speaks of how he was "gentle among" the people of Thessalonica, like a nurse caring for her children (2:7), and a little further, as "a father treats his children" (2:11). If one reads the entire passage, however, what is evident is that Paul balances these more "dialogical" images with "prophetic" ones. Paul speaks about how he came to Thessalonica after having been "insolently treated" (2:2) in Philippi. Even so, however, he "drew courage through our God to speak to you the gospel of God" (2:2). Paul talks about "being entrusted with the gospel," and so speaking in the name of God (2:4). He speaks about how he worked night and day in proclaiming the gospel, so as not to be a burden on anyone, and exhorted and encouraged the people to conduct themselves in a way worthy of the God that called them (2:9, 12). Indeed, Paul says in Romans 1:16 that he is "not ashamed of the gospel. It is the power of God for the salvation of everyone who believes." Paul preaches it gladly, joyfully, seeing his work as a priestly service making the Gentiles a worthy offering to God in the Spirit (see Rom. 15:16).

Mission is done in dialogue. Mission is done in prophecy. The two go together. While we can distinguish them to better understand the whole, we cannot and dare not separate them. Mission is prophetic dialogue. It is dialogical prophecy. The question is not "is it one or the other?" The question is rather *when* should the dialogical aspect of missionary service be emphasized or employed more fully and *when* should one act or speak prophetically in action, in words, in confrontation. Like life itself, and like any ministry, engaging in God's mission is an art. One needs to be in touch with the sources of creativity, the Holy Spirit, to know just how to proceed. It is the Spirit who opens our ears to listen, and who anoints our tongues to speak, who enflames our hearts to witness.

Chapter 4

Mission in the Twenty-first Century

Prophetic Dialogue and Contextual Theology

In a talk given at Catholic Theological Union, Chicago, several years ago, eminent Vietnamese-American theologian Peter C. Phan suggested that "mission" is "not an innocent word." There is no doubt that, in the name of mission, very much harm has been done to peoples and cultures throughout the world. "Mission Island" as depicted in the film *Australia* may have had some redeeming factors, but we also know that it was probably very much like the horrible school for Aboriginal children that we read about in novels like *Rabbit-Proof Fence*.[1] In his powerful doctoral dissertation on reconciliation in Australia, our friend Gerard Goldman speaks about the well-meaning but stifling structures in mission "dormitories" for Aboriginal boys and "convents" for Aboriginal girls.[2] Peter Matthiessen's *At Play in the Fields of the Lord* and Barbara Kingsolver's *The Poisonwood Bible* certainly strengthen the stereotype that, at least from the perspective of contextual theology, mission has *nothing* to offer the church of the twenty-first century.[3] As Native American Tink Tinker has written so bluntly: "Given the disastrous history of eurowestern mission practices — to the cultures and the peoplehood of those missionized — it would seem that there are no missiological projects that we might conceive that would have legitimacy of any kind."[4]

But for all the truth in these portrayals of mission, they are still stereotypes. Mission is certainly not unambiguously good, but neither have the efforts of mission been totally evil or destructive. Careful studies by Gambian historian Lamin Sanneh, professor of history at Yale University, have concluded that missionary efforts in West Africa to translate the Bible into local languages have actually served to preserve African languages and cultures today in the face of encroaching Westernization and globalization.[5] Scots church historian Andrew Walls writes of the various missionary societies of the nineteenth century acting as the "fortunate subversion of the Church."[6] What missionary work accomplished, despite its ambiguity, has nevertheless resulted in the rich world Christianity that we have today, with its resulting wealth of contextual theologies to provide what Steve Bevans has called new agendas, new methods, new voices, and a new dialogue.[7] Had there been no mission, there would be no contextual theologies to offer the church the new look at itself in our day. In April 2009 Steve spent Holy Week in the desert of central Australia. There he met the leading elder of the Northern Territory town of Yuendumu. The elder had been taken from his land at an early age to Darwin, where he was educated by the Marist Brothers and stayed most likely in one of those dormitories that Goldman speaks of in his work. And yet today, it is that education that enables him to be a powerful spokesperson against government efforts to take away his land for uranium mining.

Over and above these historical considerations, however — and we have indicated only a few — mission's lack of innocence and clear ambiguity should not keep us from recognizing its enduring value in Christian theology and practice. An earlier theology of mission — based often on a Western Enlightenment idea of Western superiority and a disdain for local cultures and ancient religious traditions — has been in need of radical revision, and it has found such revision in the last half century or so. Such revision has been carried out in two different directions.

The first direction of revision and renewal reaches back to the work of Karl Barth and Karl Hartenstein in the first half of the twentieth century and emphasizes mission's *trinitarian roots*. As the Willingen Conference in 1952 intimated, the church engages in mission not because it *has* a mission itself, but because *God* has a mission — or rather, because God *is* mission.[8] From this theological perspective, being a Christian means being baptized into God's very life, which is a life of radical communion, spilling forth in the world, drawing humanity and even creation itself into that communion. As is common to say today, it is not so much that the *church* has a mission. Rather *the mission has a church*. The church is the particular, concrete, sacramental — and imperfect — way that God works in the world to call all people into communion with God's self. As we read in Second Corinthians: "... in Christ God was reconciling the world to Godself, ... and entrusting the message of reconciliation to us. So we are ambassadors for Christ, since God is making ... appeal through us" (see 2 Cor. 5:19–20). Or, as Emil

Brunner has written famously: "The Church exists by mission as a fire exists by burning."[9] We share in God's mission because of God's amazing grace.

The second direction of revision and renewal of mission theology also has older roots, but we might trace these back to movements within the World Council of Churches and Roman Catholicism in the 1960s and 1970s. To trace only the Catholic side here, we see the notion of mission expanded in 1971 when the bishops of the world spoke of working for justice in the world as a "constitutive element of the preaching of the gospel."[10] Pope Paul VI, in his marvelous document on evangelization in the modern world (*Evangelii Nuntiandi*) in 1975, emphasized that although the witness to and proclamation of the gospel and the invitation to conversion is central to evangelization, evangelization includes other elements like efforts of inculturation (contextualization) and liberation. John Paul II, in his lengthy encyclical *The Mission of the Redeemer* (*Redemptoris Missio*) added the element of interreligious dialogue. Mission, as we will elaborate in the following chapter, cannot be reduced to one element, particularly to conversion efforts. It needs to include committing oneself to issues of justice, peace and the integrity of creation; it needs to proceed with cultural and contextual sensitivity; it needs to proclaim Christian convictions within the context of an honest dialogue with the world's religions.

If mission *is* about a call to conversion — and it is — that conversion has to be understood not so much as a call to abandon one's culture and deepest values but to imagine the world differently, to begin to see its possibilities with God's eyes. Canadian novelist Rudy Wiebe says it marvelously: "you repent, not by feeling bad, but by *thinking different*."[11] Helping people "think different" is the mission of the church: to call people to work with God in creating a world of justice, peace, reconciliation, harmony among religions, ecological integrity, cultural pride.

In the global, multicultural, minority status, poor, vulnerable, ecologically threatened church of the twenty-first century, the church exists by mission. But it is a very different kind of mission than was conceived by Anglicans, Baptists, Marists, Ursulines, Spiritans, and FMMs a century ago. It is a mission that needs to be lived out in "prophetic dialogue." It is to this theme that we turn next.

Mission as Prophetic Dialogue

"Prophetic dialogue" is the term that we used to describe mission in our 2004 book *Constants in Context*.[12] Actually, we were not the first to use it. In fact, the term "prophetic dialogue" was how our own missionary congregation, the Society of the Divine Word (SVD), decided to describe the way we SVDs engaged in mission. The phrase was coined at our General Chapter in 2000. The Asians in our congregation had proposed that we speak of doing mission simply as "dialogue," but the Latin Americans strenuously objected. For them, in the context of their commitment to liberation in the midst of Latin American poverty and political and cultural oppression, doing mission was closer to engaging in *prophecy.* As we argued about this, one of our members suggested that, as a compromise, we speak of "prophetic dialogue." Everyone seemed satisfied, and so we adopted the notion.

Mission as Dialogue

We have developed the idea of prophetic dialogue in our own way, however. For us, mission is first and foremost *dialogue.* One enters into mission with a profound openness to the place and to the people in which and among whom one works. Max Warren's famous dictum — "Our first task in approaching another people, another culture, another religion is to take off our shoes, for the place we are approaching is holy"[13] — should function as a basic text for missionary work. In a previous SVD General Chapter as well, we had developed a spirituality of "passing over" into other cultures and peoples. We first of all need to *leave* our homelands or our places of comfort (*leaving* is necessary; many missionaries really never *leave*), and *pass over* into people's cultures, languages, economic standards.[14] Another text that needs to be emphasized is one expressed in a talk by the great South African Catholic theologian Albert Nolan: "Listen, listen, listen. Ask questions. Listen!" Our colleague Claude Marie Barbour has coined the term "mission in reverse": we need to be evangelized by the people before we can evangelize them; we need to allow the people among whom we work to be our teachers before we presume to teach them.[15]

Mission as dialogue is the ministry of presence, of respect. It is a witness, at base, to the God who moves among us in dialogue, the Word become flesh, and to the communion in Godself who calls us to communion with our universe and with one another. Some of its great exemplars, some of whom we have noted in chapter 2, are women and men like Francis of Assisi, Pandita Ramabai in India, Charles de Foucauld, a French hermit and contemplative in Algeria, C. W. Andrews, or Bede Griffiths. Among several Scripture passages that we might offer as a foundation, one that particularly strikes us is Paul's description of himself and his work in First Thessalonians: "We were gentle among you, like a nurse taking care of her children. So, being affectionately desirous of you, we were ready to share with you not only the gospel of God but also our own selves, because you had become very dear to us (1 Thess. 2:7–8).

Mission as Prophecy

But authentic mission also involves prophecy, and this in several senses. First, the basic motivation for mission must be to share the astounding, challenging, self-convicting, amazing, *good* news about the God of Jesus Christ and God's vision for the world. The term "gospel" is translated in Pilipino or Tagalog in a marvelous way: as *magandang balita*, literally *beautiful* news. Prophecy is first of all a "telling forth," not on our own authority but on God's authority. This is why, in the powerful words of Pope Paul VI, there is no evangelization worthy of the name unless "the name, the teaching, the life, the promises, the kingdom, and the mystery of Jesus of Nazareth, the Son of God are proclaimed."[16] Engaging in mission is not simply for the physical betterment of humanity, the increase of communication among Christians, or the development of one's own personal depth — even though all these things are worthwhile. Mission is about the respectful, gentle, dialogical, and yet faithful speaking forth, in word and deed, of God's love revealed in Jesus of Nazareth.

The second way that mission is prophecy is, in the spirit of Old Testament prophets like Amos, Hosea, and Isaiah, its clear critique and exposure of any kind of injustice in the world. To allude again to that 1971 episcopal document, working for justice is a *constitutive part* of the prophetic preaching of the gospel. The gospel that Christians proclaim is a gospel of justice. It is the proclamation of a world of equality and participation, a world in which the greatest is the servant of all, a world of peace and opportunity. There is a long list of prophets in the history of the church's mission, among whom one might number Bartolomé de las

Casas, Pedro Claver, Martin Luther King Jr., Dorothy Day, and perhaps even dissenters like Roy Bourgeois.

Third, we might speak of the witness of the church community as prophetic. Gerhard Lohfink writes powerfully of the need for the Christian community to form a "contrast society," to be a demonstration to the world around it what the Reign of God might look like.[17] In Lesslie Newbigin's words, the church needs to be a "sign and foretaste"[18] of the coming Reign of God. Even if one would not fully espouse the "counter-cultural model" of contextual theology, there is indeed something in the Christian life and message that deeply challenges the status quo.[19] The way Christians care for one another, their hospitality, their involvement in the world of politics and the arts, their moral stances — all these can be gentle or not-so-gentle challenges to the world around them.

Prophecy does not have to be something serious or angry — although sometimes it may very well be. The new sense of liberation theology that Carmelo Álvarez speaks about is testimony to that.[20] Certainly the well-known exclamation of people of the Roman Empire in the early centuries of Christianity — "see how they love one another" — was a recognition of prophecy. Today we might want people to say: "see how they celebrate with one another!" or — as in the case of the Amish community several years ago — "see how they forgive!" But even when prophecy is angry — like the anger of the Old Testament prophets against Israel, or the anger of Jesus toward the Pharisees — it is an anger born out of love. It is only because the prophets and Jesus *loved* Israel that they could fulminate so strongly against it. Christians "tell it like it is" in the world not because the world is ultimately evil, but because of what it is and can be in God's sight.

Prophetic Dialogue

Mission needs to be done both as dialogue and as prophecy: in "prophetic dialogue." This idea is expressed as well in South African missiologist David Bosch's wonderful phrase of "bold humility."[21] We need boldly to proclaim the "beautiful news" of God's story in Jesus and God's vision for our world, but we need to do it in the way *God* does it: with patience, with respect, in dialogue.

We quoted from Paul's letter to the Thessalonians as an example of Paul doing mission in dialogue. In its full context, however, the text reflects much more an attitude of the bold humility or prophetic dialogue that we are advocating here.

> You yourselves know, brothers and sisters, that our coming to you was not in vain, but though we had already suffered and been shamefully mistreated at Philippi, as you know, we had courage in our God to declare to you the gospel of God in spite of great opposition. For our appeal does not spring from deceit or impure motives or trickery, but just as we have been approved by God to be entrusted with the message of the gospel, even so we speak, not to please mortals, but to please God who tests our hearts. As you know and as God is our witness, we never came with words of flattery or with a pretext for greed; nor did we seek praise from mortals, whether from you or from others, though we might have made demands as apostles of Christ. But we were gentle among you, like a nurse taking care of her children. (1 Thess. 2:1–7)

Paul certainly becomes "all things to all people," "a slave to all," but this is because "woe to me if I do not preach the gospel" (see 1 Cor. 9:16–23).

When one does mission in prophetic dialogue, one needs to be contextual, one needs to do theology contextually. This is what we will take up in our third and final section of this chapter.

Prophetic Dialogue and Contextual Theology

When does one need to be prophetic in participating in God's mission? When does one need to be dialogical? It is in discerning the answers to these questions that one needs to think contextually. In our global, multicultural, minority, poor, and vulnerable twenty-first century church, the way we live our Christian lives and witness to the gospel in mission will very much depend on the situation in which we find ourselves.

We would like to take the term "contextual theology" here as broadly as we can. Contextual theology will thus include not only a dialogue with local, particular cultures and with women and men in various social locations. It will also include dialogue with other Christians in mission and, indeed, with people of other religions. Taking this contextual theological approach to mission will also involve the reflection on and practice of reconciliation between various factions and enemies in the situation in which one lives. Finally, it will be in dialogical and prophetic conversation with situations of injustice and ecological danger.

As Christians engage in mission, our first attitude should be one of listening, respect, learning, and discernment. But as we listen and discern carefully we will experience the need, even the duty, to speak out. We will find creative ways to present the Christian message and will be impelled to oppose injustice or advocate reform. All of this will depend on a way of reflecting theologically that will guide and support us in our missional task.

It will be here that the various models that Stephen Bevans has proposed[22] — or other ones that people engaged in mission will discover — will come into play. Will the best way of presenting Christianity be a translation, a "putting the gospel into" a particular cultural value or in terms of a particular situation (translation model)? Will one's prophetic dialogue lead to amazing new discoveries in one's culture, or in another religion (anthropological model)? Will reflecting on one's practice of the gospel reveal even more effective ways of acting, more faithful to the gospel, more effective in the context (praxis model)? Will the experience of outsiders challenge or illumine the way one does mission in new ways (synthetic model)? Or will an alternate way, the way of the gospel, witness to the power of the gospel in a situation of secularity, consumerism, or overreliance on individual choice (countercultural model)?

Conclusion

When Steve first wrote his *Models of Contextual Theology,* he says he used to stress that the book was not one about *missiology* but *systematic theology* — or theological method. This is certainly true. However, as he has developed his own thinking about contextual theology on the one hand and mission on the other, he has come to realize that the book is very much a missiological work. In the same way that Christians cannot do theology that is not contextual, so Christians cannot engage in mission that is not contextual. The way we live as Christians — which is to live in mission — is constantly to live in dialogue with and discerning our context, and correlating that context with the broader and older Christian tradition. Only in this way can we dare to take up the prophetic mantle of Jesus, as God has given it through the Holy Spirit.

Chapter 5

Unraveling a "Complex Reality"

Six Elements of Mission

"Mission," writes Pope John Paul II in *Redemptoris Missio*, "is a single but complex reality, and it develops in various ways."[1] There is only *one* mission, the mission of God as such, in which the church *shares* (see e.g., Gal. 2:20; Phil. 1:21; 1 Cor. 10:16–17; Matt. 10:40; John 20:21) and *continues* (see Matt. 28:18–20; Mark 16:15–16; Luke 24:44–47; Acts 1:8) by preaching, serving, and witnessing to Jesus' Lordship and vision of the Reign of God (Acts 28:31). The church does this in four "fields" — in its pastoral work, in its commitment to the "new evangelization," in its efforts toward the transformation of society and culture, and in its movement to all peoples in the mission *ad gentes* (*Redemptoris Missio*, 34). At every level as well, there are operative six "elements": (1) witness and proclamation; (2) liturgy, prayer, and contemplation; (3) justice, peace, and the integrity of creation; (4) dialogue with women and men of other faiths and ideologies; (5) inculturation; and (6) reconciliation.

But why *six* elements? Opinions certainly vary. In 1981 the Catholic organization called SEDOS (Service of Documentation and Studies, sponsored by missionary orders headquartered in Rome) spoke of *four* elements of mission, adding dialogue, inculturation and liberation to the traditional element of proclamation.[2] In 1984, a document entitled "Dialogue and Mission" was issued by what was then known as the Secretariat for Non-Christians at the Vatican, and it named *five* elements: presence and witness; development and liberation; liturgical life, prayer, and contemplation; interreligious dialogue; and proclamation and catechesis.[3] In 1991, David Bosch's *Transforming Mission* spoke of *thirteen* "elements of an emerging ecumenical paradigm" of mission.[4] In 1999 Andrew Kirk outlined *seven* elements, as did Donal Dorr in 2000.[5]

In an effort to synthesize these various namings of elements, Eleanor Doidge and Stephen Bevans wrote an essay in 2000 in which they named the six elements on which we will reflect here.[6] For us, witness and proclamation were bound together; Andrew Kirk's important insistence on ecological concerns as integral to mission should be paired with the equally important elements of justice and peace; and Robert Schreiter's insistence on reconciliation as a new model of mission[7] needed to be fully acknowledged. In addition, unlike in contrast with the document "Dialogue and Mission," Bevans and Doidge were convinced that inculturation is an essential part of every missionary task. And so their synthesis was of six elements. What we offer here are very brief reflections on each of these six.

Witness and Proclamation

The interconnectedness of Christian witness and explicit proclamation of the gospel is perhaps expressed most clearly in the charge attributed to St. Francis of Assisi (repeated several times in this volume): "Preach always; if necessary use words." As Pope Paul VI wrote in *Evangelii Nuntiandi,* "the first means of evangelization is the witness of an authentically Christian life";[8] and the 1991 document *Dialogue and Proclamation* insists that proclamation "is the foundation, summit, and center of evangelization."[9] Witness and proclamation go together. "The deed," wrote David Bosch, "without the word is dumb; the word without the deed is empty."[10]

The church's missionary witness is of at least four kinds. At a first level, there is the witness of individual Christians. Some of these may be quite public and acclaimed, like the witness of Albert Schweitzer or Mother Teresa. But most Christian witness is given by Christians in their ordinary lives — in the patience of parents, the honesty of Christians in business, the dedication of teachers, the choices made about where to live, where to shop, how one is entertained. Second, there is the witness of the Christian community — the "hermeneutic of the gospel" as Lesslie Newbigin famously put it.[11] Third, we can speak of the church's institutional witness in its schools, hospitals, social service agencies, and orphanages. And, last but certainly not least, there is the "common witness" of Christians of various traditions committed to common prayer, common educational ventures, common work for justice, and the like. As the *Manila Manifesto* so aptly puts it: "If the task of world evangelization is ever to be accomplished, we must engage in it together."[12]

John Paul II has spoken of proclamation — the explicit proclamation of the Lordship of Jesus and of his vision of the Reign of God — as "the permanent priority of mission."[13] The task of evangelization would be empty, said Paul VI, without proclaiming "the name, the teaching, the life, the promises, the Kingdom, and the mystery of Jesus of Nazareth, the Son of God."[14] Nevertheless, proclamation needs always to be done dialogically, taking account of the situation of those to whom the good news is addressed. It can never be done apart from witness, for, "no matter how eloquent our verbal testimony, people will always believe their eyes first."[15] Moreover, proclamation is always to be given as an invitation, respecting the freedom of the hearers; it is never done in a manipulative way. *"The church proposes,"* insists Pope John Paul II, *"she imposes nothing."*[16] Finally, authentic proclamation is the answer to a question, giving "the reason for our hope" (see 1 Pet. 3:15). The first task of evangelization, mused Cardinal Francis George on a visit to the school where we teach, is to listen. To proclaim out of context, without listening to how the gospel answers people's deepest yearnings and hopes, is to proclaim in a way that is unworthy of the gospel's power.

Liturgy, Prayer, and Contemplation

The church, says Lutheran liturgist Robert Hawkins, "lives from the center with its eyes on the borders."[17] Liturgy is a dead end if it is its own end. Our colleague Richard Fragomeni said once that the goal of liturgy is *worship* — and worship is not what takes place in a church but in the world. Liturgy needs to be celebrated "inside out,"[18] as an anticipation of the "liturgy after the liturgy," as the Orthodox say. Celebration of the liturgy is an evangelizing act on several levels. It is always the evangelization of the Christian faithful who day after day, week after week make up the liturgical assembly, forming them more perfectly into Christ's body in the world and calling each individually to more authentic Christian life. But, since there are always visitors in the congregation who may be nonbelievers or the unchurched, the worthy and vital celebration of the liturgy in Eucharist, baptism, marriages or funerals can be moments when the gospel proclaimed and celebrated may find particular resonance in those who are seeking more depth in life or may even be able to break through indifference or resistance.

In 1927, Pope Pius XI declared Francis Xavier and Thérèse of Lisieux as patrons of the church's missionary activity. The Jesuit Francis Xavier was no surprise; his exploits on behalf of the gospel in India and Japan make him one of the greatest missionaries of all times. But naming Thérèse was unusual. After all, she was a strictly cloistered Carmelite nun and never left her convent in France. Nevertheless, her autobiography, published a few years after her death, revealed her to be a woman on fire for the gospel, whose heart was always beyond her convent walls, calling all humanity to faith in Christ. Her life of prayer was so intense, so universal, so missionary, that she could very justly be named patroness of the missions. The pope's action in 1927 points to the truth that commitment to the spread of the gospel is not simply a matter of heroic work in cross-cultural situations; it is a matter of allowing the missionary task to shape Christian spirituality. Prayer and contemplation is seeing and feeling with the missionary God, aligning one's needs and wants with the saving activity of God's missionary presence in the world. The British series *Dr. Who* provides a striking example of how prayer and contemplation can be missionary. Dr. Who would enter a certain telephone booth, the inside of which contained the whole world. The cloister, the parish church, one's room is like that telephone booth.

Justice, Peace, and the Integrity of Creation

"Action on behalf of justice...fully [appears] to us as a constitutive dimension of the preaching of the Gospel."[19] "If you want peace, work for justice."[20] "We discern two types of injustice: socio-economic-political injustice...and environmental injustice."[21] "The responsibility of the church towards the earth is a crucial part of the church's mission."[22] Commitment to justice, peace, and the integrity of creation weaves a seamless garment. All are constitutive of the church's missionary task.

Commitment to the poor and marginalized of the world takes shape in the first place as the church acts as a voice for the victims of injustice on the one hand and a goad to the consciences of the rich on the other. People like Oscar Romero and Desmond Tutu, and documents like the U.S. bishops' peace and economics pastorals and the Kairos Document in South Africa are shining examples of this justice ministry. Second, the church needs to work to help those who suffer injustice find their *own* voice. If the church did only the first it would ultimately only be patronizing. The goal of justice ministry is helping the poor and marginalized find their own subjectivity and hope. Third, the commitment to justice inevitably means committing oneself to a life practice that is in solidarity with the victims of this world, through a simple lifestyle, through political stances, through a constant siding with the poor and oppressed and their causes. Finally, as the 1971 Synod puts it, a church committed to justice must be just itself: "everyone who ventures to speak about justice must first be just in their eyes."[23]

In 1981, Pope John Paul II visited Hiroshima, the site of the first hostile use of the atomic bomb in 1945. "From now on," he said, "it is only through a conscious choice and through a deliberate policy that humanity can survive."[24] The mission of the church involves making sure that governments and other groups keep making that "conscious choice" and follow that "deliberate policy" toward peace. In a similar way, the church's commitment to justice cannot but be concerned for personal and institutional witness of simplicity of life, and for support of legislation and movements that promote the integrity of creation and the care of the earth. Repentance, wrote Canadian novelist Rudy Wiebe, is not "feeling bad," but *thinking different.*"[25] The Kingdom call to "repent and believe" takes on a whole new dimension in the light of today's consciousness of creation's fragility and humanity's vocation to stewardship.

Interreligious / Secular Dialogue

"Dialogue is ... the norm and necessary manner of every form of Christian mission."[26] This general norm for doing mission, however, has particular relevance as Christians encounter people of other faiths or people who have no faith at all. Mission is carried out "in Christ's way," reflective of the dialogical nature of God's trinitarian self. Dialogue is based on the conviction that "the Spirit of God is constantly at work in ways that pass human understanding and in places that to us are least expected."[27] Documents speak of four kinds of dialogue. There is, first, the *dialogue of life,* in which Christians live and rub shoulders with people of other faiths and ideologies. In this way people get to know each other, respect each other, learn from each other, and reduce the tensions that exist among people who may have radically different worldviews. Second, we speak of the *dialogue of social action,* by which women and men of differing faith commitments work together for common issues of justice. Working together for fairer immigration laws, for the abolition of the death penalty, for the sacredness of human life, and against racism and sexism are ways that committed people can learn to live with one another and be inspired by the social doctrines of the various religious and secular traditions. Third, there is the *dialogue of theological exchange.* While this may be an area for experts as they probe one another's doctrines and practices, challenging and inspiring one another, it can also take place among ordinary Christians as they read one another's sacred documents and cherished authors. Finally, there is the *dialogue of religious experience.* While there always will remain differences of content and method, this is an area where many traditions seem to converge in major ways. While perhaps people of differing faiths may not be able to pray *together,* they can — as Pope John Paul II did at Assisi in 1986 and 2002 — come together to pray in their own ways.

Inculturation

Throughout the history of the church there have been many prophetic Christians who have practiced in some way what we call today "inculturation." Peter and Paul, Justin Martyr, Francis of Assisi, Clare, Raymond Lull, Matteo Ricci, Martin Luther, Mother Teresa, Roland Allen, and Charles de Foucauld are just a few names that come to mind. Nevertheless, today there is an understanding that inculturation is not just something for a few women and men who live dangerously "on the edge." Rather, inculturation is acknowledged today as an integral part of communicating the gospel, if the gospel, indeed, is truly to be *communicated.* "You may, and you must, have an African Christianity," proclaimed Paul VI in 1969.[28] "Contextualization ... is not simply nice," writes Evangelical missiologist David Hesselgrave. "It is a necessity."[29]

The central place of inculturation in today's understanding of mission is something that has emerged only as theology and spirituality began to recognize the essential role of experience in any kind of human living. Traditionally, theology was seen as reflection in faith on Scripture and Tradition. There was one theology, always and everywhere valid.

As theology began to acknowledge the anthropological turn that has so marked Western modern consciousness, the role of experience in theology became more influential. It was not, however, that experience was just *added* to the traditional sources of Scripture and tradition; the anthropological turn revealed the fact that Scripture and Tradition themselves were highly influenced by the experiences of women and men in particular times, places, and cultural contexts. And so experience has taken on a normative value that it did not have in times past. The theology of the West, we now recognize, was itself a limited, contextual product of a particular set of experiences. Every time and every culture has to reflect on faith on its own terms, and needs to use its own lens to interpret Scripture, past doctrinal formulations, ethical practices, and liturgical customs. Today the experience of the past (Scripture and Tradition) and the experience of the present (context) may interact in various ways that are conditioned by particular circumstances and/or theological convictions, but whether Christian faith needs to engage a context authentically is simply accepted as a missiological imperative.[30]

Reconciliation

In a world of increasing violence, tensions between religions, terrorist actions and continuous threats, globalization and displacement of peoples, the church's witness to and proclamation of the possibility of reconciliation may constitute a new way of conceiving the content of the church's missionary task. Mission today recognizes that reconciliation needs to take place on a number of different levels. There is, first, the *personal* level of healing between spouses, between victims and their torturers or oppressors, among victims of natural calamities such as earthquakes or tropical storms. Then there is the reconciliation between members of oppressed cultures like Australian Aboriginals, North American First Nations, Latin American Indigenous tribes, and those who have oppressed and marginalized them for centuries. A third level of reconciliation might be called *political*. One may think of the reconciliation called for after years of Apartheid in South Africa, or by years of forced disappearances and massacres as in Argentina or Guatemala.

Reconciliation, insists Robert Schreiter, involves much more of a *spirituality* than a *strategy*.[31] In the first place, reconciliation is the work of God, a work of grace, and is offered first and foremost by the victims of injustice and violence. The church's task is not to develop strategies for this to take place, but to witness in its life and proclaim in fearless hope that God's grace *does* heal and that, through the reconciling work of Jesus Christ, the barriers of hostility can be broken down and those who are divided can be made one. For "it is he who is our peace" (Eph. 2:14). To facilitate the recognition of God's gracious working in the midst of so much violence and tragedy, the church needs to develop communities of honesty, compassion, and acceptance. Ministers of reconciliation need to hone their skills of contemplative attention and listening. Strategies might be found to employ new ways of celebrating the Sacrament of Reconciliation or of ritualizing God's reconciling action in some way.

Conclusion

Mission today needs to be understood as "a single, complex reality." While it is true that the explicit, prophetic proclamation of the gospel *of* and *about* Jesus[32] has a certain "permanent priority" (*Redemptoris Missio,* 44), it is equally true that the words of proclamation must be rooted in an authentic *being* of the church, and so rooted in what we are calling in this book *dialogue.* The church is called equally to incarnate what it says in its community life and in its engagement in the world. It does this by participating in God's mission — radically dialogical as God is in God's self, and radically prophetic as is seen especially in God's speaking forth God's Word of hope, encouragement, challenge, and, where need be, condemnation.

In a world where the Spirit is constantly manifest in social and political movements, in the riches of culture, and in the holiness of many religious ways, mission can serve that Spirit only through acts of justice, trust of human experience, and dialogue with religious difference. In a world that is torn apart by so many conflicts of religion, politics, and human tragedy, the church needs to recognize that Jesus' ministry of reconciliation and peace has been entrusted to it in turn (see 2 Cor. 5:19). Mission ultimately is witness to the hope of a new heaven and a new earth, where every tear will be washed away (Rev. 21:1–5) and every tongue from every nation (Rev. 7:9) will confess that Jesus Christ is Lord (Phil. 2:11) and that God is all in all (1 Cor. 15:28).

Chapter 6

Entering Someone Else's Garden

Intercultural Mission/Ministry

In today's global village, people of different cultural (racial, religious, economic, and political) backgrounds live and work together more and more. However, while individuals representing multicultural contexts are in fact "in the same room at the same time," this does not mean that anyone is actually sharing their "world" with someone considered "other." Peaceful co-existence and minimal cooperation for the sake of attaining a common goal — whether that is following agreed-upon traffic laws, shopping in a mall, sharing recreational facilities, or attending the same school — is one thing. However, going beyond that to actually enter a mutually enriching and challenging relationship of understanding, acceptance, and care — to the point of sharing worlds of meaning in the deepest sense — with a person of a culture different from one's own is quite another. As we know, this is fairly challenging between people of common backgrounds, but it is even more rare and difficult between those of different "worlds." In this chapter, this latter process is referred to as "crossing cultures," and it implies a mutual multidirectional movement between cultures as reflected in the use of the term "intercultural" in this chapter's title. An image of a garden and several personal narratives will be used to explore the theological and ministerial dynamics of this process for those who choose this in the name of mission/ministry.[1]

A few preliminary remarks are necessary. Reference to "culture" is intended to include the other elements mentioned earlier in parenthesis, that is, race, religion, economics, and politics, as well as social location and social change. Gary Riebe-Estrella has noted that in many contexts, racism is actually the primary barrier between people of different cultures.[2] Second, religious experiences and expressions are mutually shaped by and shape one's culture. And economic and political differences interculturally, as well as intraculturally, are determining factors within this dynamic as well. Third, while the perspective of those who attempt to cross over into other cultures as a part of their Christian mission/ministry should be assumed, these reflections will also be of interest to others who attempt to cross cultures for other reasons. For example, what will be said here might be very helpful for development workers, business people, and health care providers who have no particular Christian affiliation. Fourth, this process occurs in many different ways, to very different degrees, for very different reasons. How long, for instance, will persons be living in another culture? Are they single, celibate, or married with children? Will they be living under a repressive regime or in a flourishing democracy? Fifth, and more personally, in contrast to the other chapters in this book, much of this chapter is written in the first person. This is due to the fact that it is based on the personal and missionary experience of the original author, Roger Schroeder. Recognizing all these factors, I will now proceed to describe the general movements in intercultural mission/ministry.

Introducing the Image of the Garden

Probably due to my farming background in Ohio and significant time spent with subsistence farmers in Papua New Guinea as a missionary, an agricultural image has been very helpful for me in describing the process of crossing into the cultural world of the "other," that is, *entering into someone else's garden*. Within a subsistence agricultural economy, the garden is the place upon which one absolutely depends for one's livelihood and well-being. One realizes that life or death is dependent, first of all, on the "fruits of one's own labors," but at the same time, the forces of nature and other factors beyond one's control also determine the ultimate outcome. Within the garden, one experiences on a day-to-day basis joy and sorrow, blessing and curse, life and death, good and evil. A person and community sometimes experience the presence and absence of God in the garden. Furthermore, in many cultures one's status, identity, and world of meaning are associated with the fruitfulness of one's garden. For example, in Papua New Guinea, the size and number of large ceremonial yams grown in gardens are signs of wealth and blessing.

In every garden, a gardener or farmer cultivates those plants considered beneficial and eliminates those considered harmful. As we know, Jesus used this basic imagery of the seed and the weeds in several of his parables to talk about the Reign of God. In his explanation (Luke 8:11–15) of the parable of the sower and the seed (Luke 8:5–8), Jesus describes the seed as the "word of God," and in one of several scenarios, that seed is choked by the thorns. In the parable of the darnel (Matt. 13:24–30, 36–43), the good seed (wheat) and the weeds (darnel) co-exist in the farmer's field, but they will be judiciously separated at harvest time. Finally Jesus reminds his listeners that the seed has the power to grow on its own to full fruition (Mark 4:26–29).

Theologically, I propose referring to the "seed" as "seeds of the Word," building upon and expanding Justin Martyr's use of the term *logos spermatikos* ("seed-bearing word") for divine truth already implanted in classical Hellenistic philosophy to represent the presence of that truth in each cultural "garden."[3] The harmful elements are those elements of a culture (or philosophy) that choke the truth, love, and life of God, and that are contrary to the Reign of God. While Justin Martyr stressed the *continuity* between the Christian faith and classical philosophy of his time, that is, the presence of the "good seed," his contemporary, Tertullian of Carthage, stressed the *discontinuity* between the two, that is, the presence of the "weeds." The contrasting perspectives of these two early Christian apologists point to an issue that continues to be central to the church's understanding of itself and its mission, and in particular to the relationship between gospel and culture. In a way, this tension between continuity and discontinuity presents the same dynamic that this book refers to as "prophetic dialogue."

Why Are You Entering Someone's Garden?

Before jumping too quickly to the "how" of crossing cultures, it is extremely important to begin with the "why." While missionaries/ministers have had and continue to have a wide range of theological motivations for encountering other peoples, the perspective of this chapter reflects the idea of "mission in reverse" as developed and described by my colleague and mentor Claude Marie Barbour.

When ministry is seen as dialogical, it means that ministers become persons immersed in the world of others, like Jesus was in our world. It is *with* people, therefore, that the minister begins to ask questions; it is *with* people that basic human values are endorsed and challenged; and it is this context that shapes the way of announcing the good news and of denouncing sinful structures.[4]

Rather than a theological model of mission that is susceptible to cultural imperialism and ethnocentrism, Barbour proposes a theology that "levels the playing field" between the minister/missionary and the community so that true mutuality in mission/ministry can take place. One then approaches the "other" with an initial attitude of discerning how God is already present (dialogue) and then eventually, together *with* the people, after developing respectful and mutual relationships, confronts the "weeds" with the "good news" (prophecy). Underlying this approach is a radical trust and belief in the power of God's Spirit at work in the lives and cultures of people — people who are different from oneself, who often may be poor and marginalized, who share one's fundamental human dignity, rights, and responsibilities, and who are one's sisters and brothers created in God's image. Finally, one's own Christian faith and experience of the "good news" is the primary motivation and source behind one's commitment to and identity in mission/ministry. At the same time this faith and "good news" is shared in word and deed in a dialogical manner.

Intermingled and interrelated with our theological motivations are often a number of cultural, racial, religious, economic, and political ones. Also more "personal issues" and a personal sense of one's vocation contribute to the complex "total package" of reasons and attitudes that lead a missionary/minister to try to cross cultures. Of course, it's very important to be as aware as possible of one's motivations, attitudes, and theological foundations from the very beginning. Are you coming to save people's souls? Do you want to bring development or "civilization"? Are you coming, as a mentor of mine once asked, with your glass completely full, or with it half empty and open to receive from the local people? Usually these presuppositions will be continually clarified, revised, and challenged in the process itself of attempting to cross into another culture. Part of this challenging opportunity will take the form of an explicit or implicit question from the members of the receiving community, such as, "What are you doing in my 'garden'?" or "Why are you really here?"

How Do You Enter Someone's Garden for the First Time?

Assuming the primary motivation of "mission in reverse," one begins the process of entering someone else's "garden" by "taking off one's shoes" — the well-known image of Max Warren.[5] As Moses removed his sandals before the "burning bush," so a missionary/minister begins with a stance of respect before the presence of God in the people and their history, culture, and religion. The missionary/minister, as the "outsider," learns from the people missioned/ministered to, allowing them to choose (or not!) to begin the process of teaching the missionary/minister about the new garden just entered. Of course, there is so much to learn about someone else's garden and this is only the beginning step in developing a relationship of trust and respect. While the "outsider" is an "expert" in his or her own garden, one is like a child in the new garden. Language learning brings this point home immediately and forcefully. One is certainly a student, testing one's sense of and capacity for humility, dependency, patience, and humor.

In chapter 2, Steve Bevans and I used the image of the stranger to illustrate the dialogical attitude that one should have in mission. We borrowed this image from the work of our colleague Anthony Gittins, who has described it in marvelous detail.

> If a newcomer honestly presents herself or himself as a stranger, thus showing respect for the hosts and allowing them to take certain necessary initiatives, this facilitates the interaction, even though the price may be some uncertainty and powerlessness on the part of the stranger. But only by doing this will missionaries be able to indicate their openness, integrity, and willingness to engage in relationships.[6]

Another aspect of this process is that the newcomer will make mistakes in this new world of meaning. After completing the first stage of language learning in Papua New Guinea in 1975, I immediately spent two weeks in a village with my "guide" Benjamin Wokwanje, who had just graduated from secondary school. This was part of my introduction to the Yangoru-Boiken people,[7] with whom I would live and work as a seminarian for about twenty months. Of the many things I learned during that initiatory period, one incident is unforgettable. While Benjamin and I were spending the day doing male-designated work in the family garden, Benjamin's mother and several other women were preparing a special meal in a *mumu* — bundles of food, steam-cooked for hours from the heat of hot rocks in a covered pit, lined with banana leaves. As the extended family gathered to share in the feast, a young unmarried man, who was seated on the opposite side of the circle, asked for the towel that he had brought with him to the meal. Wanting to be helpful, I grabbed his towel and tossed it to him over the food. Immediately, all eyes turned toward me for some reason unbeknownst to me. Benjamin then explained to me that the women *now* would not be able to eat any of the food. In his culture, the powerful, life-producing "worlds" of men and women are separated by strict taboos. Tossing a man's towel, a physical possession closely identified with the essence of its owner, *over* the food, made the food part of the "men's world" and therefore dangerous to the "women's world." The women had to find food cooked in neighboring hamlets, rather than eat the food they had prepared themselves.

I was very embarrassed and sorry for the consequences of my cultural blunder. I learned that good intentions are not enough, and that mistakes are made when entering into someone else's world. I learned about their hospitality and patience with an "outsider." Benjamin and others did not berate me for this, but they made sure I understood what I had learned through it! Such a lesson should not leave the "newcomer" paralyzed with the fear of making further mistakes, but one is reminded both of one's childlike knowledge and status in the new culture and therefore the need to be an attentive learner. Furthermore, learning appropriate external behavior must be accompanied by learning the underlying internal world of meaning. Throwing the young man's towel over the food (external behavior) actually made the food part of the men's world and therefore forbidden for women (internal world of meaning).

While the above story points to a dynamic that is common for anyone seriously attempting to cross over to another cultural world, a missionary/minister in this situation needs to also be aware of the underlying theological issues and consequences. If one's initial attitude is that the other culture is a "garden" of *only* "weeds," there would not be much regard for or interest in the "cultural" understandings of sexual/food taboos and there would probably be some degree of antagonism toward other elements considered more "religious."[8] This of course is representative of the *tabula rasa* approach — that is, wiping away everything of the new culture and/or religion — which was predominant during many periods in the history of Christian mission.

However, if a missionary/minister sees that same garden containing *only* good seed, an equally dangerous theological position is hovering on the horizon. Such a tendency can dilute the "cutting edge" power of the good news for every society and make culture instead of the gospel normative. In reaction to an earlier strict *tabula rasa* perspective, many missionaries/ministers naturally swung to the opposite extreme of a utopian, overly romanticized view of culture. An appropriate theological stance, what I might call prophetic dialogue, falls in between the two extremes and recognizes the presence of both the good seed and the weeds in every garden. Of course, this likewise applies to the theological perspective of the missionary/minister regarding his or her own culture. A onesided view of one's own garden as *only* good seed or *only* weeds will of course negatively impact one's attitude and attempt in entering someone else's garden.

What Do You "Do" in Someone's Garden?

A Basic Attitude of Dialogue

After my return to Chicago from Papua New Guinea in 1977, I talked with Claude Marie Barbour about possibilities for "mission in reverse" work. She introduced me to Hattie Williams, a committed African-American Christian who was involved in many aspects of "sustaining life" on both the personal and systemic levels in her south side neighborhood of Kenwood-Oakland. I'll never forget one of the first things Hattie told me in a very caring and yet a very forceful way: "You are very welcome to work *with* us in the community, but remember that this is *our* community. We don't want you to come in with *your* solutions to *our* situation." Following this lead, I began my two-year period of collaborating with Hattie by allowing her and others to introduce me to their community. Eventually, Hattie asked me to begin getting involved in certain activities with some of the high school age young men in the neighborhood. In response to my initial question of whether this was appropriate for a white man, rather than for the black men of the community, Hattie assured me that it was fine, and that I could fulfill a real need in the neighborhood. Due to her standing in the community, Hattie's introduction of me to several high school students was the beginning step. As time went on, my relationship with Hattie and others became mutually enriching and challenging in different ways — ministerially, spiritually, and personally.

As I already insinuated earlier, we naturally tend to perceive, understand, and judge someone else's garden through the lens of our own. I would, for example, initially consider a corn-like plant in a garden in Papua New Guinea the product of good seed, as it is in Ohio, but I would later find out that it is considered a weed there. Or I could initially consider a plant, which looks like a creeping violet, to be a weed since it would choke the life out of tomato plants in Ohio, whereas in Papua New Guinea its leaves serve important medicinal purposes. Christians have made judgments about their own gardens regarding what are considered elements of the Reign of God and those things contrary to it. However, missionaries/ministers have to be very cautious about making the same kind of judgments about what are the "seeds" and the "weeds" in the contexts in which they serve. One would not walk into someone else's garden and begin, on one's own, to uproot everything that looked like a weed. In the sixteenth and seventeenth centuries, some Europeans missionaries immediately labeled the veneration of ancestors in China "idol worship" and this led to the complex and devastating "Rites Controversy."

Therefore, missionaries/ministers are challenged to understand the world of the "other" from the perspective of the "other." Furthermore, this understanding embraces both the head and the heart.

> An outsider can know more about the history, cultural externals, and even language of an ethnic group than its members and still be alien to them because of a lack of empathy. Dialogue, a consequence of empathy, is the interaction in which people seek to give of themselves as they are and to receive and know the others in their particular otherness. Dialogue presumes that one is prepared to learn from others and their cultures and to let go of attachments that interfere with the growth in mutuality.[9]

Sometimes a Prophetic Stance

In order to examine the dynamics and complexities of the "being" and "doing" of a missionary/minister in someone else's garden, I will now turn to my second experience in Papua New Guinea — three years (1980–83) in Kaugia/Mui parish with the Abelam and Arapesh peoples.[10] While I had many clear experiences of the "good seeds" from their "gardens" — such as, their shared communal care for the children, elderly and disabled — I have chosen three examples that illustrate the more challenging and ambiguous aspects of this endeavor and that call for an attitude of prophetic dialogue.

Sorcery

A number of villagers told me that sorcery was one of the biggest evils in their life. From my reading, I thought I understood sorcery. However, I didn't realize its deep and complex meaning until one of the church elders explained his dilemma to me. The elder's father had died, it was believed, because of an act of sorcery. Next to his grave the villagers had put a certain plant, signifying that the father's death has not yet been "made right," that is, had not been avenged by another act of sorcery against the alleged murderer. The elder would bear the mark of shame until he had fulfilled his duty as a son to his deceased parent, his family, and the other villagers. The belief in sorcery is deeply imbedded within the interrelated network of beliefs, behaviors, structures, and values of this particular worldview. The cultural "explanation for death" is linked both with the value of reciprocity in maintaining right relationships with the dead as much as with the living and with the strong metaphysical connection between body and spirit in that hair, food, and secretions can be used in sorcery to harm one's spirit. While it seems that the ritual act of sorcery is not often actually performed in Papua New Guinea, the sorcery mind-set is all-pervasive.

How did this church elder "feel" in this situation? I was challenged as an "outsider" in two ways. First of all, I struggled (and continue to struggle) to understand with both my head and heart the meaning of this phenomenon of sorcery, which is so foreign to my worldview.[11] Beyond that, I slowly had to discover my way as a missionary/minister to enter the conversation among the church elders and other villagers as they addressed the issue of sorcery in light of their Christian answers to basic human religious questions regarding evil, death, and "Who is my neighbor?"

Domestic Violence

One day, after I had been in Kaugia-Mui for over a year, I was driving not far from the parish center when I witnessed a man beating his wife outside their home. I stopped the car, walked over to them, and the man stopped striking the woman. After saying just a few words, I went back to the car and continued my trip. While we missionaries/ministers enter and live in someone else's "garden" as "outsiders" in a posture of respectful learning, some situations evoke an immediate response on our part to "interfere." In conscience, I could not have driven by that scene of domestic violence without doing something.

In similar situations in my own United States garden, some "prophetic" voice and action against the "weeds" of domestic violence would be just as necessary. In my own culture even I don't understand many of the interrelated issues, problems, and dynamics. How much more difficult this is when I would be an "outsider"? In the Papua New Guinea situation, the villagers themselves have the necessary knowledge and the primary right, responsibility, and power for tending to their own garden. After I got back in the car and continued on my way, I don't know what happened between that man and woman. My challenge was to find the appropriate way to present this concern to the community, which in this case could be members of the parish council, the larger parish, and/or the village community. The context for this interchange needs to be characterized by — to use the words of Arbuckle quoted earlier — empathy, dialogue, and mutuality. At the same time, one might also need to raise a prophetic voice or encourage the community to do so.

Male Initiation

When I arrived in Kaugia/Mui parish in 1980, there was a revival of their elaborate system[12] of male initiation rituals, which had basically disappeared from the public sphere for about twenty-five years. At the suggestion of several veteran missionaries and with my own pastoral interest to better understand the meaning behind this revival, I devoted a lot of my attention to this. Of course at first I had to earn the respect and trust of the local community before they would allow me to enter into their sacred space. Eventually, some of the villagers invited me to learn about the male initiation rituals by observing, listening, and conversing — similar to the anthropological methodology of participant observation. I began to learn the important role that the initiation rites played in preparing young people to be capable adults and in renewing the identity and strength of the entire village. The villagers used two images to explain their reasons for reviving the initiation rites: first of all, to restore proper order and relationships in the village, which was being threatened by chaos ("the growth of the jungle/bush was overtaking the village"), and second, to maintain proper balance within their holistic worldview with all the interconnected aspects of their cultural-religious life.

My learning came at a particular transitional and creative moment as the villagers were redeveloping the initiation rituals to prepare for the drastically new "modern" world, which included the introduction of Christian faith and values. Regarding this latter point, I would be a part of some of these discussions in which the people were discerning how various cultural/religious elements are consistent or not with the Reign of God, that is, to sort out the "good seed" from the "weeds." In one such discussion, the church elders described how certain artistic symbols within the initiation process pointed to one's primary identity within the extended family and with God, the source of all life. At the same time, they said that the drinking a particular ritual soup, which to my eyes looked like ordinary everyday soup, would be contrary to Christian values because of certain immoral activity involved in its preparation. Certainly, the people understand their own world of meaning better than an outsider does, even after he or she has been among them for many years. At the same time, as a missionary I needed to find a way to appropriately contribute the voice of Christian tradition and my local church to this conversation. It is important to remember that this process represents the ongoing challenge that every generation of Christians of every culture/society needs to face over and over again.

Of course, individuals, communities, and local churches can be at various cultural, historical, and theological points in this wider discernment process on any particular issue. The situation of Kaugia/Mui parish offers an excellent illustration of this. The parishioners on the "Kaugia side" (Abelam people) — mostly second- and third-generation Christians, a few of whom had completed tertiary education — generally encouraged me, as the parish priest, to enter the initiation enclosure and to incorporate Bible study as part of the knowledge to be handed on to the initiands. At exactly the same time in the same parish, the church elders across the ridge on the "Mui side" (Arapesh people) — mostly middle-aged and younger first-generation Christians, of whom very few had completed six years of primary school, at the most — discouraged me from entering the initiation enclosures, since such an action would be interpreted as church approval of everything associated with the initiation process. I followed the Kaugia and Mui advice in their respective contexts.

Intercultural Relationships

While an "outsider" continues to learn from many different people within the host society/culture, it is very helpful to find "advanced" mentors, that is, individuals who are able to reflect upon and articulate the meaning of their own culture (probably due to a significant experience of viewing it from another cultural perspective). Ambrose Gumbira was such a person for me during my days in Kaugia/Mui. Ambrose had left Kaugia parish to obtain a teacher's certificate and then taught in various areas of Papua New Guinea. He had returned to Kaugia shortly before my arrival as the principal of the parish primary school in order to contribute something back to his people. As our relationship developed, Ambrose helped me to gain a better "insider's view" of his people's "garden," especially in regard to the issues surrounding the male initiation rituals. Such discussions sometimes turned into real moments of "theological reflection," as Ambrose and I engaged in the dialogue of bridging the gospel and wider Christian tradition on the one side, and the daily life and the worldview of villagers on the other. In other words, we were representative of a broader inculturation process. The missiological effort would eventually branch out in two complementary directions. First, how could people of Kaugia-Mui parish celebrate and understand their traditional male initiation as Christians and members of the Roman Catholic Church? Second, how could people of Kaugia-Mui parish celebrate the process of Christian initiation in the Catholic tradition as Papua New Guineans? A more detailed description of this endeavor is not necessary here.[13] However, my examination of this case has surfaced several underlying factors in the attempt by a missionary/minister to cross cultures.

One additional point can be drawn from this example. While I treasured my intercultural relationship with Ambrose, I knew I would never be an "insider." A missionary/minister tries to cross over into the world of the "other," but never becomes the "other." One evening when I was sitting with Ambrose, his wife, Aida, and several other members of his family around the household fire after a meal, I was struck by how much I felt "at home" with them — sharing stories of pain and concern, and laughing quite naturally. And then the conversation shifted to the issue of sorcery, which (as mentioned above) was so difficult for me to understand. At that moment, I felt like I was "sitting on the moon." In other words, I was starkly reminded that I would always belong to another world. I'll never forget that evening when I was confronted with the dilemma of being an outsider, but also I valued all the more the blessing of that relationship with Ambrose, with whom I had, in spite of limitations and difficulties, crossed cultures into another world of meaning and God's presence and action.

What Happens in Your Own Garden?

Books written for people who are preparing to live for an extended period in another country — for example due to business, education, or service-oriented involvements — usually contain a section on "culture shock." Such an orientation is certainly important for preparing individuals to survive and even thrive as they face the ambiguity, awkwardness, and discomfort associated with entering a new world. On the one hand, this is extremely important for missionaries/ministers who enter other cultures, especially since they normally intend to move beyond simple coexistence to a much deeper level (as highlighted above), which in turn will have a deeper impact on them in the process. On the other hand, focusing on "culture shock" normally stresses the negative impact of living in another culture. However, truly crossing into and engaging oneself in another culture is an opportunity for positive human development through a process of transformation, that is, transforming one's cultural, racial, religious, economic, and political worldviews. Changes occur in one's attitude toward the "other," one's perspective on the economic/political systems of the world today, one's image of God, and one's "answers" to the basic human/spiritual mysteries of life. In other words, one's horizons are extended.

Theologically speaking, we return to "mission in reverse," founded on the Christian belief that God's revelation occurs within a particular time and space, not only (but certainly in a very unique form) in Jesus Christ, but also within human history and experience — in this case the human experience and history of the "other." Edward Schillebeeckx affirms that there is "an echo of the Gospel" in the depths of human experience.[14] On his own transformative missionary experience among the Maasai in East Africa, Vincent Donovan described it as *Christianity Rediscovered.*[15]

Therefore, we are enriched and challenged by God's revelation during the process of engaging in a mutual intercultural relationship *with* people. Hopefully, the good seed within our own garden will be nourished and flourish in new ways, and the weeds within our own garden will be challenged and uprooted. Also, we may even introduce a new "hybrid" — "grafting" a "shoot" from a good "fruit-bearing plant" from someone else's garden. While we never become the "other," individuals who really are transformed by the "other" often become "hybrid" persons themselves. Furthermore, the boundaries of one's own garden are often enlarged and shifted.

Since 1991, I've made a trip almost every year to spend about five days with the Lakota people of the Rose Bud and Pine Ridge reservations in South Dakota, as a co-facilitator for a group of students who participate in this traveling seminar usually as part of a ten-week course of training for cross-cultural mission and ministry through Catholic Theological Union in Chicago. Such an immersion or "seminar" is possible only due to a longstanding relationship of mutual trust and respect of my colleagues Claude Marie Barbour and Eleanor Doidge with a number of Lakota people, who teach us about their "garden." Of course, the participants learn more about themselves — who they are as they enter another culture — than they do about the Lakota in such a short time. This also holds true for me, as I am involved in the process of facilitating this group experience and reflection. It involves being attentive both to the individual issues and group dynamics for the students from Chicago as well as the powerful teachings and experiences of our Lakota teachers. I continue to be challenged to enter each time anew into that process of transformation, which is supported by the reflective, process-oriented, and intense nature of the experience. Also the dynamics and context shaped by the Lakota people, the Chicago group, and me is different and unique, to some extent, every time.

The following questions represent some of the more recent affirmations and challenges that have surfaced for me during South Dakota trips.

• How do I move beyond "guilt for" to "solidarity with"?

• How can my prayer and lifestyle become more "other-centered" as expressed by the Lakota phrases, "Pray for the people" and "Suffer for the people"?

• How is God stretching my Christian understanding of "Who is my neighbor" through a memorable sweat lodge experience with men representing the diversity of all peoples?

• How does the Lakota spirituality of *mitakuye oyas'in* ("all my relatives"), which includes the living and dead, all living creatures, and all of creation enrich and challenge my Christian response to racism, poverty, and the ecological situation today?

• How is my understanding of maleness and femaleness reflected in my spirituality and daily living?

• Where is God leading me through my experiences with the Lakota to develop a more holistic and integrated Christian life?

Conclusion

Gerald Arbuckle describes the process of interaction between people of different cultures in terms of three stages: (1) fascination with and enjoyment of cultural differences, (2) disillusionment and tension due to the difficulties of communication and interaction, and (3) movement to overcome these difficulties to reach real dialogue and mutual interaction.[16] I agree with Arbuckle's observation that most people never get beyond the second stage. This chapter points to the dynamics underlying the challenge of entering this third stage, whereby peoples of different cultures can reach the point of dialoguing with each other regarding both the seeds and the weeds of each other's gardens.

In good circular Lakota fashion, I will complete the circle by returning to the earlier quote of Barbour.

When ministry is seen as dialogical, it means that ministers become persons immersed in the world of others, like Jesus was in our world. It is *with* people, therefore, that the minister begins to ask questions; it is *with* people that basic human values are endorsed and challenged; and it is this context that shapes the way of announcing the good news and of denouncing sinful structures.[17]

As a final comment, a potentially more complete ideal and real picture of Christianity will emerge as peoples of different cultures share their expressions and experiences of the "good news." Such an enriching and challenging image of the Reign of God can enable us to listen to and participate more fully in God's mission of justice, love, and compassion today.

Chapter 7

Letting Go and Speaking Out

Prophetic Dialogue and the Spirituality of Inculturation

"You may, and you must, have an African Christianity."[1] These words of Pope Paul VI, spoken in Kampala, Uganda, in 1969, continue to be words of challenge and encouragement not only to Africans, but to women and men of every culture and social situation as well. Indeed, African Americans may, and must, have an African American Christianity; Filipinos may, and must, have a Filipino Christianity; women may, and must, have a Christianity that speaks from and to their experience; Native Americans may, and must, have a Native American Christianity. What Paul VI called for four decades ago in Africa is today recognized as the task of incarnating, contextualizing, or inculturating Christian faith, and Christians today would acknowledge that such a commitment is very much at the heart of the church's missionary vocation.[2]

But inculturation is, as Pope John Paul II pointed out on several occasions, a "lengthy," "difficult and delicate task."[3] This is because it engages in the risky business of balancing reverence for local contexts and local wisdom with faithful presentation of Christian truth and connection with the wider church. Inculturation is proving in many ways to be an exciting task, but it is also one that often causes pain — pain that is ultimately liberating and life-giving, but pain nevertheless. Those who have been the "objects" of the church's mission sometimes struggle to recover and reclaim identities that had been wrongly taken from them in the name of the gospel. Those who have worked as missionaries or official representatives of the church — many times for long years and with considerable sacrifice — may be forced to confront the fact that their understanding of Christianity has been conditioned by colonial expansionism, racism, and Western cultural superiority. If, as Bernard Lonergan attests, knowledge always makes a "slow, if not a bloody entrance,"[4] learning to know the real gospel in concrete circumstances is a particularly arduous accomplishment. It is perhaps the risk and the pain involved in the process that has made the actual results of inculturation so meager, despite many eloquent testimonies about its necessity.

This is why those who work for inculturation need a spirituality. It is not enough to know the values or key symbols of a particular culture or the nuances of a situation. Nor is it enough to have mastered the content of the Christian tradition. Like doing authentic theology, working for inculturation is an art; it certainly demands skill and knowledge and accuracy, but it demands much more than that. What makes a process of inculturation more than a mechanical activity are the more elusive qualities of insight, depth, creativity, imagination, wisdom, openness to grace, courage in the face of risk and recognition of the unexpected. Not what we are able to *do,* but who we are able to *become* is what is important.

It is this more self-involving, ascetical, prayerful aspect of ministry that this chapter will try to develop. Building on the principles of what our colleague Claude Marie Barbour has called "mission in reverse"[5] — reverence for the "other," learning from our hosts, being vulnerable — what we hope to do in these pages is to outline what might be called a "spirituality of inculturation." Such a spirituality, we are convinced, is also a spirituality that emerges from the practice of prophetic dialogue.

There are many different understandings and definitions of spirituality, but here we mean it as a kind of "framework" or "set" of values, symbols, doctrines, attitudes, and practices that persons or a community set about trying to make their own in order to be able to cope with a particular situation, to grow in the love of God and self-transcendence, and/or to accomplish a particular task in life or in the world. A spirituality in other words, is like a reservoir from which a person or a community can draw, to motivate action, to keep on track, to bolster commitment, to avoid discouragement when times get rough. When we speak of a "spirituality of inculturation," then, we mean a whole complex of ideas and practices that can open people up to the Spirit in such a way that there emerges an understanding and expression of Christianity that takes its form in a loving, creative, and sometimes critical dialogue with a particular social or cultural context.

A "spirituality of inculturation," however, might also be conceived as being of two kinds, depending on a person's position in the cultural or social context in which people are working toward a contextualized understanding of the gospel. On the one hand, there is the spirituality of the "outsider" — the stranger, the guest, the missionary. This, we believe, is a spirituality that revolves basically around the practice of "letting go": listening, observing, letting be, taking an intentional dialogical stance. On the other hand, and ultimately more important for the process of inculturation, there is the spirituality of the "insider" — the subject of a particular context, the members and leaders of a local church. Being an "insider" in the process of inculturation is to participate in a spirituality of "speaking out": attending carefully, being creative, experimenting, risking. The "insider's" stance is one of dialogue in that she or he needs to be in touch with the values and movements of the Spirit in his or her own context. On the other hand, it is one of prophecy, in that she or he needs to discern those values and movements, and "speak them forth," even in the face of opposition — from "outsiders," or even the community. Once in a while, but only after having listened closely and respectfully, having observed thoughtfully and having struggled to really "let the people be," the outsider's spirituality might call for some kind of prophetic speaking out. And once in a while, but only after having truly savored God's presence in one's own context, after having allowed oneself creative and even risky experimentation, the insider's spirituality might call for some kind of prophetic letting go.

In chapter 2 we spoke about dialogue as, ultimately, a spirituality. In chapter 3 we emphasized the fact that the prophet — and the prophetic church — must first of all be one that listens intently to God's Word before boldly and confidently living it out or proclaiming it. Living the life of a prophet too, in the final analysis, is rooted in a spirituality. It is this double-sided, dialectical spirituality of "prophetic dialogue" that this present chapter builds on. Doing mission — and engaging in contextualization in that mission — is to live out of a spirituality of prophetic dialogue: "letting go" and "speaking out."

Letting Go: The Spirituality of the Outsider

As Claude Marie Barbour and her companions have observed, "We don't need to search far to find ample literature about the damage done by

Western missions and churches to the cultures and traditional ways of indigenous peoples."[6] Indeed, anyone who is familiar with mission theology and mission literature in the last several decades knows that there has been a well-deserved focus on the negative aspects of missionary activity and missionaries. With that acknowledgement, however, we can still say that the "outsider" has and can play a vital — though definitely subordinate — role in the inculturation process.[7] An outsider might be able to see things of value in a particular context that those more familiar with it might never take as interesting or extraordinary. For example, a North American might point out the beauty of local pottery or cloth and its role in beautifying local liturgical environments — even though local people have been conditioned to think of liturgical accoutrements in terms of plated gold and watered silk. In addition, because one unfamiliar with a culture or situation can often spot inconsistencies within it more easily than those native to it, the outsider might very well offer a penetrating critique of the context in the light of his or her own understanding of the world. Living for many years in a multicultural community, for instance, has made us very aware of the antigospel values and attitudes of our own middle-class U.S. culture. And even if the outsider sees wrongly or critiques unfairly, he or she can be the catalyst that might start local people thinking in fresh ways about who they are and how they might more authentically express their faith.

As helpful as outsiders might be, however, their involvement in the inculturation process runs the distinct risk that they might hinder the development of a truly authentic expression of inculturated faith. This is why, therefore, the outsider has to practice a particular form of spirituality that revolves around the asceticism of "letting go."

What this means, in the first place, is that outsiders need *constantly* — not just in their first months or years but every year after that — to work at *really seeing* and *really listening*. A Ghanaian proverb wryly observes that "the stranger has eyes like saucers, but doesn't see anything!" and we might say as well that the stranger doesn't hear anything either, despite having huge ears! Seeing what is really there and listening to what is really being said takes a tremendous amount of self-discipline and is a genuine practice of *kenosis,* which is perhaps the most basic virtue of a missionary spirituality.[8]

Each of us sees the world through a particular set of lenses and hears others with a particular filter — and divesting ourselves of those lenses and filters is hard work, in many ways a life's work. When Steve was a new arrival in the Philippines many years ago, he was told that the best thing a missionary could do was to "keep his or her mouth shut" for the first year, and learn to both see and listen. After almost nine years there, however, he realized that he probably should not have spoken much at all, or at least that he should have spoken after listening and observing much more carefully and respectfully. The longer he was a guest within Filipino culture, the more he realized how very, very little he really understood. Bernard Lonergan once remarked regarding the five "transcendental imperatives" that need to be practiced to achieve authentic humanity — "be attentive, be intelligent, be reasonable, be responsible, and if necessary change" — that the first, attentiveness, was by far the hardest to achieve.[9] Attention takes effort, it is a real ascesis, and if it is important even in our everyday lives in our own social and cultural contexts, it is an effort that is absolutely necessary for strangers — particularly strangers who claim to *minister* in those contexts. Only when we can feel our heart, in the words of Alice Walker, "so open that the wind blows through it" can be begin to dare to make such a claim.[10]

Second, "letting go" means "letting be," and this always involves a risk for the sake of the gospel. Outsiders need to let go of their certainties regarding the content of the gospel. They need to let go of cherished ideas and practices that have nourished and sustained them in their own journeys toward Christian maturity. They need to let go of the symbols that anchor them in their human and Christian identity and let go of the order that makes them comfortable. As Vincent Donovan argues so eloquently, the role of the outsider, the missionary, is only to preach the gospel. This is done, as he illustrates, through real sensitivity and dialogue; the gospel presented is a "naked gospel," shorn of as many of the preacher's presuppositions as possible. But once this gospel is accepted, it no longer belongs to the missionary; it belongs to the people.[11] The outsider needs to believe that the people now are, like him or her, under the guidance of God's Spirit, and that the Spirit will lead them toward a faithful expression of their faith that is nevertheless *their own*.

This is a real risk, but it is a necessary one. As Mark Schultz, a Lutheran pastor, once put it so powerfully in a conversation, unless we're willing to risk *losing* the gospel in the process of inculturation, we will never see the gospel become an integral part of a culture. The Swiss missiologist Walter Hollenweger has said it powerfully. The missionary, or in his words, the "evangelist"

> gambles, as it were, with his own understanding of belief in the course of his evangelizing. He, so to speak, submits his understanding of the world and of God and of his faith to the test of dialogue. He has no guarantee that his understanding of faith will emerge unaltered from that dialogue. On the contrary, since he expects an exchange of trust with his partner in dialogue, he has himself to remain open or sensitive to the arguments of the person who is to be evangelized. How can anyone expect that the person who is listening to him should be ready in principle to change his life and way of thinking if he, the evangelist, is not...prepared to submit to the same discipline.[12]

The hardest leave-taking, says Meister Eckhart in a famous line, is taking leave of God for God — recognizing, in other words, that truth is something ultimately unable to be grasped in mere human concepts and symbols.[13] In the same way, one of the hardest and yet spiritually enriching tasks of the outsider is "taking leave of the gospel," so to speak, for the sake of the gospel — so that the gospel can be understood in a radically new and meaningful way among new peoples and in new circumstances. The outsider cannot stand in the way, even though moving aside — letting go of what to him or her seems so clear, so certain, so natural, so true — is immensely painful. But unless the outsider *does* step aside, he or she can never claim to have a part in the birth of a new and fresh understanding of Christ and his gospel.

Let us offer two images that outsiders who are committed to inculturation might bear in mind as they go through the painful process of letting go of ways of seeing, ways of hearing, and ways of understanding. The first image is one about which Steve wrote several years ago in an article about images of the missionary — the image of the "missionary as ghost."[14] His point was that a large part of being a missionary is being willing to look upon one's achievements with a certain amount of "holy indifference," being willing to leave them behind, allowing others to build on them or change them as they see fit. This is not easy; it is hard to build up a parish or a school or an organization, and then simply withdraw and leave it to another. We have known missionaries who felt quite bitter about the fact that after so many years of service their work was not fully appreciated by local folks, who, when they took over leadership, changed things according to their own vision. It seems to us, however, that such "letting go" is part and parcel of being a missionary, and that at a certain point missionaries must move on and the local community must take over. If the missionary is bitter and tries to hang on, or is bitter because he or she cannot, something is wrong. In many circumstances the best thing missionaries can do is to let go of their work, die to it so to speak, and remain present only as friendly ghosts. Perhaps it is this most difficult sacrifice of all that is required for the real fruitfulness of their labor.

A second image appears in a line from the conversion narrative of the African American ex-slave Sojourner Truth: "Oh, God, I did not know you were so big."[15] This image of the God who is "bigger" than we can ever imagine is a wonderful one for those who are struggling to "let go" of social, cultural, and theological preconceptions to "let the people be." To refer to Vincent Donovan once again, we need to admit that we really *don't* know what the whole gospel is yet, and we will know it fully only when all peoples and all cultures have appropriated the God of Jesus Christ in their own particular way.[16] This "bigness" of God is beautifully attested to in the Acts of the Apostles, which shows how the "followers of the way" move from being one of many factions within the Judaism of the day to a community that takes on a distinct identity over against the larger religion and becomes the church. As Acts unfolds, as we point out several times in this book, those who believe in Jesus are pushed by the Spirit in ways they would never have imagined as Jews; faith in Jesus showed them more and more clearly that God was indeed very big — as big as the whole world, big enough to embrace all cultures, all peoples, all races.

It is in this context of commitment to the pain and struggle of letting go that we can admit the possibility of the outsider "speaking out," voicing a critique of the context in which he or she lives, calling for that context to conform itself to the gospel. But this "speaking out," we repeat, can *only* be in the context of "letting go"; it can *never* be the result of one's own frustrations, it can *never* be done out of anger or from feelings of superiority. The prophets of the Bible present a fine example here: their critique — particularly the critique of the "outsider" prophet Amos (see Amos 7:12–15) — as vehement as it is, comes not because the prophets or the God for whom they speak hate Israel; on the contrary, their vehemence comes from the passionate love that God has for the people specially chosen as God's own.

The spirituality of inculturation expected of the outsider, in sum, is directly connected to mission in reverse. It is a spirituality that develops as guests in a particular context eschew control in relationships, grow in mutual respect and trust, begin reverencing people in the context as teachers, and open up to their hosts in real vulnerability.[17] It is tremendously hard work and will shape and stretch those who engage in it in ways almost infinitely beyond imagining. But there is another spirituality — that of the "insider," the "subject" of a culture or context — and it is a spirituality of inculturation that is just as challenging and just as transforming. It is to this spirituality that we turn in the next section.

Speaking Out: The Spirituality of the Insider

The story is told about the great sixteenth-century theologian and commentator on Thomas Aquinas, Cardinal Cajetan, that he spoke of the woman who did his laundry as not just a better believer, but a better theologian.[18] Whether Cajetan was right or not, however — whether his "laundry lady" was *indeed* better at theologizing than he was — is not as important as the intuition that his remark expresses, the intuition that theology is first and foremost the task and activity of every Christian. *"To be Christian at all is to be a theologian. There are no exceptions."*[19] In the same way, it is true that the task of inculturation is not first and foremost the work of experts — particularly "outside" experts — but the work of ordinary people, the subjects of local social and cultural contexts. As Peter Schineller wisely says, the process of inculturation is far too complex to be left only to professional theologians, and it goes without saying that such complexity can rarely if ever be grasped by outsiders.[20] Inculturation will be achieved only as ordinary "Christian members of indigenous or traditional societies... rediscover and reclaim their cultural roots and identity, including indigenous spiritual values and rituals,"[21] when people in a context who are often ignored or discounted are able to tell their stories as blacks or Hispanics or homeless, as disabled or lay people, as women, as gay or lesbian, as Asian Americans. Authentic contextualization can take place only when the "little theologies" as well as the "big theologies" are able to be articulated.[22]

As essential as it is for the real "insiders" to have a voice, the fact is that they often don't think they have anything worth saying. This is perhaps one of the worst legacies of both Western colonization and clericalism. On the one hand, years and often centuries of political domination and/or cultural denigration have left many peoples in a state of "anthropological poverty." Anthropologist Darrell Whiteman, for example, tells the story of one of his Thai students who made the astonishing discovery in his class on contextualization that she could be genuinely Thai and genuinely Christian at the same time. She had always been told that to be Christian she needed to turn her back on her Buddhist family and denounce her culture.[23] On the other hand, people have been intimidated by church leaders who saw themselves as the only authentic interpreters of the gospel. Any kind of popular expression of faith was suspect and smacked of "syncretism."

This is why the insiders of a particular social and cultural context need to practice a spirituality of "speaking out," a spirituality born of an asceticism that trusts in their culture and experience and results in a courage that gives them the energy, insight, and creativity to articulate how God is present in their lives, their work, and their struggles. Given how their faith and imaginations have been formed in the past, this will be hard work; but it will be in the stretching and the pain that it will cause that the women and men of local contexts will experience both personal growth and the breakthrough into inculturated Christianity.

Even more than outsiders, insiders need to develop the skills of really seeing and listening to the culture. What is needed is to develop a kind of "x-ray vision" by which they can begin to see the ways that God is present and active in their situation, and the values in their culture or context that might even add to the entire church's understanding of the gospel. The young woman that Darrell Whiteman refers to found a rich source of meaning for her own Christian life in the Buddhist teaching on meekness;[24] all Christians might profit from an attention to the concerns with healing and lively prayer that African Initiated Churches — especially those with a Pentecostal bent — have highlighted in recent years.

While the outsider needs to hold fast to Sojourner Truth's recognition that God is "bigger" than we might think, a dictum that the insider might follow is expressed in what might seem like a contradictory statement:

that God is actually very, very small. In other words, if God's transcendence and ineffability need to loom large in the minds and hearts of outsiders, insiders need to focus on God's immanence, God's nearness, God's presence in normal, everyday realities. One needs, in other words, to look for God in places where one might not look ordinarily; God is in the cracks, the corners, the neglected places; God is present in the very warp and woof of a context. One can, in the famous lines of William Blake, "see a World in a Grain of Sand, / And a heaven in a Wild Flower, / Hold Infinity in the palm of your hand, / And eternity in an hour."[25] The insider needs to believe that God may be found *anywhere* in his or her context — perhaps in a phrase of the local language, perhaps in an ordinary custom, perhaps in a myth or legend. Like Elijah in the cave of Mount Horeb (1 Kings 19:9–13), the insider might come to recognize God not in the places one might expect a theophany. God was not in the strong wind nor in the earthquake nor in the fire, but in a "tiny whispering sound." Like the purloined letter in Edgar Allan Poe's famous story,[26] God's presence in a context may be in the most obvious and therefore most overlooked places, and yet places where only the insider might think to look. The insider's spirituality is about the discipline of seeking and the courage to proclaim what is found.

And courage means taking risks. The great twentieth-century theologian Paul Tillich entitled his autobiography *On the Boundary* because, he said, "the boundary was the best place for acquiring knowledge."[27] The boundaries where Tillich found knowledge were those between religion and culture, between church and society, between heteronomy and autonomy, and even between faith and doubt.[28] Insiders who wish to be agents of inculturation need to live on the boundary as well — on boundaries between Christianity and other religions, between Christianity and local culture, between orthodoxy and superstition, between authentic and inauthentic syncretism.[29] As they "speak out" from these boundaries they need to have the courage to be willing to experiment, to test new formulas, to try new rituals, to explore new symbols. The spirituality of "speaking out" will also mean that insiders will be willing to come under suspicion of those in power and perhaps even be condemned for speaking their truth. Some of the great contributors in the past century to a Christianity that tried to engage the real context of people's lives were men and women like Karl Rahner, Dorothy Day, Yves Congar, Martin Luther King, Cesar Chavez, and the countless Latin American women and men, members of basic ecclesial communities, who have survived injustice and physical torture, and have often suffered martyrdom.

What might be helpful here is an analogy drawn from contemporary feminist reflection on the nature of sin. Judith Plaskow's study of sin and grace in the thought of Reinhold Niebuhr maintains that Niebuhr's theology of sin is "slanted in the direction of the experience of men."[30] For Niebuhr — and Plaskow would say for Western theology in general — the root of sin is pride, self-assertion, and self-will, and the corresponding Christian task is to undergo the discipline of humility, self-effacement and self-sacrifice. But while such *kenosis* is liberating within the lives of those who have power and prestige (that is, men in a patriarchal, androcentric culture) it is actually oppressive for women, who are thus encouraged to remain in situations in which they continue to be dominated by men and male-oriented culture.

> The problem for women has not been that they have pursued self-transcendence or the fulfillment of the image of God in an excessive and prideful way.... Rather, most women have been prone to the temptations of passivity, a resigned acceptance of the concrete contingencies which limit their lives, distractibility, and to losing themselves by defining their own identities in terms of others.[31]

What women need to recognize is that holiness for them often *entails* pride in themselves, self-assertion, and the development of an authentic sense of self. While the asceticism required of men involves the way of humility, the asceticism required of women might very well involve a discipline whereby they learn to acknowledge their own worth, dignity, and power. In the context of a spirituality of inculturation for insiders, therefore, the analogy is quite clear: while the asceticism demanded of outsiders — missionaries — is certainly in imitation of Jesus' self-emptying and patient suffering, for insiders — those who have been forced to disparage and deny their social and cultural worth — the discipline that is demanded is that of imitation of the Jesus who stood up for those on the margins of society. The discipline of insiders, in other words, is to learn to have pride in their culture and their self-identity, to practice the difficult task of articulating that identity proudly, to risk "going too far" in terms of the resources their culture or social location can bring to their Christian identity. Rather than the pain of "letting go," insiders need to school themselves in the liberating and self-constructing discipline of "speaking out."

Of course, gospel and context are never totally compatible, and insiders are the ones who will discover the areas where the values of local experience are inconsistent with the values of the gospel. They are the ones as well who will have to point them out and explain why certain traditions or practices need to be critiqued, revised, or even altogether abandoned. But this exercise of "letting go" should take place only after clearly and carefully "speaking out." Insiders' spiritual task in relation to inculturation is first of all to discern and proclaim the positive values in a context, despite what they have been told about those values in the past; their spirituality is forged in the crucible of bearing witness to the holiness of their own experience. Critique, though necessary, should come in second place. Insiders' asceticism is in the positive discernment of the presence of grace.

Conclusion: Letting Go and Speaking Out

Persons who want to be agents of inculturation need to practice a spirituality based on the discipline of "letting go" and "speaking out." This is a spirituality born of the practice of prophetic dialogue. While a dialogical "letting go" is probably the most difficult task of outsiders in a context, there will be times when that "letting go" entails as well the necessity of a prophetic "speaking out" — but only and always for the sake of the context and only and always out of love for the people among whom he or she lives as a guest. Ordinarily, however, the challenge for outsiders lies in the ascesis of close listening even when they think they know what is being said, keen observation despite seeming familiarity, and — maybe the hardest of all — suspension of judgment when they think they know how to say or do something better.

Spiritual discipline for the insider involves growing in the courage of a prophet: courage to listen in deep dialogue with his or her context, courage to think differently, courage to imagine in ways consonant with the local situation, courage to point out past mistakes, courage to see God in what may have formerly been despised, neglected, or overlooked. There will be times when insiders will be challenged to practice the discipline of "letting go" as they confront the shadow side of their comfort, or as the gospel, the Christian tradition, or the wider church sheds brighter light on their accustomed values. But such prophetic "letting go" should probably be a last resort. Insiders' spiritual challenge is to trust the conviction that God indeed has not been left "without a witness in any nation at any time"[32] (see Acts 14:17), and that the world truly is "charged with the grandeur of God."[33]

Chapter 8

Table Fellowship

Mission in the Areopagus of Today

Jesus' mission was to proclaim, serve, and witness to God's Reign of love, salvation, and justice. In the process, Jesus both affirmed and confronted certain aspects of his own context. Table fellowship was a central venue for serving the Reign of God, and it can continue to be an affirming and challenging image and practice of mission today. This chapter begins with the theological foundations of the missional nature of the church and then examines the practice of table fellowship within the mission of Jesus and the Acts of the Apostles, including Paul's encounter at the Areopagus. We then focus on the U.S. context to develop a contextualized and expanded idea of mission as table fellowship in the Areopagus of our globalized world and conclude by situating table fellowship within the spirituality of prophetic dialogue.

God's Mission, the Church, and the Second Vatican Council

At the Second Vatican Council, the Catholic Church reclaimed its original identity of being missionary by its very nature.[1] Rather than a preconciliar tendency toward an ecclesiocentric understanding of mission, the church grounded itself in a trinitarian (*missio Dei*) theology. Like an overflowing and life-giving fountain of love (*Ad Gentes*, 2), God the Father created the universe and called humanity, created in God's image, to share in the fullness of God's life. Humanity refused to live in right relationship with God and one another, but God's mission to draw humanity and all creation back into God's warm embrace was constant, like the father in the parable of the Prodigal Son. Jesus Christ, God the Son, coming in human flesh, and God the Spirit active throughout history from the beginning of time are part of that same plan (*Ad Gentes,* 3–4).

101

After the resurrection, the first men and women of the Jesus movement continued this mission. The Acts of the Apostles is a wonderful account of the Spirit leading the first disciples in mission to the foundation of the church.[2] The church exists because of and for the sake of God's mission.

The disciples continued to carry the gospel in all four directions from Israel. While the many Christians outside the Roman Empire, in places like eastern Syria, Persia, India, and Armenia, were able to practice their faith openly, those within the pre-Constantinian Roman Empire were prohibited from doing so and suffered occasional persecution. Christians gathered in the larger homes of fellow Christians, the "house-churches," to "break bread" and to break open the Word of God, to integrate more deeply their faith with daily life, to share the "good news" with acquaintances and neighbors, and to offer medical and economic assistance to those in need. The home was at the heart of Christian life and mission. Biblical scholar Wayne Meeks affirms that the individual extended household "was the basic unit in the establishment of Christianity in the city, as it was, indeed, the basic unit of the city itself."[3] Furthermore, the witness of martyrs, who professed their faith to the point of death, also nurtured and challenged the faith of the living.

Christian women and men also shared their faith outside of their homes. Michael Green describes it as "gossiping the gospel": "This must often have been not formal preaching, but the informal chattering to friends and acquaintances, in homes and wine shops, on walks, and around market stalls. They went everywhere 'gossiping the gospel.'"[4] Christianity grew at an amazing rate of perhaps 40 percent a decade within the Roman Empire,[5] primarily due to the *witness* and informal *proclamation* of the gospel by "ordinary" Christians.

The early church had a missional ecclesiology with an inseparable interconnection of church, mission, and baptism. In its rediscovery of its early foundations, the Second Vatican Council reclaimed and reaffirmed the missionary nature of the church explicitly, and one can also say that it reclaimed and reaffirmed the missionary nature of baptism in the same breath. This is reflected for example in its renewal of the liturgy, ministry, the RCIA, and sacraments in general.

Another major shift in Vatican II that greatly impacted this missional ecclesiology was the relationship of the church to the world. Rather than seeing the church as a "perfect society" and completely identifiable with the Reign of God in opposition to a world that is totally evil, the church acknowledged that God is present in the world and that grace and sin are in both the church and the world. The *missio Dei,* like that overflowing fountain, cannot be totally "contained" in the church.

Jesus Christ, the Reign of God, and Table Fellowship

Building upon the experience and deliberations of the bishops at the 1974 Synod on Evangelization, Pope Paul VI promulgated the apostolic exhortation *Evangelii Nuntiandi* the following year.[6] Rather than beginning with the trinitarian theology of mission, he began with the concrete ministry of Jesus which was centered on the Reign or Kingdom of God. "Christ first of all proclaims a kingdom, the Kingdom of God; and this is so important that, by comparison, everything else becomes 'the rest,' which is 'given in addition.' Only the Kingdom therefore is absolute, and it makes everything else relative" (*Evangelii Nuntiandi,* 8).

Jesus came not to preach himself or establish the church, but to preach, serve, and witness to the Reign of God. Jesus preached the Reign of God through his many parables; he served it through healing, exorcism, and the forgiveness of sins; and he witnessed to the Reign through his lifestyle and behavior, particularly through the boundary-breaking practice of table fellowship with sinners, tax collectors, and other people marginal to his society. Of the ten stories of meals in Luke's Gospel, beginning with the banquet at the home of Levi (5:27–32) and ending with the meal with the Eleven right before the Ascension (24:36–43), three of them were in the homes of Pharisees and three of them were with the marginalized, women, and sinners. Regarding this latter group, Filipino theologian and superior general of the Society of the Divine Word (SVD) Antonio Pernia states: "The primary image Jesus used for the kingdom was table fellowship, the subject of many of his parables and the object of many meals he shared with outcasts and sinners. Through this image Jesus announced that God ... was inviting everyone — everyone without exception — to communion with him."[7]

The Jewish cultural-religious purity laws formed a system of assigning people and objects their proper place. As anthropologist Mary Douglas illustrated in her seminal work *Purity and Danger,* impurity applies to that which was out of place.[8] "In Israel, purity and impurity, clean and unclean, holy and profane were all determined by whether things, persons, and places were 'in place' or 'out of place.' "[9] Within the Jewish integral cultural-religious worldview, the purity laws served to preserve their identity and protect their boundaries in relation to others, as well as to honor God's holiness (e.g., Lev. 10:10–11). In terms of table fellowship, certain foods and people were considered pure while others were impure. Breaking such purity laws by Jews could "expose themselves to the likelihood of ritual contamination and impurity, which isolated them from full and unrestricted participation in the social and religious affairs of the community, and...could eventually lead to such social and racial integration that their unique identity as a people could be lost."[10]

Jesus' total commitment to the Reign of God, rooted in the inclusive vision of the prophets (e.g., Isa. 2, 25, and 66:18–21), propelled him beyond the cultural-religious purity laws of table fellowship. This is most evident in Luke-Acts. Jesus breaks taboos by eating with the tax collector Levi (Luke 5:29–30), having his feet washed by the woman during a meal (Luke 7:36–38), and going into the home of tax collector Zacchaeus (Luke 19:5–6). At the reception in the house of Levi, the Pharisees asked, "Why do you eat and drink with tax collectors and sinners?" and Jesus responded, "I have come to call not the righteous but sinners to repentance" (Luke 5:30, 32). Jesus was referring to those who are open to being converted to and transformed by the Reign of God.

In John's Gospel, Jesus proclaimed, "Whoever comes to me will never be hungry, whoever believes in me will never be thirsty" (6:35). The satisfaction of hunger and thirst extended beyond any cultural boundaries. Furthermore, Jesus offered more than physical food through table fellowship; he told Zacchaeus, "Today salvation has come to this house" (Luke 19:9).

Chapter 14 of Luke elaborates on other aspects of table fellowship. Healing is more important than a strict interpretation of the law (1–6); eating is not to be an occasion for placing oneself above others (7–11); guests shouldn't be invited according to their ability to reciprocate (12–14); the parable of the banquet (15–24) illustrates that the invitation to the table is extended to the marginalized.

Acts of the Apostles, Table Fellowship, and the Areopagus

The theme of table fellowship continues through the Acts of the Apostles, the second volume of Luke's work. After Pentecost, the Spirit led the men and women disciples of Jesus in new directions as they carried on the mission of Jesus. At the beginning, they saw themselves as another Jewish sect. However, the mission of the inclusive love, salvation, and justice of God, expressed so powerfully in Jesus' inclusive practice of table fellowship, led the disciples, step-by-step, to something new: the explicit foundation of the church, distinguishing itself from (though not completely discontinuous with) the Jewish cultural-religious tradition and reaching out intentionally to Gentiles.[11]

The Greek-speaking Jewish followers of Christ took the lead in pointing in this new direction. Stephen was one of seven Hellenists appointed to assist in the fair distribution of food to widows. Before the Sanhedrin, Stephen confessed Jesus as the Just One (Acts 7:52) and the Lord (7:59), even greater than Moses, which led to his stoning. Philip, another of the seven, carried the gospel to the Samaritans or so-called "half-Jews" as Jesus had done with the woman at the well. Philip later was taken by the Spirit to preach to the Ethiopian eunuch, who was very close to Judaism, or perhaps wanted to be a Jewish proselyte. The first clear case of a Gentile becoming a Christian occurs in the incident of Peter and Cornelius, and table fellowship was a key element and symbol. New Testament scholar Luke Timothy Johnson and others consider this event "the most critical phase of the expansion of God's people."[12]

Chapter 10 of Acts opens with the devout and God-fearing Gentile Cornelius in prayer, receiving a vision to send for a man named Peter in Joppa (10:3–6). At the same time, God is appearing to Peter in a vision in which he is instructed to choose something to eat from all kinds of animals and birds (9–12). Peter states emphatically, "By no means, Lord; for I have never eaten anything that is profane or unclean" (14), to which the voice responds, "What God has made clean, you must not call profane" (15). This happened three times, and while Peter was still trying to understand its meaning, the messengers from Cornelius arrived. After listening to their message, "Peter invited them in and gave them lodging" (23). Peter invited these Gentiles as overnight guests into the house and perhaps they even shared a meal together. Whatever the case, Peter was engaging in an association that was unacceptable for a Jew.

The next day, Peter went to Caesarea to visit Cornelius and his extended household. Peter realized that "it is unlawful for a Jew to associate with or visit a Gentile," but he also acknowledged that "God has shown me that I should not call anyone profane or unclean" (28). While this incident is usually referred to as the conversion of Cornelius, it was also the conversion of Peter![13] He experienced a dramatic reversal in his cultural-religious worldview: "I truly understand that God shows no partiality, but in any nation anyone who fears God and does what is right is acceptable" (34–35). Then, as Peter was preaching the gospel, the Spirit came down upon them, and he proclaimed, "Can anyone withhold the water for baptizing these people who have received the Holy Spirit just as we have?" (47). Peter stayed with them for several days, and in light of later accusations, he certainly ate with them as well.

Upon his return to Jerusalem, the Jewish-Christian leaders criticized Peter for baptizing Gentiles, but the overriding concern was regarding table fellowship. "Why did you go to uncircumcised men and eat with them?" (Acts 11:3). After hearing the full account from Peter, the Jerusalem leadership gave its initial approval of this major development as they realized that *even* the Gentiles could receive God's "repentance that leads to life" (11:18). What occurred to a single Gentile household in Caesarea expanded in Antioch (11:19–29), where Greek-speaking Jewish followers of Jesus conducted an intentional mission to the Gentiles, and Jewish and Gentile believers lived next to each other. The break with Judaism and the birth of something new, the church, is further reflected in the use in Antioch of a new term "Lord Jesus" (11:20). This new term indicates that Jesus' significance is not only expressed in the Jewish title "Messiah" (*Christos*), but also expresses the fulfillment of Greek religious aspirations with the use of the title *Kyrios* (Lord). Finally, the recognition by others that something new, different from Judaism, was developing is that "it was in Antioch that the disciples were first called 'Christians'" (26).

Later, chapter 15 of Acts describes the watershed moment of what will be called the Council of Jerusalem, when the young church deals formally with the issues underlying the acceptance of Gentiles as Christians. After much discussion and a period of silence, James the leader of the Jerusalem community pronounced that, since God was taking from the Gentiles "a people for his name...we should not trouble those Gentiles who are turning to God" (15:14b, 19b). It is common to recognize the importance of dispensation from circumcision as a crucial part of the council's decision. However, in this context of a reflection on table fellowship, it is quite interesting to note the fact that the other major dispensations are all in the area of dietary laws and so have very much to do with a new way of eating together.

In the rest of the Acts of the Apostles (chapters 15–28), Paul is the primary figure through whom the mission to the Gentiles continues. The symbol and issue of table fellowship continues, though more implicitly. Paul and his companions stayed in the home of the Gentile woman Lydia (Acts 16:15); Paul and Silas shared a meal with the jailer's family (16:34); Paul enjoyed the hospitality of the Gentile Titus Justus possibly for much of the eighteen months he was in Corinth (18:7, 11); Paul prepared a meal for non-Jewish sailors on the ship after the storm (27:33–37). There is another key event that is related not explicitly to the *action* of table fellowship, but we propose reflects a further extension of the *meaning* of table fellowship and mission — Paul's encounter in the Areopagus.

As table fellowship points to the boundary-breaking and universal character of the Reign of God in relation to "impure" Jews and Gentiles, the author of Luke-Acts goes further by having Paul cross another boundary. He delivered his only speech to nonbelievers in the great university setting of Athens. Paul entered into discussion with Jews, Jewish sympathizers, passers-by, Epicurean and Stoic philosophers, and most likely it was the latter group, with a more positive attitude to religion and piety, who brought Paul to the Areopagus marketplace to engage some philosophers. Paul begins his speech by affirming the religiosity of his listeners and acknowledging one of the altars assigned "To a God Unknown" (17:22–23). Quickly, Paul states his purpose to make known to them the God they are worshiping in ignorance. The Creator God, who does not need a shrine or religious gifts, has ordered human life with a purpose "so that they would search for God and perhaps grope for him and find him" (17:27a). Luke's Paul contextualizes his speech by using and adapting two citations from Greek poetry — "In him we live and move and have our being" and "For we too are his offspring" (17:28). He then proclaims that God is calling all people to reform their lives and will judge the world through a man God has appointed and raised from the dead. While some sneered at Paul in response to this last point on the resurrection, others said they would like to hear more in the future, and Dionysius, Damarius, and several others became believers on the spot. This event in the Areopagus represents Luke's Paul and probably Luke's community engaging the secular philosophy and culture of the Greco-Roman world, that is, crossing another cultural and religious boundary as part of the mission of the Reign of God. Thus Luke has Paul doing at the Areopagus what Jesus' and the Christian community's boundary-breaking table fellowship signifies and implies: that mission is about moving beyond one's culture and comfort zones in order to witness to God's vision of universal inclusion.

Mission, Table Fellowship, and the Areopagus of Today

In the encyclical letter *Redemptoris Missio,*[14] Pope John Paul II drew a parallel between the Areopagus, which represented the cultural and intellectual center of Athens, and the "new sectors in which the Gospel must be proclaimed" (*Redemptoris Missio,* 37) in today's world. Building upon the theological, biblical, and cultural foundations above, we propose the image of mission as table fellowship for responding to the "Areopagus" of our globalized world. We will use key documents and the context of the Catholic Church in the United States, but this image is relevant in many other situations.

The U.S. Conference of Catholic Bishops in 2002 published a document entitled *A Place at the Table: A Catholic Recommitment to Overcome Poverty and to Respect the Dignity of All God's Children.*[15] As indicated in the subtitle, the main focus was on world poverty and human dignity. However, they also developed the idea of the "table," which can enrich the more general understanding of table fellowship as mission. The bishops point out the important links among daily life, the Eucharist, and the situation of the world. We propose formulating this interrelationship in terms of three "tables" of table fellowship — the dining room table of the domestic church, the Eucharistic table of the parish community, and the worldwide table of God's diverse peoples.

The "dining room table" is symbolic of table fellowship in the home. Jesus ate in the homes of the tax collectors Levi and Zacchaeus. These meals were moments marking the inbreaking of God's Reign. Jesus told Zacchaeus, "Today salvation has come to this house" (Luke 19:9). In the early church, the home was often the venue and origin of Christian life and mission. The Christian family setting ideally should be the initial place of inculturation, that is, where Christian faith takes root in and challenges our daily lives and relationships — our joys and sorrows, dreams and disappointments, challenges and fulfillments. The "dining room table" is not only a place for physical food, but a place of God's nourishment on many levels. A parent or grandparent teaches a child to pray, adolescents discuss the challenges of living out Christian values, a husband and wife share their worries and faith at the breakfast table, and the whole extended family gathers at Christmas, holidays, and family reunions to celebrate life and to give thanks to God. The sharing of food and faith within Christian families, however they are defined and experienced, is common in all cultures. On a human level, food is exchanged at times of reconciliation and moments of the rites of passage — birth, puberty, marriage, and death. How much more so are these opportunities for Christian faith, hope, and love to nourish and perhaps challenge our daily life "at home." Many households in the United States — and certainly elsewhere — are broken because of divorce, separation, and death, and the difficulty of having one family meal together once a week is symptomatic of social change. And many people are homeless due to poverty, mental instability, physical handicaps, and immigration status. In such cases, having a "home" is the first order of business before one can talk about table fellowship around a dining room table.

The second "table" is the Eucharist. The early church, particularly in the Roman Empire, gathered in the house churches. The link between the home and "breaking bread" was intimate. Today, there is often a great distance between the "worlds" in which Catholics actually live and in which they worship. However, theologically "the Eucharist is the sum and summary of our faith: 'Our way of thinking is attuned to the Eucharist, and the Eucharist in turn confirms our way of thinking.' "[16] Moreover, since the church, and, we would add, baptism are missionary by nature, how then are the Eucharist and worship expressions and experiences of the mission of God in real life? Lutheran theologian Thomas Schattauer[17] describes three different relationships between mission and liturgy.[18] First of all, the liturgy is "inside and out" whereby it empowers and equips the Christian community on the "inside" to be a witness and instrument of mission on the "outside." Second, the liturgy is also "outside in" in that the events and people of the neighborhood and the wider world enrich and challenge the Christian community. Finally, the liturgy as "inside out" recognizes that the liturgy itself — the Word proclaimed, meal shared, community formed, and reconciliation offered — is already God's mission in action for both the evangelized and unevangelized in a particular congregation.

In these multiple ways, the Eucharistic "table" is interrelated with both the dining room "table" of daily life and the "table" of the world. In their 1986 document *To the Ends of the Earth,* the U.S. bishops stated: "The Eucharist nourishes our mission spirituality and strengthens our commitment to give of ourselves and our resources to the development of the diocesan and universal Church as a people aware of our responsibility for, and interdependence with, all peoples of the earth."[19] Such a missionary aspect of the Eucharist is particularly evident at the moment of communion, when people of all ages, walks of life, and cultures come forward to share the one bread and the one cup. This moment eloquently symbolizes what the church is in its deepest identity and what it is called to witness to in its daily life.

The U.S. bishops' statement above reflects two overlapping aspects of the third "table" — the worldwide table of God's diverse peoples. On the one hand, it points to the communion of local churches — parishes, dioceses, and episcopal conferences — with other local churches near and far. Many Catholic parishes, institutions, and dioceses in North America have developed formal "twinning relationships" of mutuality with other parallel ecclesial communities both within and outside of North America. At the same time, there is a vision of communion with all peoples on a human level. The U.S. bishops stated the following in their document *Called to Global Solidarity: International Challenges for U.S. Parishes.* "In our parishes, the eucharist represents a central setting for discovering and expressing our commitment to our brothers and sisters throughout the world. Gathered around the altar, we are reminded of our connection to all of God's people through the mystical Body of Christ."[20] Catholic Relief Services, the official relief and development agency of the Catholic community in the United States, sponsors a Lenten Operation Rice Bowl program with a Home Calendar Guide to invite Catholic individuals and families to pray and fast "in solidarity with the hungry around the world," to learn about their situation, and assist them financially. The following statement from their program is a clear expression of the link between the three "tables." "Just as we celebrate the Eucharist on Sundays, we can use Operation Rice Bowl as a way to 'break bread' together with family and loved ones. We...learn about the joys and challenges in the lives of our brothers and sisters all around the world, and give concrete assistance to those most in need."[21] Through this and other initiatives, Catholics strive in the face of globalization to be in solidarity with others, both across the street and around the world. We remember that early Christians witnessed their faith to their non-Christian neighbors in need and they "gossiped the gospel" in their neighborhoods, along trade routes, and in other lands.

We also need to include a further extension of this third "table," which the U.S. bishops alluded to in *A Place at the Table,*[22] that is, all of creation. Our understanding of mission today is being stretched beyond a strictly anthropocentric perspective to cosmic-centric concern for the integrity of creation and ecological responsibility.

Table fellowship was a primary image of Jesus for the Kingdom and a challenging litmus test for the followers of Jesus in the Acts of the Apostles, such as Peter with Cornelius and Paul in the Areopagus. In the variety of the contexts of the Areopagus in the twenty-first century, we propose that, "table fellowship is a powerful model and motivation for mission — linking Jesus as the bread of life with our daily life (dining room table), our Christian faith (eucharistic table), and our relationship with people both near and far (the table of the 'other')."[23]

Table Fellowship and the Spirituality of Prophetic Dialogue

In *Constants in Context: A Theology of Mission for Today,* we described the ecumenical development of three strains of mission theology during and since the Second Vatican Council: mission as participation in the life and mission of the Trinity (*missio Dei*); mission as liberating service of the Reign of God; and, mission as proclamation of Jesus Christ as Universal Savior. Each of these theologies is foundational for one of the three major Catholic documents on mission in the past forty-five years, respectively: *Ad Gentes, Evangelii Nuntiandi,* and *Redemptoris Missio.* We then proposed "prophetic dialogue" as a synthesis of these three current threads and as the best expression of the theology and practice of mission today.[24] South African missiologist David Bosch used a similar expression, "bold humility," to capture the two essential dimensions of mission that we identify as prophecy and dialogue.[25] In the years since the publication of our book, we have come to see as well that prophetic dialogue expresses a spirituality of mission.

Briefly speaking, the dimension of *dialogue* draws primarily from the *missio Dei* theology with its emphasis on the holiness of the world, cultures, religions, human experience, and context in general. Acknowledging these amazing gifts of God, we respect the dignity and freedom of human beings and approach them with humility and vulnerability. The dimension of *prophecy* draws primarily from the Reign of God theology in speaking and acting against injustices and from Christocentric theology in proclaiming and witnessing to the truth of Jesus Christ and his vision of the future of the cosmos. Just as Jesus called people to conversion, Christians are called to acknowledge individual and social sin within themselves as well as within others and to be concerned with salvation in a holistic sense. The particular emphases of the three theologies of mission, although not necessarily in contradiction with each other, can lead to conflict if they would be understood in a more exclusive sense. However, when brought together into a synthesis (or a creative tension), they represent the fullness and diversity of the theology and practice of Catholic mission. All three have a foundational missional ecclesiology linking church, mission, and baptism. Speaking in eschatological terms, "dialogue" represents how the Reign of God is *already* present, and "prophecy" represents how the Reign of God is *not yet* present, or how it can be recognized. The Federation of Asian Bishops' Conferences (FABC) has expressed it clearly in this way: we dialogue with the poor, and we speak out against what keeps the poor that way; we dialogue with culture, and we critique the shadow side of culture; we dialogue with other religions and we maintain the conviction that Jesus Christ is the Way, the Truth, and the Life (John 14:6).[26] Both dimensions of dialogue and prophecy provide a necessary synthesis or balance for all forms of mission and ministry — witness and proclamation; liturgy, prayer, and contemplation; justice, peace and integrity of creation; interreligious dialogue; inculturation; and reconciliation.[27]

In our globalized world, the image of table fellowship shapes a response of mission on the interrelated levels of family, local church/parish, and all of humanity. On each level, it is necessary for Christian individuals and communities, on the one hand, to be rooted and nourished in faith and identity. On the other hand, it is also necessary to move beyond all boundaries to understand and eventually engage the world of the "other" — whether it is a family relative, a fellow Christian, or someone of another context, race, nation, or religion. In all cases, one needs to dialogue with how God's Reign is already present and to acknowledge where it is not yet present.

In the way Jesus practiced table fellowship and the early community broke bread together, especially after the breakthrough at Antioch, the dimension of prophecy was present in the call to conversion to the vision of God's Reign breaking into the world. The dimension of dialogue is represented by Jesus' and the early church's inclusion of and openness to all people as the children of God.

In the incident on the Areopagus, the dialogical dimension is reflected in the initial reference to the altar "To a God Unknown" and the use of two Greek poems. Luke's Paul speaks about God in a way that would be understandable to the Greeks. In terms of the prophetic dimension, Paul certainly was faithful in proclaiming the gospel, including Jesus Christ and the resurrection, at the end of his speech, and calling his listeners to conversion. In the words of evangelical biblical professor Lynn Allan Losie, "The speech on the Areopagus acknowledges the existence of general revelation and uses it as the basis for an evangelistic appeal."[28] Paul acknowledged that the secular intellectuals were looking for spiritual satisfaction, and he spoke to their aspirations and worldview, convinced that the gospel was the answer to what they were seeking.

Conclusion

We close with a biblical image of table fellowship: the banquet. Isaiah describes the messianic kingdom as "a feast of rich food and choice wines" (25:6). This passage is alluded to in the multiplication narratives in all four Gospels. Matthew (22:2–14) and Luke (14:16–24) both record Jesus' parable of the wedding banquet. An invitation was extended to "the poor, the crippled, the blind, and the lame" (Luke 14:21b). All are invited to the banquet, but each must be open to conversion, that is, "wearing a wedding robe" (Matt. 22:11–13). References are drawn between the heavenly banquet and the "breaking of the bread" by Jesus at the Last Supper (Luke 22:16, 18, 29–30) and as the theology of the Eucharist develops it is seen as the sacrament and foretaste of the heavenly banquet. Such development is beautifully expressed in the medieval antiphon *O Sacrum Convivium* — the sacred banquet in which a pledge of future glory is given to us.[29] In our globalized world, the banquet is a powerful and challenging image and vision of the Reign of God at all three "tables." All are invited to come to the banquet that God has prepared, and we are privileged to help God in extending that invitation through the work of prophecy and dialogue.

Chapter 9

A Short History
of the Church's Mission

Prophetic Dialogue through the Ages

The church, says Vatican II's Decree on Missionary Activity, is "missionary by its very nature," because it participates in the very life of the triune God, whose identity is self-diffusive love.[1] From the first nanosecond of creation God has been present through the Spirit, and God became concretely present in history through the Incarnation of the Divine Word. When we speak of the history of the church's mission, therefore, we are speaking of the history of the church. It used to be standard practice in historical studies of the church to speak about "church history" as distinct from "mission history," but this is becoming a distinction that is less and less valid. Works such as Dale Irvin and Scott Sunquist's *History of the World Christian Movement*, Frederick A. Norris's *Christianity: A Short Global History*, and a one-volume work currently being written by Roger Schroeder are all contributing to a reversal of perspective in the understanding of church history.[2]

Mission is not tangential to church history. It is rather at the heart of the church's life. Our story will be of the church's missionary activity and how that activity demonstrates the practice of prophetic dialogue. Because of this we will not dwell on such things as councils and popes and treaties between church and state. But the events, the movements, and the persons we will meet in the following pages will be just as important in the overall history of the church. While some of the central events and characters will be the same as in standard church history, many will not be. Such a history will certainly speak of Gregory the Great, Charlemagne, Luther, Francis, Clare, Nicea, Trent, Ignatius of Loyola, and Rose of Lima, but it will also include great missionaries like Alopen, Augustine of Canterbury, Cosmas and Damian, Raymond Lull, Matteo Ricci, and Marie of the Incarnation. Viewing the history of the church from a missionary perspective will also help us understand that our church has always been a world church, and that the Christian movement has always been a world Christian movement. The mission of the East Syrian Church on the Silk Road and into China is as important as the mission of Patrick to Ireland and Boniface to Germany. The conversion of Nubia (modern day Sudan) is as integral to the church's history as the conversion of Constantine. Down through the ages, there have been women and men committed to dialogue (Cyril and Methodius, Matteo Ricci, Anna Dengel) and women and men committed to prophecy (Francis Xavier, Bartolomé de Las Casas, Dorothy Day).

"The church exists by mission," twentieth-century Protestant theologian Emil Brunner wrote, "like a fire exists by burning."[3] We hope that these pages, although in a sketchy way, will show just that. Readers wanting more detail might want to consult our book *Constants in Context,* chapters 3 to 8.[4]

The Mission of Jesus Creates the Church

Jesus was a missionary, sent by God to preach, serve, and witness to the Reign of God. His was a message of the incredible love of God, forgiving sinners, including those usually excluded by polite religious society, healing the sick and driving out demons, challenging women and men to live in reconciliation with their neighbors, and even with their enemies. His was a vision of a new society, and his was a call to repentance, but not, as the Canadian novelist Rudy Wiebe paraphrases him, by feeling bad, but by "thinking different."[5] Everything he said in engaging parables and sayings, everything he did in works of healing and exorcism, and his very behavior of including everyone and even defying the Law for the sake of human beings helped explain his basic message: "The time is fulfilled, and the Kingdom of God is at hand; repent, and believe in the gospel" (Mark 1:15). Jesus' mission is the model for prophetic dialogue.

Jesus' challenge was to reimagine the world, to think different about God and religion and community, but it was still a challenge *within* Judaism — to imagine a new kind of Judaism, "to be Jewish in a new way," as U.S. Anglo theologian Kenan Osborne expresses it.[6] Even though he gathered a group of disciples around him and gave that group a basic structure with Peter and the Twelve, he probably had no idea (at least in the beginning of his ministry) that he was laying the foundations for what would later emerge as a "church," a community different from Judaism that would continue his mission after he was taken out of this world.

Nevertheless, Jesus was executed as a blasphemer and criminal as a direct result of the vision he lived and proclaimed. His challenge to reimagine was misunderstood by Judaism's insecure leaders as a betrayal of the Jewish tradition and as a vision that could subvert the colonial power of Rome. But the bonds of death could not bind him, and he was experienced by his timid followers as still alive. And so the community that he had formed in the time of his ministry continued to gather together in his name, to break bread in his memory as he had told them to do, and to listen to the wisdom of Peter and the Twelve. Even then, however, and even after the experience of the Spirit at Pentecost, the community still saw itself as basically Jewish. Yes, they realized that they had been called to continue Jesus' mission of preaching, serving, and witnessing to the Reign of God to the Jewish People. God had given the Jews a new chance after Jesus' resurrection, and the Jews were urged to proclaim Jesus as Messiah and repent before he would come again and reestablish the Kingdom of Israel. But they hardly understood themselves as a "church," a distinct reality from their Jewish identity and tradition.

Gradually, however, the community realized (according to the narrative in the Acts of the Apostles) that God in the Spirit had other plans for this little flock. It was only at Antioch that the Jesus community began to realize the full extent of its destiny and began to appropriate its identity. Listening to the boundary-breaking whispers of the Spirit, it recognized that it was the beginning of a new way of being religious. The people at Antioch began to speak of the community as "Christian" (Acts 11:26). The community saw itself now as "church."

It was, in other words, in the practice of mission — moving beyond the exclusive boundaries of Judaism and embracing in its community people of other nationalities and cultures — that this erstwhile Jewish sect began to recognize itself as more than Jewish in identity. The Spirit had pushed the community beyond Judaism to help it see that its faith in Jesus and its mission in his name gave it a new identity.

The Jesus community moved beyond Judaism and so became church. In the same way today, the repetition of this missionary dynamic continues to create the church. The church is missionary by its very nature, as it dialogues with the world's cultures, religions, and poor, and as it prophetically witnesses to and proclaims the gospel.

Paul and the New Testament Church

Although a kind of Jewish Christianity would continue to be a vital form of Christianity until the fourth or fifth century, especially in the area east of Palestine and in the Persian Empire, a Christianity that consisted of mostly Gentiles began to flourish in the Roman Empire, especially in Asia Minor, or what is now Turkey. One of the great missionaries of these early years of Christianity was the Jewish Christian Paul, whose missionary journeys throughout Turkey and Greece were extensive, and whose writings were so influential that some scholars have argued that it is Paul who is the real founder of the religion called Christianity. In Paul's letters we see that Paul was assisted in his missionary work by a large number of co-workers, both women and men. It seems that these early Christian missionaries made use of the vast network of Roman roads to preach the gospel in many of the major cities of the Empire, and we know from one of Paul's letters that the church was already firmly established in Rome itself. In the letter to the Romans, chapter 16, Paul mentions many of these women and men by name: the deacon Phoebe, the husband and wife team Prisca and Aquila, Epaenetus, Mary, Andronicus and Junia (whom he numbers among the apostles), Aristobulus, Persis, Hermes, and so on.

Paul's letters also give us a glimpse of some of the ministries that the early community in the Roman Empire engaged in. There were deacons, apostles, co-workers, healers, prophets, evangelists, pastors, teachers (see Rom. 16, 1 Cor. 12, Eph. 4). Other New Testament witnesses speak of presbyters or elders, often identified as overseers or bishops (e.g., 1 Tim. 3, Titus 1, James 5:14). Some of these ministries are certainly for the internal care of the community, but the constant growth of the Christian community bears witness to the fact that there must have been intentional missionary activity, even in the face of suspicion and persecution. The first letter of Peter urges people to give an account of the hope that they have within them (1 Pet. 3:15).

Gossiping the Gospel

Other early documents of the church reveal that there existed wandering apostles and prophets who, like Paul, went from town to town and city to city as they preached the gospel. These appear in one of the oldest Christian documents on record, perhaps a document older than some of our canonical texts: the Didache, or Teaching of the Twelve Apostles, dating from the beginning of the second century, most likely written in Syria. However, as Michael Green argues, perhaps the best missionaries of the early church were ordinary women and men who preached by the integrity of their lives and shared their enthusiasm with neighbors and relatives: people who "gossiped the gospel"[7] in the marketplace, while doing laundry, buying food at local shops. This informal missionary work is also attested to by sociologist of religion Rodney Stark, who writes about how most probably Christianity spread through personal and family networks, with wives convincing husbands, mothers sharing with daughters and sons, friends sharing with friends.[8]

It was a natural thing to do. The gospel was for sharing. But perhaps even more effective in terms of communicating the gospel was the witness of Christians. It is a commonplace that non-Christians at the time remarked at how Christians loved one another. Rodney Stark gives that statement credibility when he relates how people were impressed by the way Christians nursed one another during the inevitable plagues that broke out in crowded, unsanitary cities. But, he says, Christians even went beyond that. They also cared for people who were not members of their community, and many joined the church because of such witness. Ordinarily, people who got the plague were put out in the streets to die. Christians took care of other Christians and non-Christians alike. Perhaps this new religion was worth joining.

In the same way, people — especially women — were attracted by the seriousness with which Christians took marriage and parenthood. Divorce was forbidden. The killing of girl babies was forbidden, as well as abortion. The fact that being a Christian was practiced at a high cost — it could cost one her or his life — was also a kind of witness. The list of martyrs include Polycarp, Blandina, Cosmas and Damian, and Perpetua and Felicitas. The fact that people were willing to die for their beliefs and even hoped for a fuller life after death was attractive to people as well. Ultimately, Christianity grew because of the authentic, prophetic lives of ordinary people, people who lived mission in their daily lives.

Looking beyond Rome and the area north of the Mediterranean, probably the greatest area of Christian growth was in what is modern-day Turkey, Greece, Egypt and over the north coast of Africa. In north Africa was Alexandria, the intellectual center of the Roman Empire and the site of a famous catechetical school that, under the leadership of Pantaenus, Clement of Alexandria, and Origen, distinguished itself as a place of dialogue with Hellenistic culture and the Empire's mystery religions. Clement even spoke of the presence of Christ (the *logos*) in Indian religions. The Hellenistic concept of the *logos* had been used as early as the second-century philosopher and theologian Justin Martyr.

Christianity also spread quickly from Antioch through and beyond the far eastern reaches of the Roman Empire, and even into the lands of Rome's great rival, the Persian Empire. The apostles Thomas and Bartholomew and the teacher Pantaenus, following a sea route rather than one on land, are traditionally associated with the roots of Christianity in India; many Christians in southern India today still refer to themselves as "St. Thomas Christians." At the beginning of the fourth century, the king of Armenia, converted by the Cappadocian Gregory the Illuminator, declared his kingdom a Christian one, some years before the Roman Empire would do so.

Although Ethiopia traces its roots to evangelization by the anonymous Ethiopian eunuch in Acts 8, the first historical evidence of Christianity there goes back to Frumentius, a young Syrian in the fourth century. Frumentius had been sold as a slave to the king of Axum in Ethiopia; he preached the gospel and converted the king. The king sent him to the church of Alexandria in Egypt to ask for missionaries to come to the country, but instead Frumentius himself was consecrated bishop and sent back to Ethiopia in the name of the patriarch of Alexandria.

Mission and Monasticism

By the beginning of the fourth century, Christians comprised some 10 percent of the Roman Empire. According to Stark, for this to happen the rate of growth would have to have been 40 percent each decade, and at that rate by 350 Christians would number almost one-half of the Empire's population.[9] At the end of the third century Emperor Diocletian recognized this growth as a threat to Roman traditional religion and directed an Empire-wide persecution against Christians and any other religious body that did not submit to Roman religious practice. But the persecution failed to stem the tide of Christian growth. In the famous words of the Latin theologian Tertullian, the blood of martyrs was like seed, and Christian conversions continued. A new emperor, Constantine, realized that Christians were a group that could not be stopped, and so he allied himself with them. He had become sole emperor after the Battle of the Milvan Bridge outside of Rome, when he had ordered his soldiers to paint the cross on their shields. By 313 he had issued an Edict of Toleration, which at last legalized Christianity in the Empire and began to give this new religion a favored status in the Empire. By 381 Emperor Theodosius had declared Christianity the official religion of the Empire.

While this development was in some ways very beneficial to Christianity and was greeted enthusiastically by writers like Eusebius of Caesarea (who even spoke of Constantine as the thirteenth apostle!), there was a price to pay for such prosperity. Christianity had been a costly religion to join. Now it was advantageous to profess it. There began to be mass conversions to the faith, and with that there began to creep in a certain mediocrity of faith and practice.

It was in this context that a new movement began to develop in the church, that of monasticism. A number of men and women realized that a "red martyrdom" was no longer possible for Christians, but they began to seek a "white martyrdom" of more prophetic and ascetical life. One of the earliest of these white martyrs was Antony the Hermit, who lived in the desert of Egypt; he was one of countless hermits who fled the good life of the cities for the hard life of the desert. Many women, such as the famous Synlectica, were likewise a part of this movement. These men and women fled the world, but in many ways they could not succeed in doing that. They became sought-after figures to whom many people flocked for spiritual guidance and inspiration, and so their solitary and ascetical life was a new kind of witness in the world.

The shift from more individual asceticism to communal monasticism is marked by people like Pachomius and John Cassian, who began as hermits in North Africa, but around whom a community of monks soon formed. They became heads of communities of monks and wrote famous rules that are still read today for their wisdom. Both Pachomius and Cassian journeyed to Europe and established communities in what is now France. Some Egyptian monks were probably the first to bring the gospel message to Nubia, and it is said that some traveled to Ireland and were perhaps the founders of a rich Irish monasticism that flourished after Patrick converted the island in the fifth century.

Irish monasticism developed its own missionary method. As a kind of penance, individual Irish monks would set forth from Ireland in groups of twelve to what is now England and Scotland as "pilgrims for Christ" (*peregrini pro Christo*). They would preach the gospel as they traveled, and once they settled they would attract men to a monastic community, from which others would go on their own *peregrinatio*. The important monastery on the Scottish island of Iona is the foundation of the Irish monk Columba, and another monk, Columbanus, wandered as far as Italy, where he set up a monastery. Irish monasticism is famous as well for its "double monasteries" — monks and nuns living in separate quarters and yet worshiping and working together. Famous among such double monasteries were those headed by Abbess Bridget of Kildare in Ireland, by Cuthburga of Wimborne in southern England, and by Hilda at Whitby in northern England.

The monastic movement also flourished in Asia Minor (modern-day Turkey) and Greece. In Cappadocia in Asia Minor, men like Basil, his brother, Gregory of Nyssa, and his best friend, Gregory of Nazianzen, and women like Basil's and Gregory's sister, Macrina, lived at least part of their lives in monastic community, although all three men were tapped to become bishops — a common phenomenon at the time, despite their own personal opposition. All four Cappadocians drew deeply from Greek philosophy, and in this dialogue worked to defend and develop further the theology of the Trinity expressed inchoately at the Council of Nicea in 325.

Like many of the monks in the East and in the African desert, Benedict began his monastic life at the beginning of the sixth century as a hermit. Before long, however, his hermitage at Subiaco near Rome was surrounded by men who wanted to have his guidance. He soon wrote his famous Rule, moved south to Monte Cassino, and was joined by his twin sister, Scholastica, in a nearby monastery. Benedict's version of monasticism was less ascetical than that of the desert and the Irish monks. He balanced work and prayer and encouraged his monks to eat and drink properly. His version of monasticism soon became the most popular form of monasticism in Europe, and before long there were thousands of monasteries all over the continent. At a time when Europe was reeling from invasions from tribes from the north, and the Roman Empire in the West was tottering on the brink of ruin, Benedictine monks were witnesses to regularity and civilization. Their monasteries, as did the Irish monasteries before them, preserved the treasures of Western secular and religious culture. They preserved traditions of agriculture and pharmacology and educated young men in monastery schools. Their monasteries were outposts of evangelization, as evidenced by the work of the Anglo-Saxons Boniface and Leoba in what is now Germany, and Augustine of Canterbury in England. Boniface was perhaps too dismissive of local Saxon culture, but ironically his monastery was the place where the great Saxon gospel, the *Heliand,* a model of prophetic dialogue, was written in the ninth century.

Parallel to the asceticism movement in Egypt, people were drawn to the Syrian wilderness for a similar purpose, and a unique form of monasticism developed from this source. These black-robed (religious) and white-robed (secular) monks from East Syria and Persia traveled with traders on the Silk Road through the Persian Empire and on toward China. After Constantine's legitimation of Christianity in the Roman Empire, the Persian Empire began a dreadful persecution that cost the lives of tens of thousands of Christians. And after the appearance of Islam in the seventh century, Christians survived, but not always very well, under Muslim rule. But the monks continued to exist, as they established a network of monasteries that also served as places of hospitality and medical care along the Silk Road. A monument discovered in China in the seventeenth century tells us that East Syrian monks, led by a monk named Alopen, had come already by the seventh century and had traveled as far as Chang'an, the capital of the Chinese Empire under the hospitable T'ang dynasty and the largest city in the world at that time. They eventually built monasteries and churches, and they wrote the first Christian texts in Chinese. Relatively recently a collection of these Christian sutras (a literary style used by Buddhists) was discovered. The sutras are marvelous inculturations of the Christian faith, no doubt the result of serious dialogue within the multireligious context of seventh-century China. A century or so later, a bishop named Adam lived in the capital city and worked with Buddhist monks in translating both Christian and Buddhist Scriptures. Unfortunately this first great Christian period

in China came to an end at the beginning of the tenth century, when the
T'ang Dynasty fell and Christianity fell out of favor.

East Syrian monks also traveled to India, where they connected with
the "St. Thomas" Christians, and they may have traveled as far as Sri
Lanka and even Indonesia. They set up monasteries in these places,
served Christian traders and merchants, and no doubt evangelized the
indigenous population as well. Years later, when the Portuguese came
to India in the sixteenth century, they discovered a Christian community
there that had connections with the patriarchs of Persia and used Syriac
in their liturgies.

In the tenth century the monks Cyril and Methodius, two blood brothers, were sent from the Byzantine Church in the East to evangelize the
Slavs in what is now north-central Europe. In many ways we can understand them as pioneers of what we call today inculturation, since they
insisted that the gospel be preached and the Scriptures translated in the
local Slavic language. In order to do this they devised an alphabet for that
language, the alphabet that, even though it has changed over the years,
is still called by the name Cyrillic. Their efforts of adaptation, however, were fiercely opposed by missionaries from the Latin Church, and
the brothers had to journey to Rome to see the pope, who justified their
efforts. Around 1000 Russia was evangelized by monks from Byzantium.
The story is that when Russian representatives traveled to Byzantium and
experienced the splendor of the monastic liturgy, they were instantly converted and requested missionaries to Russia, who converted the czar and
the Russian people.

Mission and the Mendicant Movement

Monasticism continued to contribute to evangelization after the first millennium, as it still does today. However, another movement began to
emerge in the twelfth century that would be the primary way the gospel
was effectively preached from the thirteenth to the sixteenth centuries.
This was the mendicant movement, especially the developments of the
Order of Friars Minor under Francis of Assisi and the Order of Preachers
led by Dominic Guzmán of Caleruega.

The Franciscans and Dominicans, however, were only two examples
of movements that spread especially throughout Western Christianity at
the time. In the West, the church leadership had become powerful and,

inevitably, corrupt, and so there were many calls to return to the purity and simplicity of the gospel, and to live the *vita apostolica* or the apostolic life. Peter Waldo in France led one such movement — strongly lay in character — that called for hierarchical reform and more pastoral care of Christians. Unfortunately, Waldo's movement got on the wrong side of the church's leadership and was condemned, as were several other groups (such as the probably orthodox Humiliati and the certainly unorthodox Cathars). Francis's and Dominic's genius was to work for reform and renewal in the church while still staying faithful to the institution.

From the start, Francis's was a lay movement. The story of Francis's conversion and embrace of poverty is well known. He would go throughout Umbria in central Italy preaching the gospel wherever he could, and he soon attracted followers. At one point Francis journeyed east with one of the crusading armies and crossed the battle lines to preach to the sultan near Damietta. In what one might call a practice of prophetic dialogue, he stayed several days with the sultan, preaching, listening, and conversing. Instead of being put to death as Francis had hoped — to die a martyr's death for the faith — he preached to the sultan, who was very impressed with Francis's message and surely more with his person. Francis, in turn, was impressed by Muslim prayerfulness, and the conversation with the sultan affected a later writing of the Franciscan Rule. In that Rule, Francis talked about two kinds of preaching of the gospel — direct preaching and the preaching of witness. It may have been from these instructions that the dictum attributed to Francis has come: "Preach always. If necessary, use words."

Almost from the beginning Francis was joined by women. The first and closest to him was Clare of Assisi, who moved to a cloister with several other women in the town center, but whose ministry of prayer was not to pray for themselves but for the work that Francis and his brothers were doing. Rather than *reclusae,* or shutting out the world, they were *inclusae,* spiritually embracing the world despite being physically enclosed as prescribed by the church for women communities in those days. Clare sent many of her sisters to Muslim lands to witness to the gospel, even though most were martyred a short time after they arrived.

Two other important Franciscans need to be mentioned in this short history. Raymond Lull was a Third Order Franciscan lay brother and one of the most remarkable figures in the history of the church and its mission. His conviction was that Muslims could be converted if the gospel was presented to them in their own language and in ways that they could understand. So he spent his life learning Arabic, writing hundreds of volumes, and teaching in various places in Europe. He went on three missionary journeys to North Africa from Spain. On two of them he was almost immediately deported; on the third and last he was martyred.

The other important Franciscan of this time was John of Montecorvino, a Franciscan bishop who was sent to the court of the emperor of the Mongolian Empire in the 1200s. For a while, once again, Christianity flourished there. Pictures of John show him in episcopal attire, but with very strong Chinese accents in his dress.

Dominic Guzmán of Caleruega in Spain was a Canon Regular of Osma and traveled with his prior, Diego, now a bishop, on two diplomatic missions that would have a great impact on his later life. On one of these missions, in Toulouse in France, he encountered a Cathar and stayed up the whole night with him in conversation, trying to convince him of the church's truth and the Cathar's own error. In the end the Cathar repented and came back to the church. On another occasion, when Dominic encountered a group of inquisitors traveling in grand style, he suggested to them that they might do better to live more simply — perhaps their example would help change the heretics they wanted to root out. When Diego died and Dominic was on his own he gathered some followers to live out his own convictions of the simple life linked with piety and learning. This was the beginning of the Order of Preachers, or Dominicans, an order that took the thirteenth century by storm. The Dominicans were men of high learning, expert preachers and practitioners of simplicity of life who traveled the whole of Europe preaching and teaching reform. They also sent representatives to China.

As with the Franciscan movement, women were involved in the Dominican apostolates from the order's beginnings. Besides the cloistered order of women, the Dominicans included Third Orders of women and men who lived out the vision and spirituality of the mendicant movements within their normal daily lives. The most famous of this latter group was Catherine of Siena, who was noted in her hometown for her charitable deeds, her mystical spirituality, and her peacemaking ability among feuding families. She even traveled to Avignon to persuade the pope to return to Rome and get out from under the influence of the French king.

In the Low Countries especially there emerged a movement of women who were known by the name of Beguines (a parallel movement of men was called Beghards). These lay women lived together in communities (called Beguinages), but these were not monastic enclosures. They lived active lives of charity in the world. Especially noted among them were Mary of Oignes, Mechtilde of Magdeburg, and Mechtilde of Hackenborn. Because of their active lifestyle, however, they were always under suspicion by the church, and some of them were executed as heretics as well. But they represent women's constant efforts to live dedicated and active Christian lives in the midst of the world — efforts that would not be fully recognized and successful until the eighteenth and nineteenth centuries.

Toward the end of this era, in 1453, the great city of Byzantium (present-day Istanbul) finally succumbed to Muslim invaders, and the Byzantine Empire, which had lasted for a thousand years, beset on all sides by Muslim threats, was finally conquered. There had been sporadic missionary activity in the East even under the Muslim threat, but now mission became an impossibility. The baton of the Byzantine or Orthodox Church passed to Russia.

Mission in the Sixteenth Century and the Rise of the Jesuits

The next major development in the history of the church's mission occurred in the sixteenth century, the century when the West's horizon was indelibly altered by its initial encounter with the peoples of the Americas and by greater contact with the peoples of Asia. It was also a century when Christendom was torn apart by the schisms led by Luther, Calvin, and several other Reformers.

At the end of the fifteenth century, Christopher Columbus "discovered" or "encountered" or "invaded" (depending on one's perspective) a world that had been hitherto unknown to Europe. He and subsequent European explorers found a vast land teeming with people who had never heard of Christ or the gospel. While much of Spain's — and eventually Portugal's — motivation was that of greed, their kings and queens were also interested in converting the indigenous people of these (for Europeans) newly discovered lands. And so missionaries — Franciscans, Dominicans, Augustinians — accompanied the various explorers on their voyages of conquest and further discovery. This was the famous policy of the cross and the sword.

Converts were made, but there was much exploitation of the indigenous peoples of the Americas. In Hispaniola (the island where the Dominican Republic and Haiti are today), Dominican missionaries early on came to the defense of the indigenous peoples. Just before Christmas in 1501, the Dominican Antonio Montesinos preached a sermon in which he condemned the *encomenderos'* abuse of the local people: "You are all in mortal sin," he exclaimed, "and have as much chance of being saved as those who have not been baptized."[10]

A young priest and *encomendero* by the name of Bartolomé de Las Casas went through a major transformation as a result of the prophetic witness of these early Dominicans and the cruelty toward the local people that he witnessed. He eventually became a Dominican and for the rest of his life took up the cause of the indigenous peoples of the Americas. He made many trips back and forth across the Atlantic, defending their human rights before the king of Spain and church officials, and he wrote voluminously. Las Casas is called, rightly, the Defender of the Indians. Even though at one point he advocated the use of African slaves to take the place of the slightly built indigenous people, once he realized the inconsistency he repented of that opinion. He is one of the great "voices of compassion" of missionaries to Latin America in this era, a true prophet, deeply respectful of the humanity of the people whom he served.[11]

On the other side of the world, in the 1530s, Spain began to colonize the Philippines and, as in Latin America, Dominicans, Augustinians and Franciscans were sent to evangelize the country. At first the missionaries were quite open to the local culture. They learned the language and even translated a catechism, originally written in Mexico, into Tagalog, one of the local Filipino languages. Soon, however, the missionaries allied themselves much more with the Spanish government, owned huge tracts of land, and oppressed the local people. Some of the beautiful Spanish churches that still exist today were built with virtual slave labor, overseen by the Spanish missionaries. In the late nineteenth century, Filipino novelist and nationalist José Rizal wrote scathingly against the friars. The Philippines nevertheless is the third largest Catholic country in the world today and is known for its loyalty to the Catholic Church.

While Las Casas was desperately trying to persuade Spaniards and the pope to respect the humanity of the Latin American peoples, first Luther and then Calvin were beginning their momentous careers as the architects of Protestantism. They fought head on some of the abuses of the medieval church — corruption of the clergy, lack of pastoral care, forgetfulness of the Word of God, superstitious practices around the sacraments, the selling of indulgences — and when Rome would not listen they formed their own churches. Europe was split between Catholics and Protestants and not only was there religious turmoil but political turmoil as well. The next two hundred years would be years of senseless wars and persecution: Catholics of Protestants and Protestants of Catholics.

In this context was born the Society of Jesus, founded by Ignatius of Loyola, a former soldier who experienced conversion while recovering from a battle wound and who modeled his Society, or Company, of Jesus on a military brigade. Highly disciplined, highly educated, highly motivated, and highly mobile, the Jesuits, as they were called, embodied a completely different kind of religious life: they were *active* religious, not monks, not mendicants. They took a fourth vow to be at the pope's direct disposal, and they spread rapidly throughout Europe, using their learning and skill at preaching as strong tools to bring those who had gone over to Protestantism back to the Catholic Church.

The Jesuits were also new kinds of missionaries. They went to Latin America and started "Reductions," especially in Paraguay. These were settlements of indigenous people whom the Jesuits gathered together to protect from the exploiting Spanish and Portuguese. The film *The Mission* presented a stirring picture of the Jesuits' work in these reductions.

Jesuits also went to Asia. Perhaps the most famous was Francis Xavier, an original companion of Ignatius and his good friend. Xavier went first to India, where his zeal for conversions is legendary. He later went to Japan, and was so impressed with the culture that he spoke highly of it in a report to Ignatius. They were the best people he had encountered on his travels, he said, with a high culture, honest, and when convinced of the truth, ready to act on it. Whereas in India he had employed more of a *tabula rasa* approach to mission, which did not take the local culture into account, Xavier in Japan was much more culture conscious. He dressed like a Japanese, employed Japanese helpers, and tried to explain the gospel in ways that the Japanese could understand. It was not enough to be a prophetic preacher of the gospel. Dialogue was also necessary.

One of the most important Jesuit missionaries was the Italian Alessandro Valignano. Valignano was convinced that the missionaries had to get out from under the thumb of the Portuguese, the main European power in Asia at the time. For the Portuguese, becoming Christian meant leaving one's local culture behind and becoming European. Valignano, however, was convinced that Christianity was not tied to Europe, but could thrive in any culture. He tried to train the Jesuits under his guidance in this perspective and several stand out as models of his more dialogical approach.

The most famous of Valignano's protégés was Matteo Ricci. Ricci worked in China and became renowned for his mastery of the language, his mastery of the Confucian classics, and his knowledge of Western science. His immense learning eventually got him in contact with the emperor, and when Ricci died he was buried with the highest Chinese honors. He managed to convert a small but important group of Chinese, among whom were even men ordained as priests.

In India, the Jesuit Robert de Nobili adapted to the culture in much the same way. He dressed as a Hindu guru, or wise man, a *sannyasi,* and mastered the Sanskrit language — the first European to do so. He was learned in Hindu philosophy and sacred texts, and spoke of Christianity in terms of the Indian worldview. Sadly, he had much opposition in his life, and, while he was vindicated, his adaptations of the gospel, like Ricci's, were condemned in what is called the Rites Controversy. This was a sad, complicated chapter in the history of mission, which discouraged any real kind of taking the local culture seriously. The decisions of the Rites Controversy were reversed only around 1940.

One other Jesuit missionary in Asia should be mentioned here, although he lived later, in the seventeenth century. This was Alexandre de Rhodes, missionary to Vietnam. De Rhodes developed the alphabet for writing Vietnamese that is still used today. In a fascinating example of what we call today prophetic dialogue, he wrote a catechism that integrated Confucian principles into Christian doctrine and formed a group of men as catechists who were responsible for evangelization and teaching. He empowered the laity, including women, for leadership roles in the Christian community. He eventually was expelled from Vietnam and died as a missionary in Persia.

Jesuits also worked in North America among the Iroquois and Hurons in what is now Canada. Their work was also adapted to the local situation. They moved with the more nomadic First Nation peoples and did their best to learn their languages and customs. They were caught in the middle of tribal wars, however, and so were often looked upon with suspicion by one tribe over against the other. A number were martyred, among them Isaac Jogues and John de Brebeuf and the layman René Gupil. Marie of the Incarnation was the first woman missionary to North America. She settled in Montreal in Canada and set up schools for both French and Native American girls. Other French women came to Montreal as well. One Native American woman, Kateri Tekawitha, came to faith, inspired by the French missionaries and has been declared "blessed" by the church.

Europe at this time was being devastated by wars of religion, the aftermath of which was a great suspicion of religion and a greater trust in human reason. In this Enlightened Age there began to be, for the first time in history, a confidence in human potential, a doubt about the existence of a transcendent dimension of life, and the beginning of a secularity that led to out and out atheism.[12] As a result of many factors, not least of which were the Rites Controversy and the Jansenist controversy, the Jesuits were suppressed in 1773 (although they were never suppressed in Russia). The emotional and religious bankruptcy of Europe, the suppression of the Jesuits, and the disaster of the French Revolution of 1789 all conspired to practically put an end to mission work throughout the world. It is said that in 1800 there were only a few hundred Catholic missionaries still working around the world. This bleak picture, however, would change dramatically in the next century.

The "Great Century" of Christian Mission and the Society Model of Mission

The year 1800 was pretty much the nadir point for Catholic missionary activity around the world, but it also marked the beginning of the great surge of Protestant missionary work that marked the nineteenth and at least the first half of the twentieth century. Luther and especially Calvin had believed that there was no need for more missionary activity, since those who were destined to be saved had already had the gospel preached to them. There was some missionary activity by the Lutheran Pietists led by Count Nicholas Ludwig von Zinzendorf in the eighteenth century, but it was only after 1792, with the publication of William Carey's famous tract on the Christian obligation to convert the "heathen," that Protestant missionary work took off. And take off it did. Carey and his few companions went to India, and many others followed. Soon missionaries were going to China, and also to Africa. Mission became an important movement in the United States as well, and missionaries were also recruited for work in China, Polynesia, and Oceania. Many missionary societies like the Church Missionary Society, the London Missionary Society, and the Baptist Missionary Society in England and the American Board of Commissioners for Foreign Missions in the United States were formed.

The explosion of missionary activity in the nineteenth century coincided with interest in colonial expansion by Europe and later the United States. Colonialism made it easy for British missionaries to work in newly colonized lands like India, Kenya, and the Gold Coast (now Ghana). The colonizers were content that Christians could also be taught to be good British subjects, and mission schools educated young men and women in European languages and culture, helping to form a class of civil servants who would assist the colonizing powers in their rule. Missionaries, Catholic and Protestant, were not always intentionally the pawns of the ruling colonial powers, but they often were, consciously or unconsciously. A fine example of an indigenous missionary is Samuel Ajayi Crowther. He had been taken from his native Nigeria as a slave but was rescued by a British ship and placed in Freetown in Sierra Leone. Crowther went as a missionary to his native Yorubaland and eventually became a bishop. Even though he was passionate in preaching the gospel, his respect for Islam was great, as was his respect for African culture. He was the first African to take a lead in the translation of the Bible into an African language. In all of this he was a model of prophetic dialogue. Unfortunately his successor was not African but British.

By 1815 peace had been restored in Europe after the final defeat of Napoleon at Waterloo. The same year saw the lifting of the order of suppression of the Jesuits. Religious orders, expelled from France during the dark days of the Revolution, were beginning to be reestablished there. The papacy, which had reached its lowest point of power under Napoleon with the imprisonment of Popes Pius VII and VIII, was beginning to gain a new prestige in Europe. There had been a few missionary orders founded in the eighteenth and early nineteenth centuries: the Spiritans in 1703, the Sisters of St. Joseph of Cluny in 1807, what are today the Missionaries of the Precious Blood in 1815, the Oblates of Mary Immaculate in 1816, and the Marist Brothers in 1817. But after 1830 there was a virtual explosion of them as Catholicism achieved a new vitality and colonial expansion needed a religious dimension. The Marist Fathers were founded in 1836. In 1848, Francis Liebermann founded the Congregation of the Immaculate Heart of Mary and was asked to merge with , and take the name of, the Spiritans. The Missionaries of the Sacred Heart were founded in 1855 by Jean Jules Chevalier (1824–1907). In 1866 the Mill Hill Missionaries were founded, in 1867 the Comboni Missionaries, in 1868 the White Fathers, and in 1875 the Society of the Divine Word by Arnold Janssen. Many of these male congregations had sister congregations: Marist Sisters, Sisters of the Precious Blood, Comboni Sisters, Missionary Sisters of the Holy Spirit, Sisters of the Holy Spirit of Perpetual Adoration. The United States saw the founding of the Sisters of the Blessed Sacrament and the Sisters of the Holy Family, both of which were dedicated to working among African Americans; the former, founded by St. Katharine Drexel, also worked among Native Americans.

In the nineteenth century, and into the twentieth, there were thousands of missionaries in the field. Sixty percent of Protestant missionaries from the United States were women, according to historian Dana Robert.[13] There were also many women serving as Catholic missionaries, although not as many as Protestants. The work of mission was varied: schools, universities, hospitals, clinics, charitable services, and material aid. Most had a clear idea of the goal of mission work, the salvation of souls, and the implantation of the church. Many missionaries thought (actually contrary to the teaching of the Catholic Church) that those who died without baptism were condemned to hell, or at least sent to limbo. Local cultures and religions were considered basically evil, so the cultural and religious practices of local peoples needed to be jettisoned if they were to become true Christians. This was the age of certainty,[14] the "great century" as historian Kenneth Latourette entitled three of the volumes of his multivolume history of mission.[15] Missionaries worked in all parts of Africa, in South, Southeast, and Northeast Asia, in the islands of the Pacific, in Latin America, and in New Zealand and Australia.

In 1910 about twelve hundred delegates from all over the Protestant world met at Edinburgh, Scotland, for a great World Mission Conference. Its theme was the watchword of John R. Mott: "the evangelization of the world in this generation." Such confidence was soon to come to a crashing end.

Twentieth Century into the Twenty-first

Despite the devastation caused by the two great wars of the first half of the twentieth century, the "age of certainty" lingered for some time. But it was a certainty that was being steadily undermined by new understandings of theology, new understandings of culture, the beginning of the decolonization era, and the subsequent rise of nationalism and the renaissance of local religions. By the time of Vatican II change was in the air, ushering in what Robert J. Schreiter has called the "age of ferment" in mission within the Catholic Church.

Vatican II presented a different image of the church. Mission was part and parcel of the church's very identity, and mission was not understood so much as a territorial reality as one focused on particular people in particular circumstances. In some ways it echoed what a 1963 meeting sponsored by the World Council of Churches in Mexico described as mission today being carried out "on six continents."[16] This perspective was one of the major contributions of *Ad Gentes,* the Council's document on mission. Culture too, as presented in *Ad Gentes* and the document on the Church in the Modern World (*Gaudium et Spes*) was looked upon positively as missionaries were urged to "learn by sincere and patient dialogue what treasures a generous God has distributed among the nations of the earth."[17] The Council also acknowledged in its Declaration on Non-Christian Religions (*Nostra Aetate*) that in these religions is found "a ray of that Truth which enlightens all peoples."[18] The Council clearly taught the possibility of salvation outside explicit faith in Christ.[19]

This age of ferment that ushered in very new ideas of mission soon brought the church's understanding of mission to a crisis — one that was being felt in the Protestant churches as well as in the Catholic Church. As Anglican bishop Stephen Neil put it famously, if everything is mission, then nothing is mission. If the entire church is missionary, in other words, there is no need for a special mission across cultures, nor a need for particular people to serve as crosscultural and foreign missionaries.

If cultures are holy and good, why should Christians disturb them with a Western religion? And, perhaps most distressing of all, if women and men can be saved without explicit knowledge of Christ and without the church, why should people leave their homes and cultures to preach the gospel? In the wake of Vatican II, missionary vocations began to fall off and many missionaries left the mission field to work in their own countries. At the end of the 1960s and early 1970s there was talk of a "moratorium" on missionary activity. All foreign missionaries were urged by some people in traditional mission lands to go home and to offer the resources that supported foreign missionaries for the development of local churches.

Around the year 1975, however, after the Synod of Bishops on evangelization, with the publication of Paul VI's apostolic exhortation *Evangelii Nuntiandi* and with similar developments within Protestantism like the Nairobi meeting of the World Council of Churches and the Lausanne meeting of Evangelical Christians in 1974, mission began to undergo a "new birth." What *Evangelii Nuntiandi* did was to broaden the very idea of mission to include activities like inculturation and working for justice and liberation.

Such broadening of mission continued in John Paul II's encyclical *Redemptoris Missio* when he spoke of mission as a "single but complex reality."[20] John Paul II spoke of mission as including not only inculturation and work for justice, but also interreligious dialogue. In paragraph 37 of *Redemptoris Missio,* he also spoke of many other venues for mission: work in communications, urban ministry, youth, and science, for example.

In the years since *Redemptoris Missio* there have been several developments in the church's understanding of mission. In the aftermath of the great Medellín Conference of 1968 in Colombia, there emerged a theology of liberation. This theology developed not theoretically, but out of the practice of action/reflection of grassroots Christians committed to and working for political and social freedom, and from the personal and structural sinfulness in which institutional oppression resulted. While liberation theology focused more on the prophetic aspect of mission, it nevertheless was rooted in a dialogue with the poor and, in more recent years, with popular religiosity and indigenous cultures.

Robert J. Schreiter has articulated the need to include an understanding of working for reconciliation as an integral part of mission in today's very violent world. Especially after the fall of regimes of oppression, as in South Africa, Argentina, and Nicaragua, and after situations of genocidal slaughter, as in Rwanda and Burundi, reconciliation is no theoretical reality, but an urgent necessity. Schreiter claims that reconciliation is one of the major forms the Good News can take in the world today, and so is integral to missionary practice.

There have been cautions issued by the Vatican about a tendency in Asian churches to blur the significance of the centrality of Christ as universal savior and to minimize the prophetic or proclamation aspect of mission. While the tone of these interventions has been unfortunate, their point is certainly valid. A true dialogue with other people of faith can be possible only if we have a firm sense of Christ's unique role in salvation history. It needs to be a prophetic dialogue.

More and more the issue of migration has come to the fore as central to the church's missionary activity. In many ways the "world of the missions" has come to the "home churches." In this way, there are no more churches that are simply "sending" and "receiving," but all are both.

This last reality is true in another sense in today's church. As missionary vocations have decreased in the West, more and more missionaries from the Majority World are being sent to other traditionally "mission countries," and they are also being sent to minister to migrants in Western countries as well. In our own congregation of the Society of the Divine Word, for example, about one-fourth of our membership is Indonesian, and our largest numbers of missionaries today are coming from Indonesia, India, and the Philippines. Among Protestants, the largest number of missionaries comes from Korea. Many Majority World missionaries also see themselves as missionaries to Europe, North America, Australia, and New Zealand — sent to reevangelize cultures that have become secularized and deaf to the gospel message. This, of course, has raised its own problems.

Mission today is also being carried out in large part by laywomen and laymen, many of them on short-term mission lasting from a week (doctors going to Haiti) to several years (the Maryknoll Society of the Faithful, who sign up for five-year stints, renewable indefinitely). In some ways, today's most significant missionary work is being done by laity in these shorter terms — so much so that we could call today the era of Short-Term Lay Missionaries.

Conclusion

What is written in these few pages barely scratches the surface of the church's long history, much of which has been marked by missionary witness of both prophecy and dialogue. What we hope readers will realize, however, is how central missionary activity is and has been to the church. Missiologists and other religious writers suggest that today we are living in the era of the "world church." But those who know the church's history — its entire history — know that we have *always* lived in such an age. Christianity was born in Asia, spread East to India, Persia, and on to China, south into Ethiopia and Nubia, West across North Africa and north into what has become France, Germany, Ireland, England, and Scotland. When Europe "discovered" new lands, the church went there as well. Throughout this history, it needed to be in dialogue with Zoroastrianism, Judaism, Roman religion, Islam, the various religions of northern Europe, Hinduism, Buddhism, Confucianism, and the local religions of Indonesia and the Philippines. Many missionaries, like Alopen, Cyril and Methodius, and Alexandre de Rhodes, were in serious dialogue with local cultures. And many others, like Francis of Assisi, Bartolomé de Las Casas and Marie of the Incarnation, were always involved with the welfare of the people they served. There has also been a shadow side to mission. Missionaries like Boniface and the Spanish friars in the Americas disparaged culture and preached a Christianity that destroyed it. Many demonized local religions. Many were collaborators with the colonial expansion of the nineteenth century.

In addition to the lights and shadows, however, is another factor. In *Evangelii Nuntiandi*, Paul VI emphasized the fact that "the Holy Spirit is the principal agent of evangelization."[21] It is the Spirit that created the church in the first place, continues to equip the church for the work of mission by lavishing gifts on every Christian, and constantly challenges the church to move prophetically beyond its "comfort zone" in order to do God's purposes in the world. In a real way, the history of mission is the history of the Holy Spirit, the history of God "inside out" in creation. Our great privilege and grace as church is to somehow be participants — sacraments, actually — of that history of love, healing, liberation, and prophetic dialogue.

Chapter 10

Church Teaching, Mission, and Prophetic Dialogue

Ad Gentes, Evangelii Nuntiandi, Redemptoris Missio, *and* Dialogue and Proclamation

This chapter is a summary of the church's official teaching in the Roman Magisterium on the theology and conduct of its evangelizing mission. Rather than summarize each *document,* however, which would be quite tedious and repetitious, we will rather select the several topics of each document that present new aspects of the Magisterium's teaching on mission and harmonize them with the theme of this book: prophetic dialogue. We will start with Vatican II's Decree on the Church's Missionary Activity, *Ad Gentes,* and will include *Evangelii Nuntiandi, Redemptoris Missio*, and *Dialogue and Proclamation*, a document issued shortly after *Redemptoris Missio* by the Congregation for the Evangelization of Peoples and the Pontifical Council on Interreligious Dialogue. This last document, issued in 1991, is now twenty years old. Since then two other documents have been issued by the Roman Magisterium that are important for the church's mission — *Dominus Iesus* in 2000 and *Doctrinal Note on Some Aspects of Evangelization* in 2007, both issued by the Congregation for the Doctrine of the Faith. These, however, are more cautionary in tone and do not present any new or constructive teaching as such. We will refer to them toward the end of the chapter, but only briefly.

Ad Gentes (1965)

Ad Gentes, Vatican II's Decree on the Church's Missionary Activity, almost didn't get written. Before the Council began the Congregation for the Propagation of the Faith under the leadership of Cardinal Gregorio

Agagianian was given the task of drafting a document on the church's mission, but the result was more a summary and some revision of Canon Law as it applied to the missions rather than a theological reflection on the basis and conduct of mission. This first draft never got to the Council floor. It was a casualty of the virtual revolt of many bishops at the Council against, in the famous words of Bishop Emil de Smedt of Bruges, Belgium, the "hierarchical, clerical, and juridical" tone of the drafts that had been presented at the first session. A second draft was made, but it too was sidelined because of a ruling that called for many of the schemata to be reduced to a number of propositions. When the fifteen or so propositions were presented on the Council floor, however, they were virtually shouted down by the bishops, who called for a "full schema" that was theologically grounded. Under the leadership of SVD Superior General Johannes Schütte and with the main authorship of theologians of the caliber of Yves Congar, Joseph Ratzinger, and Karl Rahner, a draft of the present document was presented at the last session and, after a number of last-minute revisions, was unanimously approved by the Council Fathers on the last day of the Council.[1]

Ad Gentes, if not the Magna Carta of mission as it was described by Fr. Schütte, is nevertheless a remarkable document. We will focus here on only a few of its many important teachings, but these few are where the document has contributed most to the Magisterium's teaching on mission in the last half century.

The Church Rooted in the *Missio Dei*

The first aspect of the teaching of *Ad Gentes* that we would like to highlight is in paragraph 2. Here the text speaks of the ultimate foundation for the church's missionary activity: its participation in the mission of the Son and the Holy Spirit. Such participation through baptism in the very life of the Trinity, therefore, makes the church "missionary by its very nature." Here is this most important text in full: "The pilgrim Church is missionary by her very nature, since it is from the mission of the Son and the mission of the Holy Spirit that she draws her origin, in accordance with the decree of God the Father."

This is a radical statement on several accounts. First, it emphasizes the fact that mission is not just *one* thing the church does. It is rather constitutive of its very being. To be a Christian, in other words, is to be caught up in the very life of God, which is a life of reaching out and saving presence in the world. The entire church is missionary. Mission is not just something that specialists (missionaries) do. It is something that all Christians are called to. This theology, ultimately written by Congar and quite strongly fought over by the drafting commission, moves mission away from something just directed by the Roman Congregation for the Propagation of the Faith and places it squarely in the daily life of the church as such, and so it is the responsibility of every local bishop (something the decree emphasized again and again).

In his important commentary in the Unam Sanctam series Congar points to the Catholic roots of this theological foundation in the scholastics and the seventeenth-century French school of spirituality. He also acknowledges the influence of contemporary Protestant thinking on mission as participation in God's mission, the *Missio Dei*.[2] Mission, ultimately, is not something done because of a command, even the "great commission" of Matthew 28:19–20. Mission is, in its deepest identity, a privilege and a grace. The decree is not always consistent on this, but it is the logical conclusion from the church's essential missionary identity.

From Territory to People

A second rather radical implication of *Ad Gentes,* 2, follows from the first. This is that mission has now been defined not as a *territorial* concept, but as a basic attitude of the church wherever it is. Crossing boundaries, moving beyond itself, is at the center of the church's identity. While pastoral care is certainly central as well to the church's life, it must not eclipse the church's reaching out, making a difference in the world around it. Mission, then, is not about going places, but serving people — down the street or across oceans, in other cultures or one's own. While, again, the document is not totally consistent in this regard, and gradually speaks more of "younger churches" or "mission churches" implying that "missions" are in "mission countries," the seeds had been sown. This tension in the document represents the great tension in the drafting committee. Yves Congar wrote in his journal about the opposition of the "missiologists" (experts in mission law) to the "theologians."[3]

Toward Inculturation

Ad Gentes does not use the word "inculturation." This is a word that begins to appear regularly in the theological and missiological literature only in the 1970s, and is first used in a Roman magisterial document only in John Paul II's apostolic exhortation *Catechesi Tradendi* in 1979. Nevertheless, the document contains passages that certainly anticipate the discussion on inculturation in the following decade, and points to the importance of a dialogical stance in the practice of mission itself. Perhaps the most powerful expression of the need to appreciate culture and employ it in evangelization appears in paragraph 11:

> In order that they [Christians] may be able to bear more fruitful witness to Christ, let them be joined to those peoples by esteem and love; let them acknowledge themselves to be members of the group of people among whom they live; let them share in cultural and social life by the various undertakings and enterprises of human living; let them be familiar with their national and religious traditions; let them gladly and reverently lay bare the seeds of the Word which lie hidden among their fellows. At the same time, however, let them look to the profound changes which are taking place among nations, and let them exert themselves to keep modern persons, intent as they are on the science and technology of today's world, from becoming a stranger to things divine; rather, let them awaken in them a yearning for that truth and charity which God has revealed. Even as Christ Himself searched the hearts of women and men, and led them to divine light, so also His disciples, profoundly penetrated by the Spirit of Christ, should show the people among whom they live, and should converse with them, that they themselves may learn by sincere and patient dialogue what treasures a generous God has distributed among the nations of the earth. But at the same time, let them try to furbish these treasures, set them free, and bring them under the dominion of God their Savior.

This is truly a remarkable passage, and one that has hardly been improved upon in teachings on inculturation in subsequent documents. The "they" at the beginning of the passage refers to either people indigenous to a particular place or to missionaries sent to witness to the gospel. Christians are called to be real participants in the cultural and political life of the nations in which they live and are called to be people of "sincere and patient dialogue" in order to discover the treasures that God has so generously lavished on the world's cultures. But, as papal documents had pointed out even before this one, Christians are to integrate such treasures into Christian expression with a critical, we would say prophetic, sense. Still, the document is completely positive, calling for cultures to be "furbished" by setting them free to be fully what they are — which will happen as they come under the rule of Christ and of God.

A similar passage anticipating inculturation appears in paragraph 22. The passage is too long to quote, but we will try to summarize it here, with ample quotations from the text. Once again, it is a remarkable teaching, particularly in the light of the disparagement of culture that so often (but not always) took place in the exercise of Christian mission. As late as 1960, a response to a paper that tried to propose the development of an "African Theology" was responded to by a paper by a Belgian missionary entitled "First, a Real Theology" (meaning, of course, a European theology!).[4]

The passage appears in the context of chapter 3 of the decree, entitled "Particular Churches." It contains another breakthrough teaching of *Ad Gentes,* which is that no matter how "young" or fragile a church is, it is still a *church* in the proper sense and must be treated as such. Specifically, the passage deals with the importance of developing a philosophy and especially a theology in each particular church which, though connected with the wider Christian tradition, nevertheless is a product of a borrowing "from the customs and traditions of their people, from their wisdom and their learning, from their arts and disciplines, all those things which can contribute to the glory of their Creator, or enhance the grace of their Savior, or dispose Christian life the way it should be." By submitting God's revelation to a "new scrutiny," a new understanding of Christianity can be developed, relevant for that culture or context. "Thus it will be more clearly seen in what ways faith may seek for understanding, with due regard for the philosophy and wisdom of these peoples; it will be seen in what ways their customs, views on life, and social order can be reconciled with the manner of living taught by divine revelation."

If this is done carefully, the passage continues, there will be no danger of "selling out" the gospel or falling into a "false particularism." Rather, there will be a new richness added to the unity of the church throughout the world.

Missionary Qualities

Chapter 4, entitled simply "Missionaries," is hailed by many commentators as the best chapter in the entire decree.[5] The chapter is clear that being a missionary is a vocation, a particular calling from God to people who have "a suitable natural temperament," and are "fit as regards talent and other qualities." As suitable as these women and men are, however, the chapter lays out the kind of training and formation that missionaries need. The list of qualities and skills in which they are to be trained is a long one. They are to be people of perseverance, generosity, and courage — even willing to lay down their lives for the faith if necessary. They should be adaptable, prayerful, and have a knowledge of the history of the peoples to whom they are sent as well as an understanding of current issues in those particular situations. Every effort should be made to learn the local language or languages. They should be trained both in theology and missiology. Significantly, the training they receive should be given in the lands where they will work, and such training is recommended not only for foreign missionaries, but for indigenous members of particular countries and cultures who will work there as well. Simply because one is a native of a particular context, in other words, does not insure that one already has the skills to work effectively in that context.

All of this, of course, is very ideal. It may even paint an overly romantic picture of the missionary life. It does, however, provide a standard to which missionary congregations and agencies should try to measure up. Certainly in the past there have been horror stories of women and men who have been placed in cross-cultural situations with no training whatsoever, not even in language. Such situations were certainly more common in the days before the Council, and it is particularly these that the decree addresses. From our own experience and knowledge, much more can always be done, especially in the area of language study and ministerial supervision in the first months and years of a person's ministry.

In sum, the program of *Ad Gentes* lays the foundation for what we have come to speak of as an approach to missionary practice characterized as prophetic dialogue. The document emphasizes in particular the prophetic proclamation of the gospel, but it also emphasizes the need for respect and dialogue ("sincere and patient" — *Ad Gentes,* 11) with the world's cultures and religions. Subsequent documents will fill out the picture more fully.

Evangelii Nuntiandi (1975)

Paul VI's apostolic exhortation *Evangelii Nuntiandi* was written at a time when the very idea of mission was being seriously questioned. *Ad Gentes* and Vatican II in general had opened up fresh perspectives on mission (in fact, we think it can be appreciated more today than in the troubled times in which it was written). But some of these fresh perspectives also raised profound questions. If, as the document on the church had taught, women and men could be saved outside the church and without any explicit faith in Christ (see *Lumen Gentium,* 16), and if every church does mission in the context in which it exists, why should missionaries be sent abroad to convert people to Christ? If cultures are already good and holy, why should missionaries disturb them with Western ideas and Western religious forms? It was in this context that Paul VI convoked the 1974 Synod of Bishops with the theme "Evangelization in the Modern World." It was from the deliberations of the Synod and Paul VI's careful listening to the bishops of the Majority World that Paul developed his ideas for his apostolic exhortation.[6]

Interestingly, perhaps as a reflection of the rather strong aversion to the word "mission" that had emerged in the churches and in theology and (ironically!) *missi*ology, the pope uses the word "evangelization." However, the meaning of the terms is the same, and we believe that they can be used interchangeably. As we will see below, the pope does widen the idea of mission to include aspects other than simply witnessing to the faith in word and deed, but he still understands such witness to be at the heart of the evangelizing process.

The Church's Mission Continues the Mission of Jesus

The first significant teaching of *Evangelii Nuntiandi* comes in the very first chapter. Like *Ad Gentes,* the apostolic exhortation will emphasize the essential missionary nature of the church. Unlike the Council document, however, it does not begin with the grand doctrine of the Trinity. Instead, the pope begins with Jesus' prophetic mission of preaching and witnessing to the Reign of God. "As an evangelizer, Christ first of all proclaims a kingdom, the kingdom of God; and this is so important that, by comparison, everything else becomes 'the rest,' which is 'given in addition.' Only the kingdom therefore is absolute and it makes everything else relative" (*Evangelii Nuntiandi,* 8). Jesus both *taught* about God's Reign in parables and words of wisdom, and *demonstrated* its reality by his works of healing and exorcism (*Evangelii Nuntiandi,* 11–12), and those who accepted his message as good news formed "a community which is in its turn evangelizing" (*Evangelii Nuntiandi* 13). This is why "evangelizing is in fact the grace and vocation proper to the Church, her deepest identity. She exists in order to evangelize."

This section of *Evangelii Nuntiandi* is very rich and very dense — it is certainly our own favorite chapter in the document. Almost everything is worth quoting. Rather than that, however, let us highlight three things Paul VI insists on in talking about the fact that the church "is linked to evangelization in her very being" (*Evangelii Nuntiandi*, 15).

First, the pope insists that the church needs to be evangelized itself before it takes on the task of evangelization. It must constantly listen to the Word of God; it must constantly be on the road of conversion. This does not mean that the church must wait until it "gets its act together" before it moves out on mission. If this were the case it would never go! But it does mean, to use the great phrase of South African missiologist David J. Bosch, that its work of evangelization needs always to be carried out in a kind of "bold humility"[7] — bold in preaching the gospel, but humble in its realization that it too needs the repentance to which the gospel calls humanity.

Second, Paul VI insists on the strong link between Jesus' witness to the Reign of God and the church. There is real continuity between Jesus' mission and the mission of the church, "the normal, desired, most immediate and most visible fruit" of Jesus' work. In a time when the watchword was often "Jesus yes, the church no," the pope insists on the fact that evangelization is an ecclesial task through and through. Evangelization is "not accomplished without her, and still less against her" (*Evangelii Nuntiandi*, 16).

Third, the fact that the church is so essentially missionary means that *everyone* in the church is called to participate in the church's mission: "the work of each individual member is important for the whole" (*Evangelii Nuntiandi*, 15). Like *Ad Gentes, Evangelii Nuntiandi* does not want to reduce missionary work to only certain people in the church — members of missionary congregations or the hierarchy. This is a call especially to lay involvement in mission.

Evangelization a Multifaceted Reality

One of the most important teachings of the apostolic exhortation is the expansion of the church's understanding of mission to include a variety of activities other than direct proclamation of the gospel, working for conversion, and planting the church. *Ad Gentes* certainly hints at this richness in the meaning of mission, but *Evangelii Nuntiandi* moves a step farther. There had been a tendency in the past to reduce evangelization to direct proclamation of Christ to those who do not yet know him. However, says the pope, "any partial and fragmentary definition which attempts to render the reality of evangelization in all its richness, complexity and dynamism does so only at the risk of impoverishing it and even of distorting it. It is impossible to grasp the concept of evangelization unless one tries to keep in view all its essential elements" (*Evangelii Nuntiandi*, 17).

The pope then goes on to emphasize that while preaching Christ is important — indeed, there is no evangelization at all if this does not happen (*Evangelii Nuntiandi*, 22) — there are several other "essential elements." First, there is the witness of a vibrant Christian community, without which the church can have no credibility. In a famous line, the pope quotes a speech he had recently delivered: today people listen "more willingly to witnesses than to teachers, and if [they do] listen to teachers, it is because they are witnesses" (see *Evangelii Nuntiandi*, 41). Second, the pope stresses the importance of the evangelization of cultures, "not in a purely decorative way, as it were, by applying a thin veneer, but in a vital way, in depth and right to their very roots" (*Evangelii Nuntiandi*, 20).

Evangelization and Liberation

Evangelization includes a commitment to full human development and especially to social justice. Only four years before, the Synod of Bishops spoke about working for justice as a "constitutive dimension of the preaching of the gospel," and Paul VI includes this in his expanded vision of evangelization (see *Evangelii Nuntiandi*, 29). But the pope — although somewhat cautiously — carries this further, in the light of contemporary discussions of justice, particularly in Latin America. In paragraph 29, the word "liberation" (in the sense of the "theology of liberation") is used for the first time in a Roman magisterial document: "Evangelization involves an explicit message, adapted to the different situations constantly being realized, about the rights and duties of every human being, about family life without which personal growth and development is hardly possible, about life in society, about international life, peace, justice and development — a message especially energetic today about liberation."

Evangelii Nuntiandi's teaching on liberation and evangelization is quite balanced, and there are two things on which it insists. First, evangelization is not to be *reduced* to political or economic well-being. The spiritual dimension of the gospel is actually the source of humanity's deepest liberation. Second, violence is never to be sanctioned, because the church knows that "violence always provokes violence and irresistibly engenders new forms of oppression and enslavement which are often harder to bear than those from which they claimed to bring freedom" (*Evangelii Nuntiandi*, 37).

One could say much more about this Magna Carta of mission documents, but these three points will suffice. Viewing the document through the lens of prophetic dialogue, we might point out how the pope's insistence on the various dimensions of missionary activity emphasizes both the proclamation aspect of prophecy and the more critical aspect of denunciation of unjust structures involved in the theology of liberation. On the other hand, the pope implies in his call to evangelize cultures the dialogical dimension of all evangelizing activity. *Evangelii Nuntiandi*'s program is continued and expanded in the document that commemorates *Ad Gentes*'s twenty-fifth anniversary and its own fifteenth: John Paul II's massive 1990 encyclical *Redemptoris Missio*.

Redemptoris Missio (1990)

Although it was not officially published until January, 1991, Pope John Paul's encyclical *Redemptoris Missio* is dated December 7, 1990, on the eve of the twenty-fifth anniversary of *Ad Gentes* and the fifteenth anniversary of *Evangelii Nuntiandi*. The encyclical returns to the use of the term "mission," although the pope uses "evangelization" interchangeably with it, and speaks of it in a very broad and multifaceted way. *Redemptoris Missio* is the closest the Roman Magisterium has ever gotten to articulating a comprehensive and systematic reflection on mission, and while it may not be quite as inspiring as *Evangelii Nuntiandi* it represents a major step forward in the church's official teaching on what has come to be called its "evangelizing mission." A summary of the entire document would far exceed our purposes here, and so we will focus on three important aspects of *Redemptoris Missio*'s teaching: its Christocentric focus, its expansion of the understanding of mission, and its inclusion of interreligious dialogue as constitutive of the church's mission.

Christocentric Focus

At a press conference given soon after the publication of the encyclical, Cardinal Josef Tomko, then the prefect of the Congregation for the Evangelization of Peoples, explained that one of the chief reasons for the pope's writing *Redemptoris Missio* was to correct a Christology being developed by some theologians that tended to obscure Christian belief that Jesus was indeed the unique and universal savior of humanity.[8] Although he didn't mention names, it is pretty clear that he had in mind a number of Indian and other Asian theologians, and probably also the U.S. theologian Paul Knitter.

While the pope holds fast to the church's traditional teaching, clearly articulated at Vatican II, that people have the possibility to be saved outside of explicit faith in Christ (see *Redemptoris Missio,* 10), his position also reflects the Council's teaching that, nevertheless, all grace comes through Christ, and Christ alone.

> No one, therefore, can enter into communion with God except through Christ, by the working of the Holy Spirit. Christ's one, universal mediation, far from being an obstacle on the journey toward God, is the way established by God himself, a fact of which Christ is fully aware. Although participated forms of mediation of different kinds and degrees are not excluded, they acquire meaning and value only from Christ's own mediation, and they cannot be understood as parallel or complementary to his. (*Redemptoris Missio,* 5)

The pope's insistence on the centrality of Christ runs through every section of *Redemptoris Missio* and is definitely the major theological theme of the encyclical. The first chapter deals with this teaching directly, emphasizing the fact that explicit faith in Christ is what gives women and men the fullness of life. All people have a right to the truth and life that the gospel offers, although the gospel is always addressed to human beings in their freedom, and never imposed upon them (*Redemptoris Missio,* 7–8).

Chapter 2 reflects on the centrality of the Reign of God in Jesus' ministry and says clearly that the church is not an end in itself — perhaps the clearest statement of this fact in a magisterial document up to this time (see *Redemptoris Missio,* 18), but that does not mean that the Reign of God is separate from Jesus or the church. In fact, the pope insists, the

Reign of God is not a concept, a doctrine, or a program; it is a *person,* the person of Jesus of Nazareth.

Chapter 3 is on the Holy Spirit, and again, while the Spirit is understood as the "principal agent of evangelization" (see the title of the chapter), the pope insists that the Spirit is the Spirit of Jesus, and not some vague, general form of God's presence (see *Redemptoris Missio,* 29). Each of these three chapters opposes any generalizing or watering down of the specificity of Christ: mission is about proclaiming the person and work of Christ, not helping people recognize God's mysterious presence as *logos,* or in "Kingdom values," or in the pervasive presence of the Spirit. John Paul II would emphasize the prophetic aspect of mission, the proclamation of Jesus' Lordship.

"Why mission?" the pope asks. "Because to us, as to St. Paul, 'this grace was given, to preach to the Gentiles the unsearchable riches of Christ' (Eph. 3:8)" (*Redemptoris Missio,* 11).

Expanding the Idea of Mission

There are two ways in which John Paul expands the notion of mission in the encyclical. The first way is to distinguish three "situations" of the church's missionary activity. The second is to speak of mission as a "single but complex reality," composed of several elements.

The first "situation" of the church's missionary activity is mission *ad gentes,* or the direct witnessing and proclamation of Christ in situations where he is not known, or where the church is not strong enough to proclaim the gospel in a fully inculturated way (*Redemptoris Missio,* 33). This is mission, the pope says, in the proper sense of the word. However, the pope also speaks, second, about pastoral work among the established churches and, third, what he had been calling the "new evangelization" in churches "where entire groups of the baptized have lost a living sense of the faith, or even no longer consider themselves members of the Church, and live a life far removed from Christ and his Gospel" (*Redemptoris Missio,* 33). These latter are churches where the gospel has been established for a long time — like the churches of Europe or North and South America — or even churches that have only recently received the gospel — churches, for example, in urban areas of Africa or Asia.

Even though mission *ad gentes* does retain its validity as mission in the proper sense, the pope expands the notion to include particular areas like the rapidly growing urban areas of the world, particularly those in Asia, Africa, and Latin America. He also points to the world's youth, which in many countries make up half the population, and to large numbers of the world's migrants and the conditions of poverty that often makes migration necessary (*Redemptoris Missio*, 37). Referring to Paul's speech on the Areopagus in Athens, where Paul dared to present the gospel in terms that Greeks would understand, the pope also speaks about the world's new Areopagi, which call for a creative way of presenting the gospel. He singles out areas like the world of communications, the need to develop the rights of women and children, the culture of science, the situations that need liberation from any and all oppression, ecological responsibility, and the need for peacemaking. This is clearly an expansion of mission *ad gentes* far beyond how even the pope defined it earlier in the encyclical. From our perspective, the pope is calling for a missionary stance here of prophetic dialogue. On the one hand, the church is called to proclaim clearly the message of the gospel and name any and all forms of injustice. On the other, this can be done properly only after a dialogue with these new situations.

The encyclical expands the idea of mission even further, perhaps to align it with the expanded areas mentioned in paragraph 37. Although John Paul does not quite give as good a summary of a wider sense of mission as appears in a 1984 document entitled "Dialogue and Mission" (the document speaks of five aspects or elements of mission),[9] he does acknowledge that mission is indeed a multifaceted reality. In chapter 5, the pope writes about mission as witness, as explicit proclamation of the name of Christ and of the gospel, as the task of forming new communities, as inculturation, interreligious dialogue, working for development, and as works of charity.

In sum, one gets the distinct impression that mission is understood in the encyclical in a way that embraces the entire life of the church. It confirms *Ad Gentes*'s contention that the church is indeed "missionary by its very nature," or *Evangelii Nuntiandi*'s statement that evangelization is the church's "deepest identity."

Interreligious Dialogue

We have already mentioned that interreligious dialogue is included in the encyclical as part of its expanded understanding of mission. It will be important, however, to single out this aspect, both because it is relatively new in the church's teaching on mission and because in later years the idea of interreligious dialogue might seem to be called into question.

Evangelii Nuntiandi does not really deal with the question of inter-religious dialogue. It does speak of the respect that Christians have for other religions, but it does not seem to understand dialogue as part of the evangelization process itself (see *Evangelii Nuntiandi, 53*). Nine years later, in 1984, the Pontifical Council for Dialogue did issue an important statement entitled "Mission and Dialogue," in which dialogue was seen as integral to the church's evangelization efforts. This is the first time, however, that the activity of interreligious dialogue appears as part of mission in a papal encyclical. "Inter-religious dialogue," the pope writes, "is part of the church's evangelizing mission" (*Redemptoris Missio, 55*).

The pope insists that dialogue with other faiths is perfectly consistent with the church's obligation to proclaim Christ as universal savior to all peoples. While the aim of dialogue is to discover in other religions that ray of truth that enlightens all peoples (see *Nostra Aetate, 2*), each dialogue partner needs to be a person of full conviction in her or his faith. Even though Christians are called to dialogue, they must always keep in mind the uniqueness of Christ and that "the Church is the ordinary means of salvation and that she alone possesses the fullness of the means of salvation" (*Redemptoris Missio, 55*). Here we see how the notion of mission as "prophetic dialogue" has its roots in the Magisterium's teaching.

The pope insists strongly that dialogue is not some kind of tactic for eventual conversion (*Redemptoris Missio, 56*). It is born out of respect for the other religions and is done out of a sincere desire to get to know and to learn from other religious ways. Even when dialogue is difficult — say, in some Muslim areas — Christians should be open to it, despite its difficulties and despite its risks (*Redemptoris Missio, 57*). Dialogue, finally, is not just for experts or official religious leaders. The pope notes that dialogue is the task of every Christian, and he especially encourages the laity to engage in it.

As with *Evangelii Nuntiandi*, one could say much more about this virtual *summa* of mission and missiology. However, for the purpose of this overview, the three areas highlighted certainly provide an adequate picture of what the encyclical teaches. The richness of the encyclical, we believe, can very well be characterized by the term prophetic dialogue.

Dialogue and Proclamation (1991)

Reference has already been made to the 1984 document on dialogue and mission issued by the Secretariat for Non-Christians. A few months after the publication of *Redemptoris Missio,* a follow-up document to the one issued in 1984 was published by the Pontifical Council for Dialogue (the name of the Secretariat since 1988) and the Congregation for the Evangelization of Peoples. The document's title, *Dialogue and Proclamation,* points to the issue that it addresses: the relationship between direct proclamation of the gospel and the imperative, as an integral part of the church's mission, of interreligious dialogue. As Pope John Paul II indicated in *Redemptoris Missio,* there is a mutual relationship between the two aspects of mission, but that relationship had been in danger of being reduced to one or the other in the years immediately preceding *Redemptoris Missio*'s publication. Mission, he insisted over and over again in his encyclical, cannot be reduced to dialogue, as if all religions are of equal value. But he also subtly argued that dialogue is not something we can dispense with when we preach the riches of Christ. *Dialogue and Proclamation* tries to address the vital connection between the two in greater detail.

The document is developed in three parts. There is a first section that reflects on dialogue, then a second on proclamation, and finally a third on the relationship between them. The point is made, however, that, if dialogue is treated first, this does not mean that it has priority over proclamation in the document. It is treated first only because the document was first initiated by the Pontifical Council for Dialogue (*Dialogue and Proclamation,* 3). The two, rather, need to be dynamically related to one another and always exist in tension. The root of this is in God's life and saving activity itself: God offers and works for salvation in the world, and yet God works in dialogue, never forcing, but always persuading (see *Dialogue and Proclamation,* 38).

Dialogue and Proclamation presents a rather extensive theology of religions in the first part of the document. It also lays out nicely the various *forms* that interreligious dialogue can take: the dialogue of life where people simply live together and appreciate each other on a human level; the dialogue of action where members of different religions unite around some particular cause for the betterment of humanity; the dialogue of theological exchange where, especially, experts and church leaders share perspectives and study one another's traditions; and the dialogue of religious experience in which members share the richness of one another's spiritual traditions and personal spirituality and perhaps — as in Assisi in 1986 and 2002 — pray in one another's presence (see *Dialogue and Proclamation*, 42). Another interesting reflection about dialogue is the naming of a number of factors that impede dialogue, among which are insufficient grounding in one's own faith, a wrong understanding of notions like conversion, and the political climate in which one lives (see *Dialogue and Proclamation*, 52). Nevertheless, as the document says, "despite the difficulties, the Church's commitment to dialogue remains firm and irreversible" (*Dialogue and Proclamation* 54).

Focusing on the act of proclamation, *Dialogue and Proclamation* emphasizes the fact that any proclamation of the gospel is not done in a void. Rather, the Holy Spirit has gone before the one who proclaims. In fact, people "may have already been touched by the Spirit and in some way associated unknowingly to the paschal mystery of Jesus Christ (cf. *Gaudium et Spes, 22)*" (*Dialogue and Proclamation*, 68). Because of this, Christians need to learn how to present the gospel in ways that truly communicate it, illumine people's experience, and challenge them to respond. They should model themselves on Jesus (see *Dialogue and Proclamation*, 69). Any announcement of the gospel should be confident, and yet respectful and humble, dialogical and inculturated (*Dialogue and Proclamation*, 70). In the same way that it presented obstacles to dialogue, the document cites certain obstacles to a worthy gospel proclamation. There may be a gap between what one says and what one truly believes and lives out in one's life; Christians may lack respect for the religious traditions among which they proclaim the gospel; or there might exist "external difficulties," such as strong historical prejudices of a particular people against Christianity (see *Dialogue and Proclamation*, 73–74).

Paragraph 77 sums up well the close connection between two activities that the third section of the document seeks to explain. For our purposes it is enough to cite the paragraph as a whole:

Interreligious dialogue and proclamation, though not on the same level, are both authentic elements of the Church's evangelizing mission. Both are legitimate and necessary. They are intimately related, but not interchangeable: true interreligious dialogue on the part of the Christian supposes the desire to make Jesus Christ better known, recognized and loved; proclaiming Jesus Christ is to be carried out in the Gospel spirit of dialogue. The two activities remain distinct but, as experience shows, one and the same local Church, one and the same person, can be diversely engaged in both.

Once again we see how the concept of mission as "prophetic dialogue" is rooted firmly in church teaching.

Conclusion: From *Dialogue and Proclamation* to the Present

This chapter has presented a survey of the main teachings on mission that the church has presented in official Roman documents in the last half century. What has been the main missiological concern of the Roman Magisterium in the two decades since the publication of *Dialogue and Proclamation* has been the question of interreligious dialogue in relation to the uniqueness of Jesus Christ as universal savior. On two occasions, in 2000 with the declaration *Dominus Iesus* and in 2007 with a document entitled "Doctrinal Note on Some Aspects of Evangelization," the Congregation for the Doctrine of the Faith emphasized the centrality of Jesus in terms that, at least for some, seemed to neglect the equal centrality of the doctrines of grace outside Christian boundaries and the practice of interreligious dialogue (although, to be fair, these were acknowledged in both documents). Sanctions leveled against prominent theologians like Jacques Dupuis (a principal author of *Dialogue and Proclamation*) and Roger Haight, and investigations of equally prominent theologians Peter Phan and Michael Amaladoss have only underlined the fact that Rome is nervous about the correct interpretation of its own teachings.

It is precisely in these situations of conflict that the notion of mission as "prophetic dialogue" might be of help. Mission is constituted not by one or the other, but by both working together. There may be some situations in which *dialogue* may be the only way that Christians can continue to witness to the truth of their faith. Certainly, Christians must always respect the cultures, religions, and contexts in which they live, and the peoples among whom they work. Their basic attitude must be one of dialogue. On the other hand, there may be other situations — when Christians are asked about their faith, as they live in a non-Christian or secular society, or when they find themselves in situations of grave injustice — when a clear, *prophetic* proclamation of and witness to the gospel is necessary. Like mission itself, prophetic dialogue is multifaceted. It includes respect, listening, being open, on the one hand, and on the other courage to live out and speak the truth — albeit gently (1 Pet. 3:15) — in prophecy.

Theologians and missiologists have suggested that the Christological issue underlying the publication of these documents and the initiation of these investigations is the most crucial theological issue of our day. Others point to issues of inculturation as the most significant theological discussion in contemporary theology, one that is the foundation for these other Christological questions. Still others argue that much more urgent are issues of justice, peacemaking, and the care of creation. Whatever one may think, one cannot but be struck by the fact that these are *all* missiological issues, and that church teaching has dealt — at least in some sense — with every one of them in the last five decades. And whatever one may think, one cannot deny that mission is at the center of theological thought and Christian life today. In the same way that prophetic dialogue helps Christians negotiate the path between interreligious dialogue on the one hand and explicit Christian proclamation on the other, we suggest that the term "prophetic dialogue" can also help in understanding the complexity and richness of mission today.

Conclusion

In chapter 1 we spoke of God's mission as a dance, a dance in which all Christians are invited to participate. The dance begins in God's very self, and then spills forth generously, joyfully into all of creation, like a great "conga line." The Spirit leads the dance. She inspires the Lord of the Dance, and the dancers make up that "great cloud of witnesses" (Heb 12:1), among whom are Abraham and Sarah, Moses and Miriam, Deborah, Isaiah, Mary of Nazareth, Peter, Paul, Mary Magdalene, Justin, Patrick and Bridget, Alopen, Leoba, Francis and Clare, Xavier and Ricci, Marie de l'Incarnation, Samuel Crowther, Katharine Drexel, Pandita Ramabai, Charles de Foucauld, and Dorothy Day. They have danced through history, and they are inspirations for the people who are dancing now.

The name of the dance might be called "prophetic dialogue." It is based on the beautiful but complex rhythm of dialogue and prophecy, boldness and humility, learning and teaching, letting go and speaking out. It is beautiful because it is the rhythm of God's love moving through history. It is complex because it changes with time, place, creation's groaning and humanity's response. It is the rhythm of an African drumbeat, a salsa band, a Filipino tinikling, a protest march, a ballroom waltz. Learning the basic steps is fairly easy. Learning how to dance in step with the ever-changing rhythm, however, is not easy at all. When does the rhythm call for dialogue, for humility, for letting go? When does it call for prophecy, for teaching, and speaking out? The Spirit who leads the dance knows, and those of us who follow need to be attentive to her leading and to follow the example of those witnesses at the head of the line.

We began this book with God's invitation to the dance of mission. We have drawn on the church's theology, history, spirituality and practice to show how the church is challenged to join in that dance in today's world. It is a dance of prophetic dialogue. How well we dance will depend — as we dance together — on how faithful we are to the rhythms of the gospel, how responsive we are to the beat of the present, and how attentive we are to those among whom we dance.

Notes

Introduction

1. *Ad Gentes,* Vatican Council II, Decree on the Church's Missionary Activity, 2.

2. John Paul II, *The Mission of the Redeemer (Redemptoris Missio),* 41.

3. Stephen B. Bevans and Roger P. Schroeder, *Constants in Context: A Theology of Mission for Today* (Maryknoll, N.Y.: Orbis Books, 2004).

4. See, for example, the important reviews that appeared in the *International Bulletin of Missionary Research* 29, no. 2 (April 2005): 98–100, and in *Mission Studies* 22, no. 1 (2005): 135–56. See also Tim Daikin, "Discipleship: Marked for Mission," in *Mission in the 21st Century: Exploring the Five Marks of Global Mission,* ed. Andrew Walls and Cathy Ross (London: Darton, Longman and Todd, 2008), 175–200. We are grateful for discussions of our work at the Association of Professors of Mission in 2008, the Eastern Fellowship of Professors of Mission in 2005, and in various venues throughout the world.

5. Bevans and Schroeder, *Constants in Context,* 281–347.

6. Robert J. Schreiter, *The Ministry of Reconciliation: Spiritualities and Strategies* (Maryknoll, N.Y.: Orbis Books, 1998).

7. David J. Bosch, *Transforming Mission: Paradigms in Theology of Mission* (Maryknoll, N.Y.: Orbis Books, 1991), 489. See also Willem Saayman and Klippies Kritzinger, eds., *Mission in Bold Humility: David Bosch's Work Considered* (Maryknoll, N.Y.: Orbis, 1996).

Chapter 1: The Mission Has a Church

This chapter was originally written by Steve Bevans and delivered several times throughout Australia, Ireland, England, and in the United States in 2009 and 2010. An earlier version was published in the *Australian E-Journal of Theology* 14 (August 2009).

1. On this see Paul S. Fiddes, *Participating in God: A Pastoral Theology of the Trinity* (London: Darton, Longman and Todd, 2000).

2. James Chukwuma Okoye, *Israel and the Nations: A Mission Theology of the Old Testament* (Maryknoll, N.Y.: Orbis Books, 2006), 33.

3. See Thomas Aquinas, *Summa Theologiae,* Part I, Question 3, article 1.

4. Bonaventure, *De Trinitate,* 3.16. See Ilia Delio, "Bonaventure's Metaphysics of the Good," *Theological Studies* 60, no. 2 (1999): 232.

5. Mechtilde of Magdeburg, *The Flowing Light of the Godhead,* book 7, chapter 55, in *Classics of Western Spirituality,* 91, trans. Frank Tobin (New York: Paulist

Press, 1998). See Oliver Davies, "Later Medieval Mystics," in *The Medieval Theologians: An Introduction to Theology in the Medieval Period,* ed. G. R. Evans (Oxford: Blackwell, 2001), 228.

6. Leonardo Boff, "Trinity," in *Mysterium Liberationis: Fundamental Concepts of Liberation Theology,* ed. Ignacio Ellacuría and Jon Sobrino (Maryknoll, N.Y.: Orbis Books, 1993), 389.

7. This idea comes from a play on the word *perichoresis,* from the Greek *perichoreo,* meaning "cyclical movement or recurrence." "To dance around" or "dance in a ring" comes from the Greek *perichoreuo.* See Elizabeth A. Johnson, *She Who Is: The Mystery of God in Feminist Theological Discourse* (New York: Crossroad, 1992), 220–21.

8. Alfred North Whitehead, *Process and Reality: An Essay in Cosmology* (New York: Macmillan, 1929), 521, 532.

9. Benedict XVI, encyclical letter *Deus Caritas Est,* 10.

10. *Ad Gentes,* Vatican Council II, Decree on the Church's Missionary Activity, 2.

11. William P. Young, *The Shack* (Newbury Park, Calif.: Windblown Media, 2007).

12. Johnson, *She Who Is,* 127.

13. Juan Luis Segundo, *Christ in the Spiritual Exercises of St. Ignatius* (Maryknoll, N.Y.: Orbis Books, 1987), 22–26.

14. On this last parable, see Barbara E. Reid's rather unconventional but very convincing interpretation in her *Parables for Preachers, Year C* (Collegeville, Minn.: Liturgical Press, 2000), 227–36.

15. See online *http://miatorgau.melbourneitwebsites.com/page/jesus_laughing_exhibition.html.*

16. Edward Schillebeeckx, *Jesus: An Experiment in Theology* (New York: Vintage Books, 1981), 156, 158.

17. This crucial incident between Peter and Cornelius will be treated in much more detail in chapter 8 as we reflect on mission as "Table Fellowship."

18. For a more detailed treatment of the movement of Acts, see Stephen B. Bevans and Roger P. Schroeder, *Constants in Context: A Theology of Mission for Today* (Maryknoll, N.Y.: Orbis Books, 2004), 10–31.

19. See Andrew F. Walls, "Culture and Coherence in Christian History," chapter 2 of Walls, *The Missionary Movement in Christian History: Studies in the Transmission of Faith* (Maryknoll, N.Y.: Orbis Books, 1997), 16.

20. *Ad Gentes,* 2.

21. Augustine, *De Baptismo,* 5.38, quoted in Richard P. McBrien, *The Church: The Evolution of Catholicism* (New York: HarperOne, 2008), 51.

22. Gregory Augustine Pierce, *The Mass Is Never Ended* (Notre Dame, Ind.: Ave Maria Press, 2007).

23. *Gaudium et Spes,* Vatican Council II, Pastoral Constitution on the Church in the Modern World, 22.

Chapter 2: "We Were Gentle among You"

This chapter was originally written by Stephen Bevans and Roger Schroeder and was published in the *Australian E-Journal of Theology,* 7 (2006).

1. Daniel A. Lord, "For Christ (Our) King," as quoted at *http://catholicculture .org/lit/activities/view.cfm?id=912.*

2. William R. Burrows, "Concluding Reflections," in *Redemption and Dialogue: Reading* Redemptoris Missio *and* Dialogue and Proclamation (Maryknoll, N.Y.: Orbis Books, 1993), 244.

3. See, for example, Pierre Charles, SJ, *Études Missiologiques* (Tournai, Belgium: Desclée de Brouwer, 1956). This volume contains articles written by this great missiologist in the 1920s, '30s, '40s, and '50s before his death in 1954. See also the first (1964) edition of Louis J. Luzbetak, SVD, *The Church and Cultures* (Pasadena, Calif.: William Carey Library, 1970), particularly the bibliography that cites many books and articles from the first half of the twentieth century. The study of mission and mission theology will also point to examples of great missionaries in history, among whom are the brothers Cyril and Methodius, the Jesuit missionary to China Matteo Ricci, and missionaries like Vincent Lebbe, Anna Dengel, and Francis X. Ford, MM. Among friends who were missionaries of that era we count Fr. Luzbetak himself, along with great men like Alphonse Mildner, Frederick Scharpf, Richard Kraft, Charles Scanlon, Henry Sollner, Ferdie Mitterbauer — all SVDs.

4. Abbé Jean Yves Baziou, "Mission: From Expansion to Encounter," *USCMA Periodic Paper* no. 1 (Spring 2005): 2.

5. Burrows, "Concluding Reflections," 244.

6. Baziou, "Mission," 2. See David Tracy, *Dialogue with the Other: The Inter-Religious Dialogue* (Louvain and Grand Rapids, Mich.: Peeters Press and William B. Eerdmans Publishing Company, 1990), 4: "Dialogue demands the intellectual, moral, and at the limit, religious ability to struggle to hear another and to respond. To respond critically, and even suspiciously when necessary, but to respond only in dialogical relationship to a real, not a projected other."

7. Max Warren, preface to John V. Taylor, *The Primal Vision* (London: SCM Press, 1963), 10; Donal Dorr, *Mission in Today's World* (Maryknoll, N.Y.: Orbis Books, 2000), 16.

8. Gustavo Gutiérrez, *A Theology of Liberation* (Maryknoll, N.Y.: Orbis Books, 1973), 267–68.

9. See Edmund Chia, *Towards a Theology of Dialogue: Schillebeeckx's Method as Bridge between Vatican's* Dominus Iesus *and Asia's FABC Theology* (privately printed, Bangkok, Thailand, 2003), 269. Chia cites John Prior, "Unfinished Encounter: A Note on the Voice and Tone of *Ecclesia in Asia*," *East Asian Pastoral Review* 37, no. 3 (2000): 259.

10. Marcello Zago, OMI, "Mission and Interreligious Dialogue," *International Bulletin of Missionary Research* 22, no. 3 (July 1998): 98.

11. Pontifical Council for Interreligious Dialogue and the Congregation for the Evangelization of Peoples, *Dialogue and Proclamation: Reflections and Orientations on Interreligious Dialogue and the Proclamation of the Gospel of Jesus Christ* (1991), paragraph 9, in Burrows, *Redemption and Dialogue,* 96.

12. This is the term used by Leonard Swidler in "Interreligious and Inter-ideological Dialogue: The Matrix for All Systematic Reflection Today," *Toward a Universal Theology of Religion,* ed. Leonard Swidler (Maryknoll, N.Y.: Orbis Books, 1987), 5–50. Dorr uses the term "Dialogue with the Western World" for dialogue with secularists. See Dorr, *Mission in Today's World,* 56–73.

13. Eleanor Doidge and Stephen Bevans have spoken of these elements as six: witness and proclamation; liturgy, prayer, and contemplation; justice, peace, and the integrity of creation; interreligious (and secular) dialogue; inculturation; and reconciliation. See Stephen Bevans and Eleanor Doidge, "Theological Reflection," in *Reflection and Dialogue: What Mission Confronts Religious Life Today?* ed. Barbara Kraemer (Chicago: Center for the Study of Religious Life, 2000), 37–48. See also Stephen B. Bevans, "Unraveling a 'Complex Reality': Six Elements of Mission," in *International Bulletin of Missionary Research* 27, no. 2 (April 2003): 50–53; and Stephen B. Bevans and Roger P. Schroeder, *Constants in Context: A Theology of Mission for Today* (Maryknoll, N.Y.: Orbis Books, 2004), 348–95.

14. World Council of Churches, "Guidelines on Dialogue," in *New Directions in Mission and Evangelization 1: Basic Statements,* in James A. Scherer and Stephen B. Bevans (Maryknoll, N.Y.: Orbis Books, 1992), 17.

15. *Dialogue and Proclamation,* 78, in Burrows, *Redemption and Dialogue,* 114.

16. Secretariat for Non-Christians, "The Attitude of the Church toward the Followers of Other Religions: Reflections and Orientations on Dialogue and Mission," 29. Quoted in U.S. Bishops, *To the Ends of the Earth* (New York: Society for the Propagation of the Faith, 1986), par. 40, p. 22.

17. See Claude Marie Barbour, "Seeking Justice and Shalom in the City," *International Review of Mission* 73 (1984): 303–9; David J. Bosch, "The Vulnerability of Mission," in James A. Scherer and Stephen B. Bevans, eds., *New Direction in Mission and Evangelization 2: Theological Foundations* (Maryknoll, N.Y.: Orbis Books, 1994), 73–86; David J. Bosch, *Transforming Mission: Paradigm Shifts in Theology of Mission* (Maryknoll, N.Y.: Orbis Books, 1991), 489.

18. Swidler, *Toward a Universal Theology of Religion,* 5–50.

19. Bernard J. F. Lonergan, *Method in Theology* (London: Darton, Longman and Todd, 1972), xi.

20. See Jacques Dupuis, "A Theological Commentary: Dialogue and Proclamation," in Burrows, *Redemption and Dialogue,* 123 and 133–35.

21. *Nostra Aetate,* Vatican Council II, Declaration on the Relationship of the Church to Non-Christian Religions, 2; *Gaudium et Spes,* 4, Vatican Council II, Pastoral Constitution on the Church in the Modern World, and *Ad Gentes,* Vatican Council II, Decree on the Church's Missionary Activity, 11.

22. Dupuis, "A Theological Commentary," 135–36. See *Dialogue and Proclamation,* 29.

23. Pope Paul VI, *Evangelii Nuntiandi,* 20, in David J. O'Brien and Thomas A. Shannon, *Catholic Social Thought: The Documentary Heritage* (Maryknoll, N.Y.: Orbis Books, 1992), 310.

24. Pope John Paul II, letter to Cardinal Agostino Casaroli, *L'Osservatore Romano* (June 28, 1982), quoted in Aylward Shorter, *Inculturation in Africa: The Way Forward,* The Fourth Annual Louis J. Luzbetak, SVD Lecture on Mission and Culture (Chicago: CCGM Publications, 2005), 1.

25. Paul VI, *Ecclesiam Suam,* 78.

26. "Dialogue and Mission," 29.

27. See Stephen Bevans, "God Inside Out: Toward a Missionary Theology of the Holy Sprit," *International Bulletin of Missionary Research* 22, no. 3 (July 1998): 102–5.

28. See title of *Redemptoris Missio,* 28, in Burrows, *Redemption and Dialogue,* 19.

29. Preface of Christ the King.

30. *Ecclesiam Suam,* 70.

31. *Ad Gentes,* 9.

32. See *Gaudium et Spes,* 22.

33. See *Dialogue and Proclamation,* 21, in Burrows, *Redemption and Dialogue,* 99.

34. John Wood Oman, *Vision and Authority, or The Throne of St. Peter,* 2nd ed. (London: Hodder and Stoughton, 1928), 225; "God's Ideal and Man's Reality," *The Paradox of the World* (Cambridge: Cambridge University Press, 1921), 69.

35. *Dei Verbum,* Vatican Council II, Dogmatic Constitution on Revelation, 2. This translation is somewhat free. The original Latin reads: "Hac...revelatione Deus invisibilis...suae homines tamquam amicos alloquitur...et cum eis conversatur..., ut eos ad societatem secum invitet in eamque suscipiat." Our translation is an attempt to make the language more inclusive.

36. Karl Rahner, *The Trinity* (New York: Herder and Herder, 1970).

37. *Ad Gentes,* 2. Note the trinitarian context of this statement in the text.

38. *Evangelii Nuntiandi,* 14.

39. *Dialogue and Proclamation,* 69, in Burrows, *Redemption and Dialogue,* 112.

40. *Evangelii Nuntiandi,* 18; *Redemptoris Missio,* 39, in Burrows, *Redemption and Dialogue,* 27.

41. See Felix Wilfred, "The Federation of Asian Bishops' Conferences (FABC): Orientations, Challenges and Impact," in *For All the Peoples of Asia,* vol. 1, ed. Gaudencio Rosales and Catalino G. Arévalo (Quezon City: Claretian Publications, 1997), xxiii. Quoted in Chia, *Towards a Theology of Dialogue,* 230; see also 264.

42. See Chia, *Towards a Theology of Dialogue,* 228–29; Jonathan Tan, "*Missio ad gentes* in Asia: A Comparative Study of the Missiology of John Paul II and the Federation of Asian Bishops' Conferences" (Ph.D. diss., Catholic University of America, 2002), 133.

43. See Tan, "*Missio ad gentes* in Asia," 133; See also Thomas Fox, *Pentecost in Asia: A New Way of Being Church* (Maryknoll, N.Y.: Orbis Books, 2002).

44. Federation of Asian Bishops' Conferences, "Journeying Together toward the Third Millennium," Statement of the Fifth Plenary Assembly, Bandung, Indonesia, 1990, in Rosales and Arévalo, eds., 280. Quoted in Tan, 149.

45. Bevans and Schroeder, *Constants in Context.*

46. See, for example, Gustavo Gutiérrez, "Option for the Poor," in *Mysterium Liberationis: Fundamental Concepts of Liberation Theology,* ed. Ignacio Ellacuría and Jon Sobrino (Maryknoll, N.Y.: Orbis Books, 1993), 235–50.

47. Alice Walker, "A Wind through the Heart: A Conversation with Alice Walker and Sharon Salzberg on Loving Kindness in a Painful World," *Shambhala Sun* (January 1997).

48. Stephen Bevans, "Letting Go and Speaking Out: A Spirituality of Inculturation," in *The Healing Circle: Essays in Cross-Cultural Mission,* ed. Stephen Bevans, Eleanor Doidge and Robert Schreiter (Chicago: CCGM Publications, 1999), 133–46. A revised version of this article appears as chapter 7 in this volume.

49. *Redemptoris Missio,* 56, in Burrows, *Redemption and Dialogue,* 36.

50. Leonard Swidler, "Interreligious and Interideological Dialogue: The Matrix for All Systematic Reflection Today," in *Toward a Universal Theology of Religion,* ed. Leonard Swidler, 13–16; the term "dialogue decalogue" is used by Chia, *Towards a Theology of Dialogue,* 254, quoting Leonard Swidler, *After the Absolute: The Dialogical Future of Religious Reflection* (Minneapolis: Fortress Press, 1990), 42–45.

51. *Dialogue and Proclamation* 80, in Burrows, *Redemptive Dialogue,* 115.

52. Marcello Zago, "The New Millennium and the Emerging Religious Strategies," *Missiology: An International Review* 23, no. 1 (January 2000): 17.

53. Robert J. Schreiter, *The Ministry of Reconciliation: Spirituality and Strategies* (Maryknoll, N.Y.: Orbis Books, 1998), vi.

54. World Council of Churches, "Guidelines on Dialogue," 21, in Scherer and Bevans, eds., *New Directions in Mission and Evangelization 1: Basic Statements* (Maryknoll, N.Y.: Orbis Books, 1992), 14.

55. Remark by Peter Phan at the Catholic Theological Union, June 2001; see also Jeannette Rodriguez, "Response to Stephen Bevans," in *Catholic Theological Society of America: Proceedings of the Fifty-sixth Annual Convention* (Berkeley, Calif.: CTSA, 2001), 43–48.

56. Chia, *Towards a Theology of Dialogue,* 260.

57. *Ecclesiam Suam,* 81.

58. See Robert J. Schreiter, *Constructing Local Theologies* (Maryknoll, N.Y.: Orbis Books, 1985), 112–13.

59. *Ecclesiam Suam,* 81.

60. Ibid.

61. John Shea, "Theological Assumptions and Ministerial Style," in *Alternative Futures for Worship,* vol. 6, *Leadership Ministry in Community,* ed. M. A. Cowan (Collegeville, Minn.: Liturgical Press, 1987), 105–28; see also Bevans's article "Seeing Mission through Images," in *New Directions in Mission and Evangelization 2: Theological Foundations,* ed. Scherer and Bevans (Maryknoll, N.Y.: Orbis Books, 1994), 158–69.

62. Robert T. Rush, "From Pearl Merchant to Treasure Hunter: The Missionary Yesterday and Today," *Catholic Mind* 76 (1978): 6–10.

63. Anthony J. Gittins, *Gifts and Strangers: Meeting the Challenge of Inculturation* (New York and Mahwah, N.J.: Paulist Press, 1989), 132.

64. Roger Schroeder, "Entering Someone Else's Garden: Cross-cultural Mission/Ministry," in *The Healing Circle: Essays in Cross-Cultural Mission,* ed. Stephen Bevans, Eleanor Doidge, and Robert Schreiter (Chicago: University of Chicago Press, 2000), 147–61. A revised version of this essay appears as chapter 6 in this volume.

65. Galen K. Johnson, "St. Francis and the Sultan: An Historical and Critical Reassessment," *Mission Studies* 18, no. 2 (2001): 149.

66. Ibid., 157.

67. Mary Motte, "In the Image of the Crucified God: A Missiological Interpretation of Francis of Assisi," in *The Agitated Mind of God: The Theology of Kosuke Koyama,* ed. Dale Irvin and Akintunde Akinade (Maryknoll, N.Y.: Orbis Books, 1996), 79. Quoted in Bevans and Schroeder, *Constants in Context,* 143.

68. See Cajetan Esser, "Saint Francis and the Missionary Church," trans. Ignatius Brady, *Spirit and Life* 6 (1994): 22–23. Quoted in Bevans and Schroeder, *Constants in Context,* 144.

69. David Kerr, "Foucauld, Charles Eugène de (1858–1916)," in *Biographical Dictionary of Christian Missions,* ed. Gerald H. Anderson (New York: Macmillan Reference USA, 1998), 220.

70. Cathy Wright, "Nazareth as a Model for Mission in the Life of Charles de Foucauld," *Mission Studies* 19, no. 1 (2002): 36.

71. Kerr, "Foucauld," 219.

72. Quoted in Wright, "Nazareth as a Model for Mission," 37.

73. Quoted in ibid., 44.

74. Quoted in ibid.

75. Robert Ellsberg, "Pandita Ramabai: Indian Christian and Reformer (1858–1922)," in *All Saints: Daily Reflections on Saints, Prophets, and Witnesses for Our Time* (New York: Crossroad, 1997), 154.

76. Ibid., 155.

77. Ibid.

78. Eric J. Sharpe, "Ramabai Dongre Medhavi (Pandita Ramabai Sarasvati) (1858–1922)," in *Biographical Dictionary of Christian Missions,* ed. Anderson, 557.

79. Ellsberg, "Pandita Ramabai," 155.

80. Zago, "Mission and Interreligious Dialogue," 98.

81. See Bevans and Schroeder, *Constants in Context,* 281–85; 348–52. See also *In Dialogue with the Word Nr. 1* (Rome: SVD Publications, 2000) and *Prophetic Dialogue: Challenges and Prospects in India,* in L. Stanislaus and Alwyn D'Souza (Pune: Ishvani Kendra/ISPCK, 2003).

82. Bosch, *Transforming Mission,* 489.

Chapter 3: "I Am Not Ashamed of the Gospel"

This chapter was originally written by Stephen Bevans and Roger Schroeder for publication in this book.

1. *Ad Gentes,* Vatican Council II, Decree on the Church's Missionary Activity, 2.

2. Michael Amaladoss, "Mission as Prophecy," in *New Directions in Mission and Evangelization 2: Theological Foundations,* ed. James A. Scherer and Stephen B. Bevans (Maryknoll, N.Y.: Orbis Books, 1994), 64–65.

3. Paul VI, *Ecclesiam Suam.*

4. Secretariat for Non-Christians, "The Attitude of the Church toward the Followers of Other Religions: Reflections and Orientations on Dialogue and Mission" (1984), quoted in U.S. Bishops, *To the Ends of the Earth,* 40 (New York: Society for the Propagation of the Faith, 1986), 22.

5. See Edward Schillebeeckx, *Interim Report on the Books* Jesus *and* Christ (New York: Crossroad, 1981), 64–74; and N. T. Wright, *Jesus and the Victory of God* (Minneapolis: Fortress Press, 1996), 147–97.

6. Larry Nemer, "Prophetic Dialogue: A New Way of Doing Mission?" See *www.instrumentsofpeace.ie/Prophetic%20Dialogue.pdf.*

7. Gregory Nazianzen, *Discourse on Moderation in Disputing,* 29. Quoted in Brendan Leahy and Michael Mulvey, *Priests Today: Reflections on Identity, Life, and Ministry* (Hyde Park, N.Y.: New City Press, 2010), 42.

8. *Evangelii Nuntiandi,* 41.

9. Ibid.

10. Ibid., 21.

11. Juan Luis Segundo, *Christ in the Spiritual Exercises of St. Ignatius* (Maryknoll, N.Y.: Orbis Books, 1987), 22–26.

12. Roger Haight, *Jesus, Symbol of God* (Maryknoll, N.Y.: Orbis Books, 1999), 16.

13. William Placher, *The Triune God: An Essay in Postliberal Theology* (Louisville: Westminster John Knox, 2007), 44. The quotation is from Gregory of Nyssa, *An Address on Religious Instruction,* 24. *Christology of the Later Fathers,* ed. R. Hard, trans. Cyril C. Richardson, Library of Christian Classics (Philadelphia: Westminster, 1954), 301.

14. Gerhard Lohfink, *Jesus and Community* (Philadelphia: Fortress, 1984), 168.

15. Stanley Hauerwas and William Willimon, *Resident Aliens: Life in the Christian Colony* (Nashville: Abingdon Press, 1989).

16. Craig van Gelder, *The Essence of the Church: A Community Created by the Spirit* (Grand Rapids, Mich.: William B. Eerdmans, 2000), 99–100.

17. John Paul II, *Evangelium Vitae,* 95.

18. U.S. Catholic Bishops, *The Challenge of Peace: God's Promise and Our Response* and *Economic Justice for All,* in *Catholic Social Thought: The Documentary Heritage,* ed. David J. O'Brien and Thomas A. Shannon (Maryknoll, N.Y.: Orbis Books, 1992), 492–680.

19. Appalachian Bishops, *This Land Is Home to Me* and *At Home in the Web of Life, www.osjspm.org/majordoc_this_is_home_to_me.aspx;* and *www.ncrlc.com /1-pfd-files/At%20Home%20in%20the%20Web%20of%20Life.pdf.*

20. Cardinal Francis George, *Dwell in My Love: A Pastoral Letter on Racism* (Chicago: New Catholic World, 2001).

21. Gustavo Gutiérrez, *A Theology of Liberation* (Maryknoll, N.Y.: Orbis Books, 1973), 265–72.

22. *Evangelium Vitae,* 1.

23. See the 1971 Synod of Bishops, *Justice in the World,* Introduction, in O'Brien and Shannon, eds., *Catholic Social Thought,* 289.

24. See Stephen Bevans, "Seeing Mission through Images," in *New Directions in Mission and Evangelization 2: Theological Foundations,* ed. James A. Scherer and Stephen B. Bevans (Maryknoll, N.Y.: Orbis Books, 1994), 158–69, and "Images of Priesthood in Today's Church," *Emmanuel* 102, no. 7 (September 1996): 389–98. The idea of "seeing through images" comes from John Shea, "Theological Assumptions and Ministerial Style," in *Alternative Futures for Worship* 6, ed. M. A. Cowan (Collegeville, Minn.: Liturgical Press, 1987), 105–28.

25. See Paulo Freire, *The Pedagogy of the Oppressed* (New York: Seabury, 1968) and Parker J. Palmer, *The Courage to Teach: Exploring the Inner Landscape of a Teacher's Life* (San Francisco: Jossey-Bass Publishers, 1998), 89–113.

26. Frank Delaney, *Ireland* (New York: HarperCollins Paperback, 2008).

27. McIntyre's definition is quoted in Delwin Brown, *Boundaries of Our Habitations: Tradition and Theological Construction* (Albany: State University of New York Press, 1994), 84–85.

28. Robert Ellsberg, *All Saints: Daily Reflections on Saints, Prophets, and Witnesses for Our Time* (New York: Crossroad, 1997).

29. Ibid., 528–29.

30. Ibid., 79–80.

31. Ibid., 519–21.

Chapter 4: Mission in the Twenty-first Century

This chapter was originally written by Stephen Bevans and delivered as a paper at a conference on contextual theology at United Theological College, Sydney, Australia. A slightly different version appears as "A Theology of Mission for the Church of the 21st Century: Mission as Prophetic Dialogue," in *Contextual Theology for the 21st Century,* ed. Stephen Bevans and Katalina Tahaafe-Williams (Eugene, Ore.: Pickwick Publications, 2011).

1. Doris Pilkington, *Rabbit-Proof Fence* (New York: Miramax Books, 2002).

2. Gerard Goldman, "Remembering Ian, Alan Goldman, and Memela: Using Narrative as an Approach to Aboriginal Reconciliation in Australia," D.Min. thesis project, Catholic Theological Union, Chicago, 1999.

3. Peter Matthiessen, *At Play in the Fields of the Lord* (New York: Random House, 1965); Barbara Kingsolver, *The Poisonwood Bible: A Novel* (New York: HarperFlamingo, 1998).

4. Tink Tinker, "The Romance and Tragedy of Christian Mission among American Indians," in *Remembering Jamestown: Hard Questions about Christian Mission,* ed. Amos Yong and Barbara Brown Zikmund (Eugene, Ore.: Pickwick Publications, 2010), 26–27.

5. Lamin Sanneh, *Translating the Message: The Missionary Impact on Culture, Twentieth Anniversary Edition* (Maryknoll, N.Y.: Orbis Books, 2009).

6. Andrew F. Walls, "Missionary Societies and the Fortunate Subversion of the Church," in *The Missionary Movement in Christian History* (Maryknoll, N.Y.: Orbis Books, 1996), 241–54.

7. See Stephen Bevans, "What Does Contextual Theology Have to Offer the Church of the Twenty-first Century?" in *Contextual Theology for the 21st Century,* ed. Bevans and Tahaafe-Williams.

8. See the Willingen document in *Classic Texts in Mission and World Christianity,* ed. Norman Thomas (Maryknoll, N.Y.: Orbis Books, 1994), 103–4. See also what we have written in chapter 1.

9. Emil Brunner, *The Word in the World* (London: SCM Press, 1931), 11.

10. 1971 Synod of Bishops, "Justice in the World," Introduction, in *Catholic Social Thought: The Documentary Heritage,* ed. David J. O'Brien and Thomas A. Shannon (Maryknoll, N.Y.: Orbis Books, 1992), 289.

11. Rudy Wiebe, *The Blue Mountains of China* (Toronto: McClelland and Stewart, New Canadian Library Edition, 1995), 258.

12. Stephen B. Bevans and Roger P. Schroeder, *Constants in Context: A Theology of Mission for Today* (Maryknoll, N.Y.: Orbis Books, 2004).

13. Max Warren, Preface to John V. Taylor, *The Primal Vision* (London: SCM Press, 1963), 10.

14. *Following the Word Nr. 1, Mission, Spirituality, Formation* (Rome: SVD Publications, 1988), 43–60.

15. See Claude Marie Barbour, "Seeking Justice and Shalom in the City," *International Review of Mission* 73 (1984): 303–9.

16. Pope Paul VI, *Evangelii Nuntiandi,* 22.

17. Gerhard Lohfink, *Jesus and Community* (Philadelphia: Fortress Press, 1984), 168.

18. For reference to Newbigin's works on this phrase, see George Hunsberger, *Bearing the Witness of the Spirit: Lesslie Newbigin's Theology of Cultural Plurality* (Grand Rapids, Mich.: William B. Eerdmans, 1998), 167.

19. Stephen B. Bevans, *Models of Contextual Theology,* revised and expanded edition (Maryknoll, N.Y.: Orbis Books, 2002), 117–37.

20. Carmelo E. Álvarez, "A Future for Liberation Theology," in *Contextual Theology for the 21st Century,* ed. Stephen Bevans and Katalina Tahaafe-Williams (Eugene, Ore.: Pickwick Publications, 2011).

21. David J. Bosch, *Transforming Mission: Paradigm Shifts in Theology of Mission* (Maryknoll, N.Y.: Orbis Books, 1991), 489.

22. See Bevans, *Models of Contextual Theology.*

Chapter 5: Unraveling a "Complex Reality"

This chapter was originally written by Stephen Bevans and published in the *International Bulletin of Missionary Research* 27, no. 2 (April 2003): 50–53.

1. John Paul II, *Redemptoris Missio,* 41.

2. "Agenda for Future Planning, Study, and Research in Mission," in *Trends in Mission: Toward the Third Millennium,* ed. William Jenkinson and Helene O'Sullivan (Maryknoll, N.Y.: Orbis Books, 1991), 399–414.

3. Secretariat for Non-Christians, "The Attitude of the Church toward the Followers of Other Religions: Reflections and Orientations on Dialogue and Mission," *Bulletin Secretariatus pro non Christianis* 56, no. 2 (1984): 13.

4. David J. Bosch, *Transforming Mission: Paradigms in Theology of Mission* (Maryknoll, N.Y.: Orbis Books, 1991).

5. J. Andrew Kirk, *What Is Mission: Theological Explorations* (London: Darton, Longman and Todd, 1999); Donal Dorr, *Mission in Today's World* (Maryknoll, N.Y.: Orbis Books, 2000).

6. Stephen Bevans and Eleanor Doidge, "Theological Reflection," in *What Mission Confronts Religious Life in the U.S. Today?* ed. Barbara Kraemer (Chicago: Center for the Study of Religious Life), 37–48.

7. See, for example, Robert J. Schreiter, "Globalization and Reconciliation: Challenges to Mission," in *Mission in the Third Millennium,* ed. Robert J. Schreiter (Maryknoll, N.Y.: Orbis Books, 2001), 121–43.

8. Paul VI, *Evangelii Nuntiandi,* 41.

9. Pontifical Council for Interreligious Dialogue and Congregation for the Doctrine of the Faith, *Dialogue and Proclamation,* 10.

10. Bosch, *Transforming Mission,* 420.

11. Lesslie Newbigin, *The Gospel in a Pluralist Society* (Grand Rapids, Mich.: William B. Eerdmans, 1989), 222–33.

12. *The Manila Manifesto,* in *New Directions in Mission and Evangelization 1: Basic Statements,* ed. James A. Scherer and Stephen B. Bevans (Maryknoll, N.Y.: Orbis Books, 1992), 301.

13. *Redemptoris Missio,* 44.

14. *Evangelii Nuntiandi* 22.

15. San Antonio 1989, "Mission in Christ's Way: Your Will Be Done," in *New Directions in Mission and Evangelization 1: Basic Documents,* ed. James A. Scherer and Stephen B. Bevans (Maryknoll, N.Y.: Orbis Books, 1992), 78.

16. *Redemptoris Missio,* 39.

17. Robert D. Hawkins, "Occasional Services: Border Crossings," in *Inside Out: Worship in an Age of Mission,* ed. Thomas H. Schattauer (Minneapolis: Fortress Press, 1999), 201.

18. See ibid.

19. 1971 Synod of Bishops, "Justice in the World," in *Catholic Social Thought: The Documentary Heritage,* ed. David J. O'Brien and Thomas A. Shannon (Maryknoll, N.Y.: Orbis Books, 1992), 289.

20. Paul VI, "Message for World Day of Peace," *Origins* 1, no. 29 (January 6, 1972): 491.

21. Leonardo Boff, "Social Ecology: Poverty and Misery," in *Ecotheology: Voices from South and North,* ed. David G. Hallman (Maryknoll, N.Y.: Orbis Books, 1994), 243.

22. Frederick R. Wilson, ed., *The San Antonio Report: Your Will Be Done, Mission in Christ's Way* (Geneva: WCC Publications, 1990).

23. 1971 Synod of Bishops, "Justice in the World," 295.

24. John Paul II, "Moral Choices for the Future," *Origins* 10, no. 39 (March 12, 1981): 621.

25. Rudy Wiebe, *The Blue Mountains of China* (Toronto: McClelland and Stewart, 1995), 258.

26. "Dialogue and Mission" 29.

27. World Council of Churches, "Ecumenical Affirmation: Mission and Evangelism," in *New Directions in Mission and Evangelization 1,* ed. Scherer and Bevans, 43.

28. Paul VI, "The African Church Today," *The Pope Speaks* 14, no. 3 (1969): 219.

29. David J. Hesselgrave, *Communicating Christ Cross-Culturally: An Introduction to Missionary Communication* (Grand Rapids, Mich.: Zondervan, 1978), 85.

30. See Stephen Bevans, *Models of Contextual Theology* (Maryknoll, N.Y.: Orbis Books, 2002), 3–15.

31. Robert J. Schreiter, *The Ministry of Reconciliation: Spirituality and Strategies* (Maryknoll, N.Y.: Orbis Books, 1997).

32. Mortimer Arias, *Announcing the Reign of God: Evangelization and the Subversive Memory of Jesus* (Philadelphia: Fortress Press, 1984).

Chapter 6: Entering Someone Else's Garden

This is a slightly revised version of an earlier article published by Roger Schroeder in *The Healing Circle: Essays in Cross-Cultural Mission,* ed. Stephen Bevans, Eleanor Doidge, and Robert Schreiter (Chicago: CCGM Publications, 2000), 147–61.

1. Throughout this chapter, the terms "mission/ministry" and "missionaries/ministers" will be used to include people and situations under both categories, in whatever way one understands the difference.

2. Gary Riebe-Estrella, "On the Threshold: How the Present Is Shaping the Future of Ministry," in *Word Remembered, Word Proclaimed,* ed. Stephen Bevans and Roger Schroeder (Nettetal, Germany: Steyler Verlag, 1997), 175–88.

3. For further theological treatment and references to the primary sources of Justin Martyr and Tertullian, see Stephen B. Bevans and Roger P. Schroeder, *Constants in Context: A Theology of Mission for Today* (Maryknoll, N.Y.: Orbis Books, 2004), 84, 95–97.

4. Claude Marie Barbour, "Seeking Justice and Shalom in the City," *International Review of Mission* 73, no. 291 (1984): 305.

5. M. A. C. Warren, introduction to John V. Taylor, *The Primal Vision: Christian Presence amid African Religion* (Philadelphia: Fortress Press, 1963), 10.

6. Anthony Gittins, *Gifts and Strangers: Meeting the Challenge of Inculturation* (New York and Mahwah, N.J.: Paulist Press, 1989), 132.

7. See Patrick Gesch, *Initiative and Initiation, Studia Instituti Anthropos* 33 (St. Augustine, Germany: Anthropos Institute, 1985), 11–26.

8. Many societies do not have a separate category for "religion/religious" within their more holistic worldview. For example, most if not all of the eight hundred languages spoken in Papua New Guinea do not have a word for "religion." Therefore, even such categories as "cultural" and "religious" reflect images and concepts from one's own "garden" which may not be appropriate in someone else's.

9. Gerald Arbuckle, "Multiculturalism, Internationality, and Religious Life," *Review for Religious* 54, no. 3 (May–June, 1995): 329.

10. See Roger Schroeder, *Initiation and Religion: A Case Study from the Wosera of Papua New Guinea, Studia Instituti Anthropos* 46 (Fribourg, Switzerland: University Press, 1992), 57–80.

11. See Gesch, *Initiative and Initiation,* 189–97; Schroeder, *Initiation and Religion,* 107–10.

12. In the past, the initiation system consisted of eight named stages over a thirty-year period as a male moved from childhood to elderhood. In the process of accommodating to a new situation, such as a formal school year, the length and sequence of these stages are changing as well.

13. See Schroeder, *Initiation and Religion,* 235–42, 246–48.

14. Quoted in Joseph Healey and Donald Sybertz, *Towards an African Narrative Theology* (Maryknoll, N.Y.: Orbis Books, 1996), 33.

15. Vincent Donovan, *Christianity Rediscovered* (Maryknoll, N.Y.: Orbis Books, 1982).

16. Arbuckle, "Multiculturalism, Internationality, and Religious Life," 330.

17. Barbour, "Seeking Justice and Shalom in the City," 305.

Chapter 7: Letting Go and Speaking Out

This chapter is a revised version of an essay originally written by Stephen Bevans and published as "Letting Go and Speaking Out: Toward a Spirituality of Inculturation," in *The Healing Circle: Essays in Cross-Cultural Mission,* ed. Stephen Bevans, Eleanor Doidge, and Robert Schreiter (Chicago: CCGM Publications, 2000), 133–46.

1. Paul VI, "Closing Discourse to All-Africa Symposium," quoted in Aylward Shorter, *African Christian Theology* (Maryknoll, N.Y.: Orbis Books), 20.

2. See World Council of Churches, "Report from the Ecumenical Conference on World Mission and Evangelization, Salvador de Bahia, Brazil," in *New Directions in*

Mission and Evangelization 3: Faith and Culture, ed. James A. Scherer and Stephen B. Bevans (Maryknoll, N.Y.: Orbis Books), 42–43; John Paul II, *Redemptoris Missio,* 52–54.

3. *Redemptoris Missio,* 52; John Paul II, *Ecclesia in Asia,* 62.

4. Bernard Lonergan, *Insight: A Study in Human Understanding* (New York: Philosophical Library, 1957), 187.

5. Claude Marie Barbour, Kathleen Billman, Peggy DesJarlait, and Eleanor Doidge, "Mission on the Boundaries: Cooperation without Exploitation," in *Beyond Theological Tourism: Mentoring as a Grassroots Approach to Theological Education,* ed. Susan B. Thistlethwaite and George F. Cairns (Maryknoll, N.Y.: Orbis Books, 1995), 82–83.

6. Ibid., 135.

7. See Stephen B. Bevans, *Models of Contextual Theology,* revised and expanded edition (Maryknoll, N.Y.: Orbis Books, 2002), 18–21.

8. Yves Raguin, *I Am Sending You: Spirituality and the Missioner* (Manila, Philippines: East Asian Pastoral Institute, 1973).

9. David Tracy, address on the occasion of the inauguration of the Catholic Theological Union Project on Spirituality and the Vocation of the Theological Educator, and the installation of Gary Riebe-Estrella as academic dean of Catholic Theological Union, October 17, 1996. The reference to Lonergan was an "off the cuff" remark and not found in the text as such. For the published text of the address, see David Tracy, "Traditions of Spiritual Practice and the Practice of Theology," *Theology Today 55,* no. 2 (July 1998): 235–41.

10. Alice Walker, "A Wind through the Heart: A Conversation with Alice Walker and Sharon Salzberg on Loving Kindness in a Painful World," *Shambhala Sun* (January 1997): 1–5.

11. Vincent Donovan, *Christianity Rediscovered* (Maryknoll, N.Y.: Orbis Books, 1982).

12. Walter J. Hollenweger, "Evangelization in the World Today," *Concilium* 114 (1979): 40–41.

13. Joseph Campbell (with Bill Moyers), *The Power of Myth* (New York: Doubleday, 1998), 49.

14. Stephen Bevans, "Seeing Mission through Images," *Missiology: An International Review* 19, no. 1 (January 1991): 45–57.

15. Sojourner Truth, "Document 3. Sojourner Truth: The Conversion of a Female Slave," in *In Their Own Voices: Four Centuries of American Women's Religious Writing,* ed. Rosemary Radford Ruether and Rosemary Skinner Keller (San Francisco: HarperCollins, 1995), 173.

16. Vincent Donovan, *The Church in the Midst of Creation* (Maryknoll, N.Y.: Orbis Books, 1989), 119.

17. Barbour et al., "Mission on the Boundaries," 82–83.

18. See Thomas Gilby, "Theology," in *Encyclopedic Dictionary of Religion,* volume O-Z, ed. Paul Kevin Meagher, Thomas C. O'Brien, Sister Consuelo Maria Aherene (Washington, D.C.: Corpus Publications, 1979), 3498.

19. Howard W. Stone and James O. Duke, *How to Think Theologically* (Minneapolis: Fortress Press, 1996), 2. Original emphasis.

20. See Peter Schineller, "Inculturation and Modernity," *Sedos Bulletin* 2 (February 15, 1988): 47.

21. Claude Marie Barbour, Peggy DesJarlait, Eleanor Doidge, and Amy Carr, "Gospel, Culture, Healing and Reconciliation: A Shalom Conversation," *Mission Studies* 16, no. 2/32 (1999): 135.

22. Clemens Sedmak, *Doing Local Theologies: A Guide for Artisans of a New Humanity* (Maryknoll, N.Y.: Orbis Books, 2002), 119–57.

23. Darrell Whiteman, "Contextualization: The Theory, the Gap, the Challenge," in *New Directions in Mission and Evangelization 3: Faith and Culture,* ed. James A. Scherer and Stephen Bevans (Maryknoll, N.Y.: Orbis Books, 1999), 43.

24. Ibid.

25. William Blake, "Auguries of Innocence, in *The Viking Book of Poetry of the English Speaking World* (New York: Viking Press, 1962), 621.

26. Edgar Allan Poe, "The Purloined Letter," in *The Complete Tales and Poems of Edgar Allan Poe,* introduction by Wilbur S. Scott (Edison, N.J.: Castle Books, 2002), 185–97.

27. Paul Tillich, *On the Boundary: An Autobiographical Sketch* (London: Collins, 1967), 13.

28. Paul Tillich, *Dynamics of Faith* (New York: Harper Torchbooks, 1958), 16–22.

29. On the complex discussion surrounding syncretism, see Robert J. Schreiter, *Constructing Local Theologies* (Maryknoll, N.Y.: Orbis Books, 1985), 144–58.

30. See Judith Plaskow, *Sex, Sin, and Grace: Women's Experience and the Theologies of Reinhold Niebuhr and Paul Tillich* (Lanham, Md.: University Press of America, 1980).

31. Tina Allik, "Human Finitude and the Concept of Women's Experience," *Constructive Christian Theology in the Worldwide Church,* ed. William R. Barr (Grand Rapids, Mich.: William B. Eerdmans, 1997), 225.

32. M. A. C. Warren, Introduction to John V. Taylor, *The Primal Vision: Christian Presence amid African Religion* (Philadelphia: Fortress Press, 1963), 10.

33. Gerard Manley Hopkins, "God's Grandeur," in *Modern American Poetry and Modern English Poetry,* combined new and enlarged edition, ed. Louis Untermeyer (New York: Harcourt, Brace and World, 1958), 2:42.

Chapter 8: Table Fellowship

This chapter is a revision of a paper authored by Roger Schroeder and originally delivered at the conference of the International Association of Catholic Missiologists (IACM) held in Tagaytay City, the Philippines, July 2010. It is published here for the first time.

1. *Ad Gentes,* Vatican Council II, Decree on the Church's Missionary Activity, 2.

2. See Stephen B. Bevans and Roger P. Schroeder, *Constants in Context: A Theology of Mission for Today* (Maryknoll, N.Y.: Orbis Books, 2004), 10–31.

3. Wayne A. Meeks, *The First Urban Christians: The Social World of the Apostle Paul* (New Haven: Yale University Press, 1983), 29.

4. Michael Green, *Evangelism in the Early Church* (Grand Rapids, Mich.: William B. Eerdmans, 1970), 173.

5. Rodney Stark, *The Rise of Christianity* (San Francisco: HarperCollins, 1996), 6.

6. Paul VI, Evangelization in the Modern World (*Evangelii Nuntiandi*).

7. Antonio Pernia et al., *The Eucharist and Our Mission, Following the Word 7* (Rome: SVD Publications, 1996), 38.

8. Mary Douglas, *Purity and Danger: An Analysis of the Concepts of Pollution and Taboo* (London: Routledge & Kegan Paul, Ark Paperbacks edition, 1984 [1966]).

9. Thanh Van Nguyen, "The Legitimation of the Gentile Mission and Integration: A Narrative Approach to Acts 10:1–11:18," Doctoral diss., Pontificia Università Gregoriana, 2004, 80–81.

10. Glenn Rogers, *Holistic Ministry and Cross-Cultural Mission in Luke-Acts* (Mission and Ministry Resources, 2003), 93; see P. F. Esler, *Community and Gospel in Luke-Acts: The Social and Political Motivation of Lucan Theology* (Cambridge: Cambridge University Press, 1987), 86.

11. Bevans and Schroeder, *Constants in Context,* 10–31.

12. Luke Timothy Johnson, *The Acts of the Apostles.* Sacra Pagina 5 (Collegeville, Minn.: Liturgical Press, 1992), 186.

13. See C. E. Van Engen, "Peter's Conversion: A Culinary Disaster Launches the Gentile Mission, Acts 10:1–11:18," in *Mission in Acts: Ancient Narratives in Contemporary Context,* ed. R. Gallagher and P. Hertig (Maryknoll, N.Y.: Orbis Books, 2004), 133–43.

14. John Paul II, The Mission of the Redeemer (*Redemptoris Missio*).

15. United States Conference of Catholic Bishops, *A Place at the Table: A Catholic Recommitment to Overcome Poverty and to Respect the Dignity of All God's Children* (Washington, D.C.: USCCB, 2002).

16. *Catechism of the Catholic Church,* 2d ed. (Vatican City: Libreria Editrice Vaticana, 1997), 1327, quoting Irenaeus.

17. T. H. Schattauer, "Liturgical Assembly as Locus of Mission," in *Inside Out: Worship in an Age of Mission,* ed. T. H. Schattauer (Minneapolis: Fortress Press, 1999), 1–21.

18. See Bevans and Schroeder, *Constants in Context,* 362–66.

19. United States Conference of Catholic Bishops, *To the Ends of the Earth: A Pastoral Statement on World Mission* (Washington, D.C.: USCCB, 1986), 58.

20. United States Conference of Catholic Bishops, *Called to Global Solidarity: International Challenges for U.S. Parishes* (Washington, D.C.: USCCB, 1997), 8.

21. Catholic Relief Services, "Home Calendar Guide," 2006.

22. *A Place at the Table,* section V, "A Tradition: The Biblical Vision."

23. Roger Schroeder, *What Is the Mission of the Church? A Guide for Catholics* (Maryknoll, N.Y.: Orbis Books, 2008), 8.

24. Bevans and Schroeder, *Constants in Context,* 348–95.

25. David Bosch, *Transforming Mission: Paradigm Shifts in Theology and Mission* (Maryknoll, N.Y.: Orbis Books, 1991), 489.

26. Bevans and Schroeder, *Constants in Context,* 349.

27. See ibid., 348–95.

28. L. A. Losie, "Paul's Speech on the Areopagus: A Model of Cross-Cultural Evangelism. Acts 17:16–34," in *Mission in Acts: Ancient Narratives in Contem-*

porary Context, ed. R. Gallagher and P. Hertig (Maryknoll, N.Y.: Orbis Books, 2004), 232.

29. *"O Sacrum Convivium"* as quoted in *www.preces-latinae.org/thesaurus/Euch/SacrumConv.html.*

Chapter 9: A Short History of the Church's Mission

This chapter was originally written by Stephen Bevans for a gathering of members of the Missionaries of the Precious Blood in Salzburg, Austria in July 2009. Bevans and Roger Schroeder subsequently thoroughly revised it for publication in this volume.

1. See *Ad Gentes,* Vatican Council II, Decree on the Church's Missionary Activity, 2.

2. See Dale Irvin and Scott Sunquist, *History of the World Christian Movement* (Maryknoll, N.Y.: Orbis Books, 2001); and Frederick A. Norris, *Christianity: A Short Global History* (Oxford: OneWorld Publications, 2002). Schroeder's work is in progress and will be published by Orbis Books within the next several years.

3. Emil Brunner, *The Word in the World* (London: SCM Press, 1931), 11.

4. Stephen B. Bevans and Roger P. Schroeder, *Constants in Context: A Theology of Mission for Today* (Maryknoll, N.Y.: Orbis Books, 2004).

5. Rudy Wiebe, *The Blue Mountains of China* (Toronto: McClelland and Stewart, New Canadian Library Edition, 1995), 258.

6. Kenan Osborne, *A Theology of the Church for the Third Millennium: A Franciscan Approach* (Leiden: Brill, 2009).

7. Michael Green, *Evangelism in the Early Church* (Grand Rapids, Mich.: William B. Eerdmans, 1970), 173.

8. Rodney Stark, *The Rise of Christianity* (San Francisco: HarperCollins, 1996).

9. Ibid., 3–27.

10. Original text in Gustavo Gutiérrez, *Las Casas: In Search of the Poor of Jesus Christ* (Maryknoll, N.Y.: Orbis Books, 1993), 29.

11. See Justo L. González, "Voices of Compassion," *Missiology: An International Review* 20, no. 4 (1992): 163–73.

12. For a detailed history of this development, see Charles Taylor, *A Secular Age* (New York: Oxford University Press, 2006).

13. Dana L. Robert, *American Women in Mission: A Social History of Their Thought and Practice* (Macon, Ga.: Mercer University Press, 1996), 37.

14. Robert J. Schreiter, "Changes in Roman Catholic Attitudes toward Proselytism and Mission," in *New Directions in Mission and Evangelization 2: Theological Foundations,* ed. James A. Scherer and Stephen B. Bevans (Maryknoll, N.Y.: Orbis Books, 1994), 113–25.

15. Kenneth Scott Latourette, *A History of the Expansion of Christianity* (New York: Harper & Brothers, 1937–45). Vols. 4, 5, and 6 cover the "Great Century," which he speaks of as from 1800 to 1914.

16. Conference on World Mission and Evangelism (CWME), Mexico City, 1963.

17. *Ad Gentes,* 11.

18. *Nostra Aetate,* 2.

19. See *Lumen Gentium,* 16.

20. John Paul II, *Redemptoris Missio,* 41.

21. *Evangelii Nuntiandi,* 75

Chapter 10: Church Teaching, Mission, and Prophetic Dialogue

This chapter is a revised version of a presentation given by Stephen Bevans for the Missionaries of the Precious Blood in Salzburg, Austria, in July 2009. An earlier version was published in *The Cup of the New Covenant* (Newsletter of the Missionaries of the Precious Blood), 29 (October 2009): 1–5.

1. For a more detailed account of the remarkable history of *Ad Gentes* see Part I, Section I of Stephen Bevans, SVD, and Jeffrey Gros, FSC, *Evangelization and Religious Freedom:* Ad Gentes *and* Dignitatis Humanae (New York: Paulist Press, 2009).

2. Yves Congar, "Principes doctrinaux," in *Vatican II: L'activité missionnaire de L'Église,* Unam Sanctam 67, ed. Johannes Schütte (Paris: Éditions du Cerf, 1967), 186.

3. Yves Congar, *Mon journal du concile* (Paris: Éditions du Cerf, 2002), 2:348, March 24, 1965.

4. The story is related in Bénézet Bujo, *African Theology in Its Social Context* (Maryknoll, N.Y.: Orbis Books, 1992), 58–62.

5. See, for example, the commentary of William R. Burrows in Timothy E. O'Connell, *Vatican II and Its Documents: An American Reappraisal* (Wilmington, Del.: Michael Glazier, 1986), 180–96.

6. For a fuller explanation of the background of the apostolic exhortation, see Stephen Bevans, "Witnessing to the Gospel in Modern Australia," *Australian E-Journal of Theology* 6 (2006).

7. David J. Bosch, *Transforming Mission: Paradigm Shifts in Theology of Mission* (Maryknoll, N.Y.: Orbis Books, 1991), 489.

8. Cardinal Josef Tomko, "Proclaiming Christ the World's Only Savior," *L'Osservatore Romano,* April 15, 1991, 4.

9. Secretariat for Non-Christians, "The Attitude of the Church towards the Followers of Other Religions: Reflections and Orientations on Dialogue and Mission," AAS 75 (1984), 816–28; see also *Bulletin Secretariatus pro non Christianis* 56 (1984/2), no. 13. The five elements are presence and witness; commitment to social development and human liberation; liturgical life, prayer and contemplation; interreligious dialogue; and proclamation and catechesis.

Select Bibliography

Allik, Tina. "Human Finitude and the Concept of Women's Experience." In *Constructive Christian Theology in the Worldwide Church,* ed. William R. Barr, 214–33. Grand Rapids, Mich.: William B. Eerdmans, 1997.

Amaladoss, Michael. "Mission as Prophecy." In *New Directions in Mission and Evangelization 2: Theological Foundations,* ed. James A. Scherer and Stephen B. Bevans, 64–72. Maryknoll, N.Y.: Orbis Books, 1994.

Anderson, Gerald H., ed. *Biographical Dictionary of Christian Missions.* New York: Macmillan Reference USA, 1998.

Appalachian Bishops. *This Land Is Home to Me.* 1975.

————. *At Home in the Web of Life.* 1995.

Arbuckle, Gerald. "Multiculturalism, Internationality, and Religious Life." *Review for Religious* 54, no. 3 (May–June 1995): 326–38.

Arias, Mortimer. *Announcing the Reign of God: Evangelization and the Subversive Memory of Jesus.* Philadelphia: Fortress Press, 1984.

Barbour, Claude Marie. "Seeking Justice and Shalom in the City." *International Review of Mission* 73, no. 291 (1984): 303–9.

Barbour, Claude Marie, Kathleen Billman, Peggy DesJarlait, and Eleanor Doidge. "Mission on the Boundaries: Cooperation without Exploitation." In *Beyond Theological Tourism: Mentoring as a Grassroots Approach to Theological Education,* ed. Susan B. Thistlethwaite and George F. Cairns, 72–91. Maryknoll, N.Y.: Orbis Books, 1995.

Barbour, Claude Marie, Amy Carr, Peggy DesJarlait, and Eleanor Doidge. "Gospel, Culture, Healing, and Reconciliation: A Shalom Conversation." *Mission Studies* 16, nos. 2–32 (1999): 135–50.

Baziou, Abbé Jean Yves. "Mission: From Expansion to Encounter." *USCMA Periodic Paper* no. 1. (Spring 2005).

Benedict XVI. Encyclical letter *Deus Caritas Est,* 2006.

Bevans, Stephen B. "Seeing Mission through Images." *Missiology: An International Review* 19, 1 (January 1991): 45–57.

————. "Images of Priesthood in Today's Church." *Emmanuel* 102, no. 7 (September 1996): 389–98.

————. "God Inside Out: Toward a Missionary Theology of the Holy Spirit." *International Bulletin of Missionary Research* 22, no. 3 (July 1998): 102–5.

————. *Models of Contextual Theology.* Rev. exp. ed. Maryknoll, N.Y.: Orbis Books, 2002.

————. "Witnessing to the Gospel in Modern Australia." *Australian E-Journal of Theology* 6 (2006).

Bevans, Stephen, and Eleanor Doidge. "Theological Reflection." In *What Mission Confronts Religious Life in the U.S. Today?* ed. Barbara Kraemer, 37–48. Chicago: Center for the Study of Religious Life, 2000.

Bevans, Stephen, and Jeffrey Gros. *Evangelization and Religious Freedom:* Ad Gentes *and* Dignitatis Humanae. New York: Paulist Press, 2009.

Bevans, Stephen B., and Roger P. Schroeder. *Constants in Context: A Theology of Mission for Today.* Maryknoll, N.Y.: Orbis Books, 2004.

Blake, William. "Auguries of Innocence." In *The Viking Book of Poetry of the English Speaking World,* ed. Richard Aldington, 621. New York: Viking Press, 1962.

Boff, Leonardo. "Trinity," in *Mysterium Liberationis: Fundamental Concepts of Liberation Theology,* ed. Ignacio Ellacuría and Jon Sobrino, 389–404. Maryknoll, N.Y.: Orbis Books, 1993.

————. "Social Ecology: Poverty and Misery." In *Ecotheology: Voices from South and North,* ed. David G. Hallman, 235–47. Maryknoll, N.Y.: Orbis Books, 1994.

Bosch, David J. *Transforming Mission: Paradigm Shifts in Theology and Mission.* Maryknoll, N.Y.: Orbis Books, 1991.

————. "The Vulnerability of Mission." In *New Directions in Mission and Evangelization 2: Theological Foundations,* ed. James A. Scherer and Stephen B. Bevans, 73–86. Maryknoll, N.Y.: Orbis Books, 1994.

Brunner, Emil. *The Word in the World.* London: SCM Press, 1931.

Bujo, Bénézet. *African Theology in Its Social Context.* Maryknoll, N.Y.: Orbis Books, 1992.

Burrows, William R., ed. *Redemption and Dialogue: Reading* Redemptoris Missio *and* Dialogue and Proclamation. Maryknoll, N.Y.: Orbis Books, 1993.

Campbell, Joseph (with Bill Moyers). *The Power of Myth.* New York: Doubleday, 1988.

Catechism of the Catholic Church. 2d ed. Vatican City: Libreria Editrice Vaticana, 1997.

Charles, Pierre. *Etudes Missiologiques.* Tournai, Belgium: Desclée de Brouwer, 1956.

Chia, Edmund. *Towards a Theology of Dialogue: Schillebeeckx's Method as Bridge between Vatican's* Dominus Iesus *and Asia's FABC Theology.* Bangkok: Privately printed, 2003.

Congar, Yves. *Mon journal du concile.* Paris: Éditions du Cerf, 2002.

Cowan, M. A., ed. *Alternative Futures for Worship.* Vol. 6: *Leadership Ministry and Community,* 105–28. Collegeville, Minn.: Liturgical Press, 1987.

Daikin, Tim. "Discipleship: Marked for Mission," in *Mission in the 21st Century: Exploring the Five Marks of Global Mission,* ed. Andrew Walls and Cathy Ross, 175–91. London: Darton, Longman and Todd, 2008.

Davies, Oliver. "Later Medieval Mystics." In *The Medieval Theologians: An Introduction to Theology in the Medieval Period,* ed. G. R. Evans, 221–32. Oxford: Blackwell, 2001.

Delaney, Frank. *Ireland.* New York: HarperCollins Paperback, 2008.

Delio, Ilia. "Bonaventure's Metaphysics of the Good." *Theological Studies* 60, no. 2 (1999): 228–46.

Donovan, Vincent. *Christianity Rediscovered.* Maryknoll, N.Y.: Orbis Books, 1982.

———. *The Church in the Midst of Creation.* Maryknoll, N.Y.: Orbis Books, 1989.

Dorr, Donal. *Mission in Today's World.* Maryknoll, N.Y.: Orbis Books, 2000.

Douglas, Mary. *Purity and Danger: An Analysis of the Concepts of Pollution and Taboo.* London: Routledge & Kegan Paul: Ark Paperbacks edition, 1984 (1966).

Dupuis, Jacques. "A Theological Commentary: Dialogue and Proclamation." In *Redemption and Dialogue: Reading* Redemptoris Missio *and* Dialogue and Proclamation, ed. William R. Burrows, 119–58. Maryknoll, N.Y.: Orbis Books, 1993.

Ellacuría, Ignacio, and Jon Sobrino, eds., *Mysterium Liberationis: Fundamental Concepts of Liberation Theology.* Maryknoll, N.Y.: Orbis Books, 1993.

Ellsberg, Robert. *All Saints: Daily Reflections on Saints, Prophets, and Witnesses for Our Time.* New York: Crossroad, 1997.

Esler, Philip F. *Community and Gospel in Luke-Acts: The Social and Political Motivation of Lucan Theology.* Cambridge: Cambridge University Press, 1987.

Fiddes, Paul S. *Participating in God: A Pastoral Theology of the Trinity.* London: Darton, Longman and Todd, 2000.

Following the Word, Nr. 1. Mission, Spirituality, Formation. Rome: SVD Publications, 1988.

Fox, Thomas. *Pentecost in Asia: A New Way of Being Church.* Maryknoll, N.Y.: Orbis Books, 2002.

Freire, Paulo. *The Pedagogy of the Oppressed.* New York: Seabury, 1968.

George, Cardinal Francis. *Dwell in My Love: A Pastoral Letter on Racism.* Chicago: New Catholic World, 2001.

Gesch, Patrick. *Initiative and Initiation.* Studia Instituti Anthropos 33. St. Augustine, Germany: Anthropos Institute, 1985.

Gittins, Anthony. *Gifts and Strangers: Meeting the Challenge of Inculturation.* New York: Paulist Press, 1989.

Goldman, Gerard. "Remembering Ian, Alan Goldman, and Memela: Using Narrative as an Approach to Aboriginal Reconciliation in Australia." D.Min. thesis project. Catholic Theological Union, Chicago, 1999.

González, Justo L. "Voices of Compassion." *Missiology: An International Review* 20, no. 4 (1992): 163–73.

Green, Michael. *Evangelism in the Early Church.* Grand Rapids, Mich.: William B. Eerdmans, 1970.

Gutiérrez, Gustavo. *A Theology of Liberation.* Maryknoll, N.Y.: Orbis Books, 1973.

———. *Las Casas: In Search of the Poor of Jesus Christ.* Maryknoll, N.Y.: Orbis Books, 1993.

———. "Option for the Poor." In *Mysterium Liberationis: Fundamental Concepts of Liberation Theology,* ed. Ignacio Ellacuría and Jon Sobrino, 235–50. Maryknoll, N.Y.: Orbis Books, 1993.

Haight, Roger. *Jesus, Symbol of God.* Maryknoll, N.Y.: Orbis Books, 1999.

Hauerwas, Stanley, and William Willimon. *Resident Aliens: Life in the Christian Colony.* Nashville: Abingdon Press, 1989.

Hawkins, Robert D. "Occasional Services: Border Crossings." In *Inside Out: Worship in an Age of Mission,* ed. Thomas H. Schattauer, 181–99. Minneapolis: Fortress Press, 1999.

Healey, Joseph, and Donald Sybertz, *Towards an African Narrative Theology.* Maryknoll, N.Y.: Orbis Books, 1996.

Hesselgrave, David J. *Communicating Christ Cross-Culturally: An Introduction to Missionary Communication.* Grand Rapids, Mich.: Zondervan, 1978.

Hopkins, Gerard Manley. "God's Grandeur." In *Modern American Poetry and Modern English Poetry,* ed. Louis Untermeyer, 42. New and enlarged ed. New York: Harcourt, Brace and World, 1958.

Hunsberger, George. *Bearing the Witness of the Spirit: Lesslie Newbigin's Theology of Cultural Plurality.* Grand Rapids, Mich.: William B. Eerdmans, 1998.

In Dialogue with the Word Nr. 1. Rome: SVD Publications, 2000.

Irvin, Dale T., and Akintunde Akinade, eds. *The Agitated Mind of God: The Theology of Kosuke Koyama.* Maryknoll, N.Y.: Orbis Books, 1996.

Irvin, Dale T., and Scott W. Sunquist. *History of the World Christian Movement.* Vol. 1. Maryknoll, N.Y.: Orbis Books, 2001.

Jenkinson, William, and Helene O'Sullivan, eds. *Trends in Mission: Toward the Third Millennium.* Maryknoll, N.Y.: Orbis Books, 1991.

John Paul II. "Moral Choices of the Future." *Origins* 10, no. 39 (March 12, 1981): 621–23.

———. *Redemptoris Missio,* 1990.

———. *Ecclesia in Africa,* 1995.

———. *Evangelium Vitae,* 1995.

Johnson, Elizabeth A. *She Who Is: The Mystery of God in Feminist Theological Discourse.* New York: Crossroad, 1992.

Johnson, Galen K. "St. Francis and the Sultan: An Historical and Critical Reassessment." *Mission Studies* 18, no. 2 (2001): 146–64.

Johnson, Luke Timothy. *The Acts of the Apostles.* Sacra Pagina 5. Collegeville, Minn: Liturgical Press, 1992.

Kerr, David. "Foucauld, Charles Eugéne de (1858–1916). In *Biographical Dictionary of Christian Missions,* ed. Gerald H. Anderson, 219–20. New York: Macmillan Reference USA, 1998.

Kingsolver, Barbara. *The Poisonwood Bible: A Novel.* New York: HarperFlamingo, 1998.

Kirk, J. Andrew. *What Is Mission: Theological Explorations.* London: Darton, Longman and Todd, 1999.

Latourette, Kenneth Scott. *A History of the Expansion of Christianity.* New York: Harper & Brothers, 1937, 1945.

Lohfink, Gerhard. *Jesus and Community.* Philadelphia: Fortress Press, 1984.

Lonergan, Bernard J. F. *Insight: A Study in Human Understanding.* New York: Philosophical Library, 1957.

———. *Method in Theology.* London: Darton, Longman and Todd, 1972.

Losie, L. A. "Paul's Speech on the Areopagus: A Model of Cross-Cultural Evangelism. Acts 17:16–34." In *Mission in Acts: Ancient Narratives in Contemporary Context,* ed. Robert Gallagher and Paul Hertig, 221–38. Maryknoll, N.Y.: Orbis Books, 2004.

Luzbetak, Louis J. *The Church and Cultures.* Pasadena, Calif.: William Carey Library, 1970 (1964).

Matthiessen, Peter. *At Play in the Fields of the Lord.* New York: Random House, 1965.

McBrien, Richard P. *The Church: The Evolution of Catholicism.* New York: HarperOne, 2008.

Mechtilde of Magdeburg. *The Flowing Light of the Godhead.* In Classics of Western Spirituality. trans. Frank Tobin. New York: Paulist Press, 1998.

Meeks, Wayne A. *The First Urban Christians: The Social World of the Apostle Paul.* New Haven: Yale University Press, 1983.

Motte, Mary. "In the Image of the Crucified God: A Missiological Interpretation of Francis of Assisi." In *The Agitated Mind of God: The Theology of Kosuke Koyama,* ed. Dale T. Irvin and Akintunde Akinade, 73–87. Maryknoll, N.Y.: Orbis Books, 1996.

Nemer, Larry. "Prophetic Dialogue: A New Way of Doing Mission?" See online *www.instrumentsofpeace.ie/Prophetic%20Dialogue.pdf.*

Newbigin, Lesslie. *The Gospel in a Pluralist Society.* Grand Rapids, Mich.: William B. Eerdmans, 1989.

Nguyen, T. V. "The Legitimation of the Gentile Mission and Integration: A Narrative Approach to Acts 10:1–11:18." Doctoral diss., Pontificia Università Gregoriana, 2004.

Norris, Frederick A. *Christianity: A Short Global History.* Oxford: OneWorld Publications, 2002.

O'Connell, Timothy E. *Vatican II and Its Documents: An American Reappraisal.* Wilmington, Del.: Michael Glazier, 1986.

Okoye, James Chukwuma. *Israel and the Nations: A Mission Theology of the Old Testament.* Maryknoll, N.Y.: Orbis Books, 2006.

Oman, John Wood. "God's Ideal and Man's Reality." In *The Paradox of the World,* 60–72. Cambridge: Cambridge University Press, 1921.

———. *Vision and Authority or the Throne of St. Peter.* 2nd ed. London: Hodder and Staughton, 1928.

———. *"O Sacrum Convivium."* See online *www.preceslatinae.org/thesaurus/Euch/ SacrumConv.html.*

Osborne, Kenan. *A Theology of the Church for the Third Millennium: A Franciscan Approach.* Leiden: Brill, 2009.

Palmer, Parker J. *The Courage to Teach: Exploring the Inner Landscape of a Teacher's Life.* San Francisco: Jossey-Bass Publishers, 1998.

Paul VI, Encyclical Letter *Ecclesiam Suam,* 1964.

———. "The African Church Today." *The Pope Speaks* 14, no. 3 (1969): 214–23.

———. "Closing Discourse to All-Africa Symposium." *Gaba Pastoral Paper* 7 (1969).

———. "Message for World Day of Peace," *Origins* 1, no. 29 (January 6, 1972): 490–91.

———. *Evangelii Nuntiandi,* 1975.

Pernia, Antonio et al. *The Eucharist and Our Mission. Following the Word* 7. Rome: SVD Publications, 1996.

Pierce, Gregory Augustine. *The Mass Is Never Ended.* Notre Dame, Ind.: Ave Maria Press, 2007.

Pilkington, Doris. *Rabbit-Proof Fence.* New York: Miramax Books, 2002.

Placher, William. *The Triune God: An Essay in Postliberal Theology.* Louisville: Westminster John Knox, 2007.

Plaskow, Judith. *Sex, Sin, and Grace: Women's Experience and the Theologies of Reinhold Niebuhr and Paul Tillich.* Lanham, Md.: University Press of America, 1980.

Poe, Edgar Allan. "The Purloined Letter," in *The Complete Tales and Poems of Edgar Allan Poe,* intro. Wilbur S. Scott, 185–97. Edison, N.J.: Castle Books, 2002.

Pontifical Council for Interreligious Dialogue and Congregation for the Evangelization of Peoples, 1991. *Dialogue and Proclamation.* In *Redemption and Dialogue: Reading* Redemptoris Missio *and* Dialogue and Proclamation, ed. William R. Burrows, 93–118. Maryknoll, N.Y.: Orbis Books, 1993.

Prior, John, "Unfinished Encounter: A Note on the Voice and Tone of *Ecclesia in Asia." East Asian Pastoral Review* 37, no. 3 (2000): 256–71.

Raguin, Yves. *I Am Sending You: Spirituality of the Missioner.* Manila: East Asian Pastoral Institute, 1973.

Rahner, Karl. *The Trinity.* New York: Herder and Herder, 1970.

Reid, Barbara E. *Parables for Preachers, Year C.* Collegeville, Minn.: Liturgical Press, 2000.

Riebe-Estrella, Gary. "On the Threshold: How the Present Is Shaping the Future of Ministry." In *Word Remembered, Word Proclaimed,* ed. Stephen Bevans and Roger Schroeder, 175–88. Nettetal, Germany: Steyler Verlag, 1997.

Robert, Dana L. *American Women in Mission: A Social History of Their Thought and Practice.* Macon, Ga.: Mercer University Press, 1996.

Rogers, Glen. *Holistic Ministry and Cross-Cultural Mission in Luke-Acts.* Mission and Ministry Resources, 2003.

Rosales, Gaudencio, and Catalino G. Arévalo, eds. *For All the Peoples of Asia,* vol. 1. Quezon City: Claretian Publications, 1997.

Rush, Robert T. "From Pearl Merchant to Treasure Hunter: The Missionary Yesterday and Today." *Catholic Mind* 76 (1978): 6–10.

Saayman, Willem, and Klippies Kritzinger, eds. *Mission in Bold Humility: David Bosch's Work Considered.* Maryknoll, N.Y.: Orbis Books, 1996.

Sanneh, Lamin. *Translating the Message: The Missionary Impact on Culture.* 20th anniv. ed. Maryknoll, N.Y.: Orbis Books, 2009.

Schattauer, Thomas H. *Inside Out: Worship in an Age of Mission.* Minneapolis: Fortress Press, 1999.

Scherer, James A., and Stephen B. Bevans, eds. *New Directions in Mission and Evangelizaton 1: Basic Statements.* Maryknoll, N.Y.: Orbis Books, 1992.

———. *New Directions in Mission and Evangelization 2: Theological Foundations.* Maryknoll, N.Y.: Orbis Books, 1994.

———. *New Directions in Mission and Evangelization 3: Faith and Culture.* Maryknoll, N.Y.: Orbis Books, 1999.

Schillebeeckx, Edward. *Interim Report on the Books* Jesus *and* Christ. New York: Crossroad, 1981.

———. *Jesus: An Experiment in Theology.* New York: Vintage Books, 1981.

Schineller, Peter. "Inculturation and Modernity." *Sedos Bulletin* 2 (February 15, 1988): 43–47.

Schreiter, Robert J. *Constructing Local Theologies.* Maryknoll, N.Y.: Orbis Books, 1985.

———. "Changes in Roman Catholic Attitudes toward Proselytism and Mission." In *New Directions in Mission and Evangelization 2: Theological Foundations,* ed. James A. Scherer and Stephen B. Bevans, 113–25. Maryknoll, N.Y.: Orbis Books, 1994.

———. *The Ministry of Reconciliation: Spirituality and Strategies.* Maryknoll, N.Y.: Orbis Books, 1998.

Schreiter, Robert J., ed. *Mission in the Third Millennium.* Maryknoll, N.Y.: Orbis Books, 2001.

Schroeder, Roger. *Initiation and Religion: A Case Study from the Wosera of Papua New Guinea.* Studia Instituti Anthropos 46. Fribourg, Switzerland: University Press, 1992.

———. *What Is the Mission of the Church? A Guide for Catholics.* Maryknoll, N.Y.: Orbis Books, 2008.

Schütte, Johannes, ed. *Vatican II: L'activité missionnaire de l'Église.* Unam Sanctam 67. Paris: Éditions du Cerf, 1967.

Secretariat for Non-Christians, "The Attitude of the Church toward the Followers of Other Religions: Reflections and Orientations on Dialogue and Mission." *Bulletin Secretariatus pro non Christianis* 56, no. 2 (1984).

Sedmak, Clemens. *Doing Local Theology: A Guide for Artisans of a New Humanity.* Maryknoll, N.Y.: Orbis Books, 2002.

Segundo, Juan Luis. *Christ in the Spiritual Exercises of St. Ignatius*. Maryknoll, N.Y.: Orbis Books, 1987.

Sharpe, Eric J. "Ramabai Dongre Medhavi (Pandita Ramabai Sarasvati) (1858–1922)." In *Biographical Dictionary of Christian Missions,* ed. Gerald H. Anderson, 557. New York: Macmillan Reference USA, 1998.

Shea, John. "Theological Assumptions and Ministerial Style." In *Alternative Futures for Worship*. Vol. 6: *Leadership Ministry and Community,* ed. M. A. Cowan, 105–28. Collegeville, Minn.: Liturgical Press, 1987.

Shorter, Aylward. *African Christian Theology: Adaptation or Inculturation?* London: Geoffrey Chapman, 1975.

———. *Inculturation in Africa: The Way Forward*. The Fourth Annual Louis J. Luzbetak, SVD Lecture on Mission and Culture. Chicago: CCGM Publications, 2005.

Stanislaus, Lazar, and Allwyn D'Souza, eds. *Prophetic Dialogue: Challenges and Prospects in India*. Pune: Ishvani Kendra / ISPCK, 2003.

Stark, Rodney. *The Rise of Christianity*. San Francisco: HarperCollins, 1996.

Stone, Howard W., and James O. Duke. *How to Think Theologically*. Minneapolis: Fortress Press, 1996.

Swidler, Leonard. "Interreligious and Interideological Dialogue: The Matrix for All Systematic Reflection Today." In *Toward a Universal Theology of Religions,* ed. Leonard Swidler, 5–50. Maryknoll, N.Y.: Orbis Books, 1987.

Synod of Bishops, 1971. "Justice in the World." In *Catholic Social Thought: The Documentary Heritage,* ed. David J. O'Brien and Thomas A. Shannon, 287–302. Maryknoll, N.Y.: Orbis Books, 1992.

Tan, Jonathan. "*Missio ad Gentes* in Asia: A Comparative Study of the Missiology of John Paul II and the Federation of Asian Bishops' Conferences." Ph.D. diss., Catholic University of America, 2002.

Taylor, Charles. *A Secular Age*. New York: Oxford University Press, 2006.

Thomas, Norman, ed. *Classic Texts in Mission and World Christianity*. Maryknoll, N.Y.: Orbis Books, 1994.

Tillich, Paul. *Dynamics of Faith*. New York: Harper Torchbooks, 1958.

———. *On the Boundary: An Autobiographical Sketch*. London: Collins, 1967.

Tinker, Tink. "The Romance and Tragedy of Christian Mission among American Indians." In *Remembering Jamestown: Hard Questions about Christian Mission,* ed. Amos Yong and Barbara Brown Zikmund, 13–27. Eugene, Ore.: Pickwick Publications, 2010.

Tomko, Cardinal Josef. "Proclaiming Christ the World's Only Savior." *L'Osservatore Romano,* April 15, 1991.

Tracy, David. *Dialogue with the Other: The Inter-Religious Dialogue*. Louvain and Grand Rapids, Mich.: Peeters Press and William B. Eerdmans, 1990.

———. "Traditions of Spiritual Practice and the Practice of Theology." *Theology Today* 55, no. 2 (July 1998): 235–41.

Truth, Sojourner. "Document 3. Sojourner Truth: The Conversion of a Female Slave." In *In Our Own Voices: Four Centuries of American Women's Religious*

Writing, ed. Rosemary Radford Ruether and Rosemary Skinner Keller, 172–74. San Francisco: HarperCollins, 1995.

United States Conference of Catholic Bishops. *The Challenge of Peace: God's Promise and Our Response.* Washington, D.C.: USCCB, 1983.

———. *Economic Justice for All.* Washington, D.C.: USCCB, 1986.

———. *To the Ends of the Earth: A Pastoral Statement on World Mission.* Washington, D.C.: USCCB, 1986.

———. *Called to Global Solidarity: International Challenges for U.S. Parishes.* Washington, D.C.: USCCB, 1997.

———. *A Place at the Table: A Catholic Recommitment to Overcome Poverty and to Respect the Dignity of All God's Children.* Washington, D.C.: USCCB, 2002.

Van Engen, Charles E. "Peter's Conversion: A Culinary Disaster Launches the Gentile Mission. Acts 10:1–11:18." In *Mission in Acts: Ancient Narratives in Contemporary Context,* ed. Robert Gallagher and Paul Hertig, 133–43. Maryknoll, N.Y.: Orbis Books, 2004.

Van Gelder, Craig. *The Essence of the Church: A Community Created by the Spirit.* Grand Rapids, Mich.: William B. Eerdmans, 2000.

Vatican Council II. *Ad Gentes,* Decree on the Church's Missionary Activity, 1965.

———. *Dei Verbum,* Dogmatic Constitution on Divine Revelation, 1965.

———. *Gaudium et Spes,* Pastoral Constitution on the Church in the Modern World, 1965.

———. *Nostra Aetate,* Declaration on the Relationship of the Church to Non-Christian Religions, 1965.

Walker, Alice. "A Wind through the Heart: A Conversation with Alice Walker and Sharon Salzberg on Loving Kindness in a Painful World." *Shambhala Sun* (January 1997): 1–5.

Walls, Andrew F. *The Missionary Movement in Christian History: Studies in the Transmission of the Faith.* Maryknoll, N.Y.: Orbis Books, 1996.

Warren, M. A. C. Introduction to *The Primal Vision: Christian Presence amid African Religion* by John V. Taylor. Philadelphia: Fortress Press, 1963.

Whitehead, Alfred North. *Process and Reality: An Essay in Cosmology.* New York: Macmillan, 1929.

Whiteman, Darrell. "Contextualization: The Theory, the Gap, the Challenge." In *New Directions in Mission and Evangelization 3: Faith and Culture,* ed. James A. Scherer and Stephen B. Bevans, 42–53. Maryknoll, N.Y.: Orbis Books, 1999.

Wiebe, Rudy. *The Blue Mountains of China.* Toronto: McClelland and Stewart, 1995 (1970).

Wilfred, Felix. "The Federation of Asian Bishops' Conferences (FABC): Orientations, Challenges and Impact." In *For All the Peoples of Asia,* vol. 1, ed. Gaudencio Rosales and Catalino G. Arévalo, xxiii–xxx. Quezon City: Claretian Publications, 1997.

Wilson, Frederick R., ed. *The San Antonio Report: Your Will Be Done, Mission in Christ's Way.* Geneva: World Council of Churches Publications, 1990.

World Council of Churches. "Ecumenical Affirmation: Mission and Evangelism." In *New Directions in Mission and Evangelization 1: Basic Statements,* ed. James A. Scherer and Stephen B. Bevans, 36–51. Maryknoll, N.Y.: Orbis Books, 1992.

———. "Guidelines on Dialogue." In *New Directions in Mission and Evangelization 1: Basic Statements,* ed. James A. Scherer and Stephen B. Bevans, 12–17. Maryknoll, N.Y.: Orbis Books, 1992.

———. "Report from the Ecumenical Conference on World Mission and Evangelization." Salvador De Bahia, Brazil. In *New Directions in Mission and Evangelization 3: Faith and Culture,* ed. James A. Scherer and Stephen B. Bevans, 196–234. Maryknoll, N.Y.: Orbis Books, 1992.

Wright, Cathy. "Nazareth as a Model for Mission in the Life of Charles de Foucauld." *Mission Studies* 19, no. 1 (2002): 36–52.

Wright, N. T. *Jesus and the Victory of God.* Minneapolis: Fortress Books, 1996.

Yong, Amos, and Barbara Brown Zikmund, eds. *Remembering Jamestown: Hard Questions about Christian Mission.* Eugene, Ore.: Pickwick Publications, 2010.

Young, William P. *The Shack.* Newbury Park, Calif.: Windblown Media, 2007.

Zago, Marcello. "Mission and Interreligious Dialogue." *International Bulletin of Missionary Research* 22, no. 3 (July 1998): 98–101.

———. "The New Millennium and the Emerging Religious Strategies." *Missiology: An International Review* 28, no. 1 (January 2000): 5–18.

Index

185